The Use and Abuse of Social Science

edited by

Frank Heller

⑤ SAGE Publications

London · Beverly Hills · Newbury Park · New Delhi

Grateful acknowledgement is made to *The Journal of Higher Education*, 53,
November/December 1982 who published the article 'Policy Research in the Context
of Diffuse Decision Making', upon which chapter 15 is based.

SAGE Publications Ltd
28 Banner Street
London EC1Y 8QE

SAGE Publications Inc.
275 South Beverly Drive
Beverly Hills, California 90212
and 2111 West Hillcrest Drive
Newbury Park, California 91320

SAGE Publications India Pvt Ltd
C-236 Defence Colony
New Delhi 110 024

British Library Cataloguing in Publication Data

The Use and abuse of social science.
   1. Social sciences — Research
   I. Heller, Frank A.
   300'.72   H62

ISBN 0-8039-8016-7
ISBN 0-8039-8017-5 Pbk

Library of Congress catalog card number 86-061923

Printed in Great Britain by
J.W. Arrowsmith Ltd, Bristol

To Florence Anne

Contents

Acknowledgements

This book discharges many debts. In the first place I must acknowledge the encouragement and financial support of the Economic and Social Research Council (ESRC) and the initiative of Chris Caswill, then Secretary of the Council's Management and Industrial Relations and Industry and Employment Committees.

Interest in this topic by the Council goes back to the days when it was called the Social Science Research Council (SSRC) and when its Management and Industrial Relations Committee set up a group to study the complex and always less than satisfactory relations between producers and consumers of research. For two years I chaired this group and we produced an interim report based in part on a conference to which several of the present chapter writers made important contributions. Professor David Chambers, from the London Business School, took over the chairmanship of the group which further refined the analysis and finalized the report with the intention of submitting it to the Council.

My second debt is due to the Netherlands Institute for the Advanced Study of the Humanities and Social Sciences (NIAS) which allowed me to spend a year in aesthetically and academically congenial surroundings during which I was able to finalize my own thoughts on this topic and persuade the chapter authors to make their contributions within an agreed format.

During the year in the Netherlands, a number of NIAS Fellows made useful contributions. Bob Haveman and Ansgar Weyman happened to be working on relevant topics and agreed to interrupt their schedules to write chapters for this book. Bob Blackburn, Pjotr Hesseling, Ypre Portinga and Nicholas Rupke read and helpfully commented on various drafts which Ann Simpson patiently put on her computer.

Chris Caswill had intended to write a chapter, but eventually contented himself with up-dating the information on the current position of the Economic and Social Research Council's Open Door Policy in Gill's chapter.

George Strauss and Desmond Graves suggested a number of stylistic and content improvements, and Pamela Hattingh, my assistant at the Tavistock Institute, had the painstaking task of checking references and establishing effective communication with chapter authors in their several countries.

Many imperfections remain for which I am alone responsible. There is one further admission I would like to make; this is a book I really enjoyed putting together and writing for. I hope that enjoyment and utility are reconcilable outcomes in this case.

Frank Heller

Introduction and overview

Frank Heller

Introduction

This book addresses the issue of social science and its uses. While only a few people would argue specifically against making use of existing social science knowledge, it should not be assumed too readily that a broad-based advocacy of more utilization is either logical or practical. The contributions have therefore been assembled with the objective of examining the scope as well as the limitations of the utilization thesis. One does not want to fall into the trap of thinking that the expenditure of money on social science is sufficient reason for demanding practical outcomes, let alone utilization of these outcomes. Such a cost-benefit thesis is destructive of knowledge creation and unfair to other disciplines which will always retain their importance without imposing the utilization burden on themselves: for instance, history (particularly ancient history), the history of science, philosophy, literature and literary criticism, the sociology of knowledge, experimental and animal psychology, and archaeology, to mention only some.

These wider considerations came to mind very naturally in the setting in which this book was assembled and edited. In 1984–5 I was able to enjoy a Fellowship at NIAS, the Netherlands Institute for Advanced Study in the Humanities and Social Sciences, which each year brings together about forty scholars for twelve months' uninhibited thinking, writing or whatever intellectual activity seems appropriate. The Fellows come from different parts of the world, East and West, and from a wide variety of disciplines. Although there has been pressure on NIAS to assemble groups with some similarity of background, luckily they did not succeed in this barbaric objective. I was therefore privileged to share my daily lunchtable with an invigorating variety of scholars, most of whom were doing important work — one husband and wife team in Armenian and biblical archaeology, for instance — without being worried about utilization in the sense in which this word is often used in discussions on the role of social science. This caveat must always be remembered, but it does not prevent many of us from believing that social science can often make a very important contribution to the

1

understanding of social phenomena and may be able to suggest options
and even solutions to problems that need to be resolved.

This is the spirit which led to this book. The writers are all social
scientists who have given considerable thought to the utilization issue
and cover a very wide range of experiences. They come from seven
countries. Some work in government, others in industry or commerce,
several are associated with giving funds for research, and one has spent
most of his working life in a major international agency. The academic
disciplines cover economics, political science, accountancy, law,
psychology, sociology, systems science and industrial relations. While
each writer gives examples of successes or failures in making use of
research, there are also several important theoretical contributions
which help us to understand the implications of the debate. The writers
were chosen for the experience they could contribute to our topic and
they were free to interpret the meaning of the term 'utilization' as they
liked. They were asked to write for an audience which, apart from other
researchers, would include potential users of research in every kind of
organization and at every level, including government.

The debate about the use and abuse of research has a long history
and a substantial literature, as the review chapter by Karapin shows, but
a large part of it is concerned with what are called evaluation studies.
These are designed to assess the impact of a particular piece of work,
often by somebody outside the research project and frequently against
specified criteria. With one exception, the contributions to this book do
not take this approach and, unlike most of the previous literature, our
cases come from a number of countries and a wide variety of topics.
Nevertheless, as I hope to show in the final chapter, both successes and
failures share some common features.

The utilization process
The utilization of research should be seen as part of a wider inquiry into
the function of knowledge. Such a topic is clearly beyond the scope of
this book, although we will come back to it briefly to argue that under-
utilization and even misuse of knowledge is endemic in all civilizations
and should make us accept relatively humble objectives and realizable
expectations.

Whatever the level of expectations, I see utilization as a process which
has four phases. In the first place it is necessary to create *access*, that is
to say diffusion to people with a potential interest in the topic. This is in
part a matter of creating channels of communication and using appropriate language. The second requirement is to enable the available
knowledge to be *seriously considered* by those who could benefit from
it. This requirement poses enormous problems of motivation and of
definition of those most likely to benefit. Potential users of information

have to be motivated to give more than superficial attention to what is available. This is only partly a matter of presentation. There are often deep-seated non-intellectual obstacles that prevent serious consideration of new findings or ideas. As to the range of potential audiences, the reader is invited to keep this question in mind when considering the various examples produced by chapter writers. Very frequently, the client for a particular piece of research is only one of several who could derive benefit from it.

Thirdly, after having achieved access and serious consideration, the client has to *make a decision* either to accept, reject or adopt some intermediate position, such as postponement or a request for further research work on the subject. Finally, if and when a positive decision to accept and use the research findings is made, there remains the need for *implementation.* Many things can go wrong at each phase of this cycle of events, which may take place over a considerable time from start to finish. The phases may not always be as clearly differentiated as my description has implied. In what is called 'action research', for instance, the four phases are extensively integrated.[1] Access is assured through the act of commissioning and the client's motivation is likely to be high, since he is usually the initiator. The implications or recommendations of the action research still have to be accepted, and this is by no means a foregone conclusion. If the client accepts, then the action-research process usually continues into the implementation phase. Nevertheless, many problems can emerge at various unexpected times (see, for instance, Clark, 1976).

A variety of problem-solving approaches

Most researchers would probably agree that they aim at solving problems: theoretical or practical, hypothesis inspired or bottom-up empirical. Nevertheless, from the point of view of a client who has a problem to solve, research is not always the first or the only option. For the purpose of this book and to give the reader a framework to approach the contributions which follow, I will briefly describe twelve fairly clearly differentiated varieties of problem-solving, nine of which use a research approach directly, and three of which use it in varying degrees indirectly. The twelve methods of approach can be grouped into five modules as shown in Table 1:

I.   The traditional approach: 'science only'
II.   Building bridges between researcher and user
III.   Researcher-client equality
IV.   Client-professional exploration
V.   Client-dominated quest.

Moving from I to V is not simply to move from pure to applied research; there are important distinctions within and between the modules that relate to methods of finance, channels of diffusion, expected audiences, language used and other facets that overlap the modules. For my present purpose I shall indicate only the most usual diffusion channels and language choice (in the right-hand margin).

TABLE 1
Five problem-solving modules

I. The traditional approach: 'science only'	Diffusion channels and language
1. Basic research in the social sciences is inevitably different from basic research in the physical sciences. For most people it is more an aspiration than a reality. Where it is thought to apply, it includes work in physiological and animal psychology; mathematical modelling; epistemology and statistical theory. Application to problem-solving in the real world is not usually seen as an objective.	Diffusion is entirely through academic channels. Language is highly specialized, abstract and with a tendency to use symbols.
2. Less basic research may still be thought to be 'pure' or theoretical. It consists of model-building, the development of methodological refinements or theories. The researcher may use laboratory tests or strictly controlled situations. Application is not a high priority and is usually left to other people.	Diffusion is through academic channels. Language is highly specialized, often condensed and abstract.
3. Research on practical problems where, at least in theory, application would seem feasible. Laboratory research and controlled field experiments with careful pre-testing and scientific criteria for sampling and evaluation. Application is seen as a possible but not a necessary outcome and is often left to other people.	Diffusion is through academic channels. Language is specialized, often condensed and abstract.
II. Building bridges between researcher and user	Diffusion channels and language
4. The researcher believes that the work has practical implications and should be used. To this end he or she takes steps to disseminate the results in simple language and as widely as possible, in addition to the usual academic channels.	Diffusion is through academic and more popular channels. Two languages tend to be used: one for academic and the other for popular dissemination.
5. The researcher obtains client or client-group collaboration on a project designed by him or herself based on own interests and/or extant literature. The researcher would like the client or client-group to be influenced by any research outcome.	Diffusion is through academic and more popular channels. Abstract language for academic use; simple language with careful explanation of terms for popular channels.

TABLE 1 (continued)

II. Building bridges between researcher and user	Diffusion channels and language
6. The same as 5, but in addition steps are taken to give the client or client-group regular feed-back on the progress of the research, problems and outcomes. During feed-back, the client has an opportunity to check on the interim findings and contribute his own analysis and interpretation of the results. The researcher attempts to help in the implementation phase.	Diffusion is through feed-back meetings, popular as well as academic channels. Language as above.

III. Researcher-client equality	Diffusion channels and language
7. The researcher and client together discuss one or several problem areas and a research design is jointly formulated. The research involves active collaboration and some measure of control on the part of the client system (a difficulty here may be to define the boundary of the client system). Implementation, or working through with the help of the researcher, is part of the collaborative design. This method can be called 'research-action', since fact-finding takes precedence over implementation.	Diffusion is through feed-back and frequent contact with client, plus popular and possibly also academic channels. Permission to publish usually has to be negotiated. Use of fairly simple language predominates but includes definitions and may include theory.
8. The same approach as in 7, except that the initiative is taken by the client who identifies the problem. This problem is taken by the researcher to be the 'presenting problem' and the early stages of the research process are designed to ascertain whether beyond or behind the 'presenting problem' lie other issues which should receive primary attention. This method can be called 'research action' or 'action research', depending on how much emphasis is put on the fact-finding phase.	Diffusion is expected through the client and his network based on feedback and written reports to client, with possibly other publications not excluding academic channels. Usually permission to publish has to be obtained. Language as above.
9. The same as in 8, but the problem identified by the client is not questioned and the research proceeds on that basis. If the researcher is involved in implementation, the method is 'action research', because fact-finding occupies a subsidiary role.	As above.

IV. Client-professional exploration	Diffusion channels and language
10. A client with a problem requests help from a researcher/academic. No new data (or very little) are collected. The advice or recommendation will be based on the researcher's past experience	Diffusion beyond the client and the client network is unlikely but some case descriptions are

TABLE 1 (continued)

IV. Client-professional exploration	Diffusion channels and language
and his/her knowledge of the field. If the exploration takes place in an organization, then training or organization development is frequently an outcome or one of the outcomes of this method. This approach can also be called 'action research' if the investigator uses past experience to help with the implementation.	occasionally published in a fairly popular medium, often under some disguise. Language tends towards the popular but may include definitions and theoretical distinctions.

V. Client-dominated quest	Diffusion channels and language
11. A client requests help from a specialist or staff person (for instance, a personnel manager or a consultant with a social science background). The specialist is familiar with the social science literature and is prepared to bring him/herself up to date if necessary. The specialist will examine the problem and, using his/her interpretation of what is 'best current knowledge' and personal experience, will make a diagnosis and suggest a line of action.	Diffusion is minimal and usually by word of mouth. If a report is written it is confidental to the client. Language is popular and tends to avoid definition and theory.
12. A client requests help from a non-specialist (meaning a person who has no formal training or qualifications in social science but who may have read some of the more popular literature). The non-specialist may be a personnel manager or consultant, for instance in the field of management, where he/she may cover several areas like finance, marketing and organizational design. The procedure is as in 11. Best current knowledge, however, will be interpreted at second or third hand heavily influenced by personal experience and 'common sense'. The ideas used in sections 11 and 12 will derive from 'Do It Yourself Social Science' or DYSS, which will be discussed in the final chapter.	Diffusion is to the client system or to a single client, often by word of mouth or in a confidential report. In professional consultancy, diffusion is through aggregation of experience which will be transferred to other clients. Occasionally books or articles are written or lectures are given to conferences. Language is popular to simplistic and carefully avoids theory. Instead, checklists are preferred.

There is no need to use the word research to apply to all twelve approaches, particularly in places where the term is not very popular. There is much to be gained by using alternatives like *investigation* to describe more routine data collection, such as regular surveys by distributed questionnaires; and terms like *inquiry, search, quest* and *exploration* to cover different ways of reaching conclusions from experience or the scrutiny of evidence.[2]

I said at the outset that the twelve variations of problem-solving do not include all available alternatives. Two in particular have to be added. One is *replication research,* the relative scarcity of which is criticized by several authors. Replication studies could be undertaken by means of any of the options 1 to 9. The second omission is research on research (sometimes called *meta-research* or, less flatteringly, *secondary research*) which analyses an existing body of knowledge, either by description or statistical re-analysis, to extract (where possible) seminal conclusions. Igor Ansoff would like to see more meta-research and, since it is economical, one must assume that its lack of popularity, even among funding bodies, is due to its low place in the pecking order of academic prestige. The same applies to replication research.

There is another important issue that needs to be considered in any analysis of the various research approaches and their potential impact on utilization. Who pays for the work? In options 10 to 12 it is almost always the client who pays,[3] but in other cases the source of funds can vary and can be a critical influence on the development, objectivity and outcome of the research. If the client pays for the work, particularly in large-scale consultancies where considerable sums can be involved, acceptance of recommendations and their implementation is reinforced by the cash nexus. The apocryphal story of a company which paid for a large survey and then offered more money to have it suppressed illustrates an exceptional problem. When independent sources pay for research, the incentive to use the outcome appears to be reduced.

Most professional researchers and academics engaged on work which falls within options 4 to 9 or even 10 are likely to prefer independent funding for a number of reasons. They would claim that while nobody is quite unbiased and completely impervious to value judgements and sectional pressures, the possibility of severe distortions and prejudgements on the part of a researcher is less than those that operate on a client. This case is not easy to sustain and the reader would do well to bear this in mind in each case. Lévy-Leboyer's study of telephone-box vandalism and Wilkins's work on war medals and hearing aids would support the contention of client bias, but others may not be as clear-cut.

But even if human frailty operated equally on both sides, client funding can create difficulties since power relationships are always present within the client system. On whose behalf is the work being done? Is one group's diagnosis more relevant than another's? Organizations always have hierarchies and their views on most issues are starkly different. These disparities are well documented in the literature and have to be faced. When there are organized interest groups like trade unions or employers' confederations, suppressed antagonisms quickly come to the surface and the quality of the information available to the researcher will be a function of the neutrality and confidentiality he or she can convey in his work. Finally, there is the delicate question of the extent to which a research analysis can be critical of people or issues closely associated with the piper who pays for the tune.

In terms of research utilization, these circumstances point to a dilemma. Modules II (Building bridges between researcher and user) and III (Researcher-client equality) present the range of research opportunities that most frequently figure in the literature on utilization, and this applies also to the present compilation. These are areas where independent funding is most desirable and most likely to appeal to funding bodies. At the same time, the self-interest dynamic for utilization is lower than for modules IV (Client-professional exploration), and V (Client-dominated quest). These last options are, however, much less likely to yield interesting scientific findings. The dilemma is reinforced if the reader looks at the column on diffusion channels next to the various options. He/she will notice that the widest range of popular as well as academic writings takes place through options 4 to 9, although permission to publish may have to be obtained from the client system in cases 7 to 9. The later options (10 to 12), which are much more heavily client-centred and client-financed, tend to yield only small additions to general knowledge and little diffusion.

'Action research' or 'research action'?

This brings us to the issue of action research which is raised by many authors, many of whom favour this approach. Action research has been variously defined (see, for instance, Sanford, 1976 or Rapoport, 1970) and refers to a process stressing action or implementation in which the researcher or consultant plays an active part. There are, of course, many variations but, by and large, the academic community and the more academically-oriented funding bodies have been very critical. Action research is accused of being long on action but short on research and to give understanding of individual cases but no useful generalizations. In any case, the purists argue that the scientist's objectivity is reduced if he or she enters the action arena. These arguments have been challenged, notably by Argyris (1970; 1976; 1980), but nevertheless continue, as Karapin's chapter shows.

However, something like this method is favoured by the authors in this book, who describe a fair degree of success in the utilization of research outcomes: Lévy-Leboyer, Gustavsen, Wilkins (Guidelines for Parole Boards), Heller (the Shell and Glacier projects) and Gill (Open Door scheme). It is also close to van de Vall's empirical findings. Looking through these projects it becomes clear that a distinction must be made between work which is strongly oriented towards fact-finding and then uses the outcome in the implementation phase, and the alternative approach, which puts the dominant stress on implementation. I will call the first *research action* and the second *action research*. This distinction becomes clear when we go back to the five modules and twelve methods described earlier. Both research action and action research fall mainly within module II (Building bridges between researcher and user) and module III (Researcher-client equality). Methods 6, 7 and to some extent 8, can be described as research action. The research emphasis need not diminish the intensity of the researcher's participation in implementation, but in method 9 and in 10 (which falls within the client-professional exploration module), the fact-finding research phase is severely restricted or left out altogether.

The more consultancy-oriented action research often relies on evidence from previous research and/or on the experience and judgement of the consultant. In many cases, the client faces a crisis or feels he has to make a rapid decision which precludes extensive fact-finding. In such a situation, the consultant may have no real choice. He is either content with writing a report including recommendations or insisting that he is involved in implementing the report.

Of course, the ideal type of distinction between research action and action research may become unclear in some cases (in method 8, for instance, in the schema) but the absence of this distinction in the literature has led to quite unnecessary shadow-boxing with indiscriminate attacks on imaginary targets. Research action at its best produces evidence that can be generalized beyond the experience of a single case (Heller, 1976).

One has to be aware that research findings, irrespective of the method used, may be an embarrassment to the host. This is demonstrated by Berry et al. in the case of the National Coal Board, and Eldridge in the case of the British Broadcasting Corporation. Lengyel's analysis is unlikely to appeal to Unesco, for the moment at least, and even Wilkins's remarkable success in many American states is most unlikely to produce a clamour among the legal profession in other countries to have such a research-based aid at their disposal. I shall come back to some of these issues in the final chapter which will attempt to reach a few conclusions based on available evidence.

Which is the best method?
During the last two decades, social science research has moved sharply towards a situational or contingency model, having abandoned the search for solutions which were thought to be applicable in all situations. Contingency research seeks to specify the conditions under which certain findings apply. Recommendations about how to reduce poverty, for instance, may be contingent on the prevailing rate of inflation and economic growth. Contingency models have become a mini-paradigm among the research fraternity, although most clients still cherish a preference for the simple universal solution. However, when it

comes to the researcher's own preference of method there is little evidence of a contingency approach. Researchers tend to prefer one method to all others, for instance a client-researcher equality model using an action-research method. I believe that evidence is building up to show that this option has indeed great strength and often leads to very satisfactory solutions. This is well demonstrated by Lévy-Leboyer's three examples, by the history of development in Scandinavian research described by Gustavsen, and Wilkins's account of legal sentencing procedures in the United States. Nevertheless, it can be a gross over-simplification to conclude that any one model is best under all circumstances. I will content myself by putting forward one argument against such a universal preference and some examples to illustrate its limitation.

The main limitation of depending on client-researcher equality or client-professional exploration models is their emphasis on *current* issues. Social science should also consider the future and has done much too little of this. For instance, research on the effect of the media on imitative behaviour should not wait for an increase in violence or political misgivings. Research on trade-union decision-making practices should not wait until there is a political demand for change; social cost research should precede redundancy crises; and research on the effect of participative industrial relations practices should not wait until the legislature appoints a commission to make major policy recommendations within less than twelve months (see the chapter by Brannen). Future-oriented research, however, is unlikely to attract much interest and even less finance from clients whose main preoccupation is — quite understandably — with the here-and-now.

There are other arguments in favour of an eclectic contingency model from which researchers can choose the approach most suitable to the subject they wish to develop.

If one looks at the most widely known and influential theories in the present century, it becomes obvious that they were produced by many starkly different approaches. Twentieth-century literature would be very different without the work of Sigmund Freud and his followers. Economics has not been the same since Keynes's 'General Theory' or Marx's '*Kapital*'. On a less elevated level, Weyman et al. show in their chapter that different social science terminologies have pervaded policy-making over a wide area and probably influenced policy thinking. In the field of management and organizational behaviour, the most extensively used concepts and 'buzz words' range from consensus decision-making (based on Likert's research) via McGregor's Theory X and Y and Maslow's hierarchy to motivational analysis (influenced by Herzberg and others). Some of these notions are now superseded by more refined findings but in their day they were the best that was on offer. Will more recent research have the same impact? In any case, the point I want to repeat is that the most utilized social science concepts derive from several of the twelve options described in the preceding paragraphs.

Policy can operate at several levels

Most contributions to this book are concerned with what can be called 'policy issues', but of course this is a fairly vague term and can operate on several levels. Many analysts reserve the term 'policy' for more or less integrated propositions, ideas or measures oriented towards action at the national, local government or community level. But the same process can operate at lower and in-between levels. An organization can have coherent ideas, propositions and preferences which are intended to act as guidelines for action. Finance, marketing and personnel departments can have policies and so can a profession, like medical practitioners.

If the hallmark of a policy is its relatively developed coherence and integration between diverse considerations, then there is plenty of scope for non-policy problems and non-policy decisions which could also receive help from research. Two of the three examples given by Wilkins (assessing the demand for war medals and hearing aids), and two cases from Lévy-Leboyer (telephone-box vandalism and choices of work schedules) are cases of socially important problems which do not necessarily require a policy-oriented treatment.

As with so many other distinctions in social science, the one between policy and more specific and isolated decision-making is one of degree, and the reader will find several examples of borderline cases (see also Bulmer 1978; 1982).

Policy covers, and attempts to integrate, several distinct areas of issues and preferences and often involves power clashes between interest groups. Therefore one might on a priori grounds expect that research would be less likely to influence action when it is related to policy-oriented problems than when it is concerned with non-policy problems. John Eldridge gives several examples of the difficulty of accepting and implementing findings which affect policy at national level. Research in this area is controversial and can often be criticized for the values which separate researcher and users.[4]

Overview

The arrangement of this book does not follow the usual academic schema. Although it starts with a short scene-setting theoretical piece by Ansoff, the rest of Part I is given over to a variety of specific cases of evidence of failure and of use or abuse of research. Part II covers a broader picture. It concentrates on accumulated experiences and theoretical contributions, though there is some overlap and several authors in Part I would probably claim that their methodological and theoretical work is at least as important as the specific evidence they cite. The chapters by Eldridge and Gill provide a bridge between Part I and Part II.

The justification for this arrangement is the belief that the reader who moves from specific examples to the more general evidence will be able to test whether a scenario based on theories and surveys of experience is sufficiently robust to warrant the conclusions that are drawn.

Setting the scene

Igor Ansoff's short chapter poses some deceptively simple questions, such as why we do social research and why funding bodies give grants. Are we guided by personal value preferences, by our own reservoir of skills, or by the convenient availability of statistical data? The moment the question is posed, it becomes obvious that for a large body of research, social relevance receives little attention. He goes on to argue that even where relevance is considered in the choice of subject — in leadership research for instance — false priorities which are out of touch with social reality lead investigators to put forward mistaken priorities. For instance, they have been known to stress consensual behaviour when this is no longer important in most organizations. For similar reasons, researchers often assume that most people want to maximize self-determination, when the real organizational problems revolve round the distribution of power. Methodological choices, he complains, follow a similar pattern of self-indulgence, leading to the use of static tools like factor analysis instead of methods that can capture the flow of dynamic change. Excessive complexity, the language barrier and a mistaken concentration on perfection and novelty instead of market needs, rounds up his sombre diagnosis from which he concludes that the world of potential research users does not 'beat its way to the new mousetrap'.

Examples

Part I strikes a fair balance between successes and failures of research as assessed by the authors. Some of the accounts in the early chapters deal with research on relatively well-defined problems, like Lévy-Leboyer's action project on alcoholism. The French agency charged with reducing alcoholism had come to believe that fear-arousing advertising is counter-productive, but this was based on a misinterpretation of previous findings. The action project was able to establish that alcohol habits could be changed when youngsters were exposed to fear-arousing information, as long as it also gave hope. Adoption and implementation was immediate and successful. Two of her other three examples also yielded clear results but in one case (telephone-box vandalism) the client refused to give up his original hypothesis, though incorrect, and therefore refused to implement the result.

On a more general level, Lévy-Leboyer argues that social science research is often too easily accepted and applied without adequate evidence. She believes that misuse of our theories and techniques is more serious than non-use.

Wilkins gives three examples of successful research implementation; two were market research type issues but required unusual methods of assessment. The third example shows how an important breakthrough in predicting recidivism grew out of a complex combination of perseverence and serendipity. In Britain the research was very successful in terms of impact on the literature and future research, but had no effect on policy. In the United States various circumstances allowed a similar approach to be extensively applied to help judges make better decisions.

Wilkins shows that success sometimes grows out of previous failures and in any case usually requires a careful build-up of antecedents. Even so the 'creative mix' often has to include luck and propitious timing.

Haveman asks the question whether social scientists and economists in particular respond to changes in public thinking and policy. He uses a major American social policy initiative called the 'War on Poverty', which received very considerable research funding, to examine this issue. He finds that the 'War on Poverty' programme had a substantial impact on the reorientation of research, particularly of economists who published in the more prestigious journals. The implication is that major national policy initiatives can be stimulated by deliberate funding priorities and this in turn presumably helps to initiate policy redesign.

Weyman et al.'s chapter also deals with national policy and research. It seems that German governments believe that when scientific findings are available, they should be used. Consequently, a number of major research programmes on utilization are supported and carefully scrutinized by government departments, but the results are uneven. Optimism about social science research reached a peak in the 1960s and then declined, although relatively heavy financial investment continues. One of the most extensive and prolonged German research programmes deals with the 'Humanization of Work' and is briefly described by Heller. It started in 1974, has been continued by successive governments of different political persuasions, and even in 1985 spent about DM100 million a year (about £30m or $46m at July 1986 values). However, it has attracted as much criticism as praise from practitioners as well as academics.

The chapter by Berry et al. is written by four academic teachers of accountancy and describes the complex problems facing an industry which has to make critical policy decisions about closures and redundancy. The authors were able to examine the accounts of the National Coal Board in Britain at a time when the closure decisions had led to the most extended and ferocious industrial relations dispute in Britain's twentieth-century strike history. The academic analysis was critical of the accountancy conventions used by the Coal Board for purposes of the public debate and in justification of certain pit closures. In an atmosphere heavily imbued with emotion and political considerations, such a research-based critique cannot be expected to produce immediate favourable consideration from the industry, but the methods used to attack the findings are well worth closer examination. In the long run the authors' technical arguments may well have an effect on accountancy theory and practice in public sector organizations.

A much more clear-cut negative picture emerges from Lengyel's forensic analysis of Unesco's mismanagement of research opportunities. There were many culprits: personalities, national value patterns, political in-fighting, ineptitude and structural inadequacies. Some of these shortcomings exist in all large-scale organizations, but Lengyel points to the major cause of missed opportunities as Unesco's failure to develop a distinctive area of competence in social science, and he explains what kind of policy would have served Unesco well. Unesco's weakness in this respect is not unique. There is much duplication and overlap in social science work within the family of United Nations agencies and most of their individual projects are grossly under-financed and consequently superficial.

The reasons for the low prestige and poor utilization of the social sciences are examined by several writers, including Gill. The fact that some of these issues (like the unintelligibility of the literature) have often been brought up before, strengthens rather than weakens the need for discovering the main causes for these alleged weaknesses. It is only then that remedial action becomes possible. If it is true that unnecessarily turgid language correlates with academic prestige, then the flight of potential research users into the arms of popularizers becomes understandable. Everything then depends on whether the popularizer has the ability and the inclination to use real evidence or spurious, glib generalizations. Unfortunately, the temptation to have a quick, easy answer for every problem often triumphs over the more painstaking responsible alternative. Several authors point their finger at this problem, but fail to provide an answer. Our authors are senior members of the institutions whose promotion policy provides the incentives that probably encourage the very behaviour they criticize. Do academics take note of their own theories and utilize their own evidence?

One could also ask whether social scientists choose their topics in relation to the merit of the problem or for some more self-serving priorities. Ansoff has provided his own sceptical answer based on extensive experience. Is research by accountants, organizational psychologists and members of business schools too heavily influenced by concern with higher-level employees?[5]

The concentration on managerial rather than employee problems in social science research agenda was one of the reasons which led to the 'Open Door Policy' initiative by the Social Science Research Council[6] and is briefly described by Gill. Potential users of research who lack financial resources (like trade unions) are encouraged to apply to the Research Council, who will appoint a qualified person to examine the feasibility of the idea. If possible the idea is converted into a research proposal which will then be judged on its merits and supported if funds are available. It is a potentially important innovation which has not always received as much support as it deserves.

An example of a controversial research topic (on behalf of a consumer without funds) is used by Eldridge to illustrate the twin problems of relevance and power in sociological research. Among the several examples he gives to illustrate his thesis, one casts the general television-viewing public in the role of consumer. Eldridge and his team asked whether, over a substantial period of time, there is balance or bias in the presentation of industrial relations issues. At the same time he comes out strongly against the belief that researchers and their topics can or should achieve 'ethical neutrality'.[7] The uneasy distinction between bias and lack of neutrality requires more attention than it has so far received.

Social scientists are generally in agreement that strict value neutrality is not feasible and many, like Eldridge, believe it is not desirable. At the same time, we are all aware that deliberate bias, as alleged in the television research, is undesirable. The ethical problems do not stop at this stage. Does an excess of everything become a vice? I will comment on this in the final chapter.

The last chapter in Part I gives a number of examples which remind us of the danger of becoming excessively committed to a 'cause' to the point where integrity is abandoned for the blind pursuit of an obsession. Two examples show what happens when elitism becomes an obsession in the minds of scientists who want to prove the superiority of one class of humanity over others. One researcher doctored intelligence test results, the other falsified the data of skull dimensions.

Heller's chapter briefly describes five projects and illustrates the difficulty of a straight evaluation of success or failure in research utilization, at least in the case of four of the projects. The fifth is an interesting example because it started off with the avowed intention of making policy relevance and follow-through to implementation its main preoccupation. Furthermore, it is one of the few projects sponsored and financed by business and organized outside academe. Regrettably it failed, partly because of the somewhat uneven quality of the data, partly because most of the available funds were distributed without a clear plan and on the basis of ad hoc consultancy rates, but above all because the commercial sponsors were more concerned with their own publicity than with the relevance of the research outcome.

Experience and theory

Part II contributions cover too large an area of experience and theory to be summarized adequately here and I will content myself with a number of illustrations which will also include a few of the theoretical positions from chapters in Part I.

Many of the Part II contributors, as well as several of the early chapter writers, stress the great and at times decisive importance of the party political dimension in policy-relevant social science research.

Haveman makes this point in his analysis of the American 'War on Poverty' programme. Weymann et al. show that in Germany, in spite of a minimum measure of continuity between different governments, the intensity of investment and utilization fluctuated with the political persuasion of the party in power. Brannen and Cherns both show that changes in the political climate affect sponsorship of social research in Britain and give several specific instances. In one notorious case, a Minister of the Crown had commissioned a piece of research on an important social issue. The outcome clashed with the Minister's own value perspective and this episode almost had disastrous consequences for the Social Science Research Council, which had to endure an extensive and many say punitive inquiry that might have led to its demise.

Brannen also raises the issue of national differences in attitudes towards research and utilization by comparing Swedish enthusiasm with Britain's scepticism in relation to a specific policy issue. Cross-national comparisons on utilization should receive much more research attention (see, for instance, Nowotny and Lambiri-Dimaki, 1985).

Several writers in Part II produce taxonomies or schemas. The most detailed, and also the most complex one, is presented by van de Vall, who distinguishes between external and internal investigators and between research issues arising from inside or outside the organization. Using a sample of 120 research projects, he concludes that these dimensions have empirical value. The distinction of internal versus external researchers is useful, principally because internal workers have a much higher frequency of communication with the client both during and after the presentation of the results, and because they are much more active in helping the client translate research data into feasible policy decisions.

The positive results achieved by internal organization researchers in the Netherlands' sample coincides with Weymann et al.'s finding that in

Germany academic social scientists are losing out against independent research institutes and in-house units. Are differences in methodology responsible for this trend? Van de Vall shows that time and effort spent on methodological refinement is less effective than using frequent feedback communication and assisting with implementation.

Notes

1. 'Action research' is a term given to a variety of practices which deliberately involve the researcher in implementation of results. Action research and its variant 'research action' will be described later.

2. In 1975 the British government set up a group within the Department of Employment called the Work Research Unit. The name was probably influenced by the very successful Oslo Work Research Institute, a pioneer in European organization research. The British unit was always an under-financed reflection of the Oslo Institute but its birth was seen as a positive step. *The Times* newspaper (12 October 1975) praised the initiative but claimed that the word 'research' in its title would be a severe handicap to it. The article was written by an experienced industrial journalist who assumed, correctly I believe, that in the mind of the average business person the term 'research' has 'academic undertones which are apt to repel the down-to-earth industrialist'. (Note the implied deprecation in the word 'undertones' rather than 'overtones'.) Nobody can tell how successful the unit might have been if it had used the word 'inquiry' or 'exploration' in its title. In 1985 the Department of Employment considered privatizing the unit, but eventually handed it over to a semi-autonomous body, ACAS (Advisory, Conciliation and Arbitration Service).

3. In most cases, including those covered in this book, the client is the government or one of its departments, or the management of an organization. It is rarely a trade union, although in some Scandinavian countries, unions are given funds to engage consultants on their behalf and the Stockholm Work Research Centre specializes in investigations on behalf of problems identified by Swedish unions. The consumer of goods and services is almost never in a position to commission research or even to have an influence over projects, the outcome of which affects consumers.

The Economic and Social Research Council in Britain has a scheme called 'The Open Door' which could widen the range of research beneficiaries (see chapter by Gill).

4. The research by Eldridge and his Scottish media team has been criticized for its values and methodology. I will refer to the important value issue again in the final chapter.

5. See Hopwood's (1985) analysis for the accountancy profession and Heller's (1986) for organizational psychology.

6. Now called the Economic and Social Research Council.

7. On Eldridge, see note 4 above.

References

Argyris, Chris (1970) *Intervention Theory and Method: A Behavioral Science View.* Reading, Mass.: Addison-Wesley.
Argyris, Chris (1976) 'Problems and New Directions in Industrial Psychology', in M. D. Dunnette (ed.), *Handbook of Industrial and Organizational Psychology.* Chicago: Rand, McNally.

Argyris, Chris (1980) *Inner Contradictions of Rigorous Research.* London: Academic Press.

Bulmer, Martin (ed.) (1978) *Social Policy Research.* London: Macmillan.

Bulmer, Martin (1982) *The Use of Social Research: Social Investigation in Public Policy Making.* London: Allen and Unwin.

Clark, A.W. (ed.) (1976) *Experimenting with Organizational Life: The Action Research Approach.* New York: Plenum Press.

Heller, F.A. (1976) 'Group Feed-back Analysis as a Method of Action Research', in A.W. Clark (ed.), *Experimenting with Organizational Life: The Action Research Approach.* New York: Plenum Press.

Heller, F.A. (1986) 'At the Crossroads: An Examination of Content and Values of Organization Psychology'. Invited address, West European Conference on the Psychology of Work and Organization, Aachen, Germany, April 1985. Amsterdam: Elsevier.

Hopwood, Anthony (1985) 'The Tale of a Committee that Never Reported: Disagreements on Intertwining Accounting with the Social', *Accounting, Organization and Society,*10:361–77.

Nowotny, Helga and Jane Lambiri-Dimaki (eds) (1985) *The Difficult Dialogue between Producers and Users of Social Science.* Vienna: Eurosocial.

Rapoport, R..N. (1970) 'Three Dilemmas in Action Research', *Human Relations,* 23:499–513.

Sanford, Nevitt (1976) 'Whatever Happened to Action Research?', in A.W. Clark (ed.), *Experimenting with Organizational Life: The Action Research Approach.* New York: Plenum Press.

I

EVIDENCE

1

The pathology of applied research in social science

H. Igor Ansoff

In making brief comments about research utilization it would have been equally easy to take a normative or a descriptive approach. Since my comparative advantage comes from having spent many years as a buyer as well as a seller of social and management science research, and since the record of successes in the field is far from brilliant, I felt that I might contribute my experience by dealing broadly with pathology, rather than narrowly with a prescription.

On the use of social science research

To start with, I want to recognize that a substantial body of social science research is not applied for the simple reason that it is not intended to be applicable. Unlike the natural scientists, social scientists have paid relatively little attention to the distinctions between applicable and inapplicable research. I shall therefore borrow from the natural sciences a taxonomy which has served it well for recognizing and maintaining such distinctions. There are four categories:

1. *Basic research* which seeks to increase the general understanding of reality
2. *Applied research* which advances general propositions applicable to a class of practical problems
3. *Technology* which develops procedures for resolving particular classes of problems
4. *Problem-solving* which resolves a particular practical problem.

I would like to suggest that, in the absence of such taxonomy, researchers in social sciences are frequently unclear about the level on which they are working. This leads to three kinds of confusion:

1. Much work that is being done is treated as if it were basic research, whereas the narrowness of the questions asked precludes the results from being an interesting contribution to fundamental knowledge
2. When engaged in applied research, the researchers are frequently unclear either about the particular class of practical problems they are trying to treat, or about the social importance of the problems they are treating
3. Very little attention is paid in social sciences to doing 'research on research' or what we pejoratively call 'secondary research'. Rather than seek to interpret for practical purposes the basic insights produced by previous researchers, we either seek insights alternative to theirs, or seek to enlarge the basic insights developed by them.

All this can be summed up by saying that in starting a piece of research we typically fail to ask ourselves, or our doctoral students, two simple questions:

1. Will the proposed project contribute significantly to a theoretical understanding of reality?
2. And if not, what class of practical problems will it help solve and how important is that class in the world of the people to whom the solution is addressed?

If we don't ask these questions, what criteria *do* we use in applying for grants, or approving doctoral research proposals? My experience is that the following four criteria are dominant:

1. The personal values and the professional interests of the researcher
2. The applicability of the personal skills of the researcher to the proposed topic
3. The values and the accepted methodologies of the research community to which the researcher belongs
4. The availability of data which will permit a statistical validation of results.

In yesterday's world, when research costs were modest and impact of research on human lives mostly beneficial, it was accepted that the ethic of research was the business of the researchers and that this ethic was pursuit of knowledge for its own sake. But, as Alfred North Whitehead pointed out some thirty years ago, even within the scientific community this ethic was challengeable because, by the middle of the twentieth century, it began to breed scientific orthodoxy and conservatism.

In today's world of 'big science', research is costly and no longer has a uniformly beneficial impact. The ethic of basic research for the sake of research is being challenged on the basis of both economics and social relevance. On the level of applied research there is the additional challenge of the utility of projects which consume large amounts of money but produce no visible benefits for society.

There are numerous examples of research which is out of touch with social priorities. Thus, much of the recent research on leadership has been on consensual behaviour, which is appropriate to conditions of a stable culture in a uni-ideological organization. But even a casual look outside the windows of academia would show that a majority of organizations are going through a cultural shock and at the same time are becoming ideologically polarized.

Much of the research on organizational behaviour is still being done in the grand old tradition of static multiple correlation and factor analysis, while the burning problems are dynamic change and a redefinition of the *raison d'être* of organizations in the post-industrial society. A majority of research on participation is done in the psycho-sociological tradition which assumes that all individuals share a common ideology and seek a maximum of self-determination in decision-making, whereas the practical problem is how to deal with the very pressing phenomena of ideological polarization and redistribution of power. Perhaps the most dramatic example of the gap between researchers' choices and society's needs is in the fact that most research is being done from the vantage point of single disciplines, whereas the key social problems are multi-disciplinary.

Thus, I would like to suggest that the second basic difficulty with application of social science research is that we select our research projects according to our scientific value systems and not according to societal relevance and importance of the problems.

The last issue that I would like to consider is the way in which research results that are relevant to social problems find their way into organizations. Here we must distinguish between two customer populations. One is organizations, such as the business firms, in which there is a group or groups with enough power to serve as a conduit between the research findings and the organization. These are the managers who are in a position to decide what research results will be used and to disseminate the results throughout the organization.

The other customer population is organizations in which power is distributed and which are ideologically polarized. In such organizations, such as the body politic, there is no clearly visible powerful target group to which one can 'sell' the results of the research. Application of research in such distributed power organizations presents special and more difficult problems than in the purposive, ideologically uniform organizations. Because of limitations of time I shall deal only with dissemination of research in the latter organizations. For such organizations we can regard the problem as one of *marketing* our results to a potential and well-identified customer.

For an insight into the problem we might take advantage of the experience of management scientists who have been concerned for some thirty years with the very low market penetration of the great profusion of mathematical decision models. The failure to make a market penetration is more serious for the management scientists than it is for the social scientists, because the former frankly and admittedly work on the last two levels of knowledge enlargement: technology and problem-solving. Therefore, it is more difficult for them to salvage their pride, conscience and, indeed, their jobs by pretending that they are in basic research business which need not be directly applicable.

As mentioned above, the experince of the management scientists has not been a happy one and the major reason, in my opinion, is that they generally assume that virtue attracts its own rewards; or to use an American idiom, that the world will beat its way to a new mousetrap. As a result, management scientists have been living with what in business we call a *production mentality.* They have focused on the perfection of their products, without much attention being paid to the needs of the market, or any attempt made to market the product.

There is enough human experience as well as research (such as technology diffusion studies, for example) to prove conclusively that the world does not wait with bated breath for acts of innovation. Very few new products sell themselves, even if they present great advantages to potential customers. I think the experience of management scientists is increasingly being duplicated by social scientists: the results do not 'sell' but we make precious little effort to market them.

Let us review briefly why it is that the results do not sell. One reason which was perceived early by management scientists was the incomprehensibility of the offer to the customer. Some years ago, C. West Churchman diagnosed this as a communication gap between the scientist and his client. Churchman suggested that they should learn to speak each other's language. There were two difficulties in this prescription. First, as in any commercial situation, there is usually no incentive for the client to learn the seller's language. This placed the burden of learning on the scientist and I regret to say that both social and management scientists have not risen to the occasion. Instead of learning the practitioner's languages they prefer enriching the highly specialized jargon of their own professions.

The second difficulty with Churchman's prescription, which we have learned to appreciate recently, is that learning the saleable language is not enough. To be saleable, an offering must appear practical, attractive and valid withn the culture of the customer (some would say within his 'model of reality'). And the culture of practising managers is typically distinctive and different from that of the scientist. Typically, and almost definitionally, science offers products which in the culture of the client are both incomprehensible and too advanced technologically to be acceptable.

Another difficulty in marketing research is that, as we have already mentioned, the products frequently have a low potential interest to the client. For example, the professional criteria of social scientists have in the past typically led them to focus on the *average* behaviour of managers and organizations. The reasons are clear: the average is easier to observe and offers samples of data which lend themselves to statistical analysis.

What most scientists do not seem to realize is that: (1) an *average* manager is a very unlikely customer for the research results, unless they serve to confirm his security in mediocrity; (2) the manager who is potentially the 'hottest' customer is the aggressive one who has very little interest in average behaviour. What he wants is useful research on the extremes: first on behaviour which leads to success and second on behaviour which will help him to avoid failure.

Thus the priorities of the customer population are (1) success, (2) failure and (3) mediocrity as a poor third. The research priorities are in precisely the reverse order!

I would like to summarize briefly the main points I have been trying to make.

The first is that in doing social science research we typically do not pause long enough to ask ourselves what type of research we are attempting and what is its potential applicability.

Second, we do not do enough secondary research which attempts to convert basic research into applied research and technology.

Third, we select research topics according to our introverted professional criteria and not according to the needs of our potential customers.

Fourth, we take very little trouble to market our research to potential customers.

It seems to me that these critical remarks are sufficiently operational to suggest immediate directions for improvements in the utilization of social science research.

2

Applying psychology or applied psychology

Claude Lévy-Leboyer

Since Lewin said that there is 'nothing so practical as a good theory', psychologists have questioned the truthfulness of his statement, wondering how many of their theoretical outcomes are actually practical and how many are practised. Most of the time when approaching such an issue, psychologists do not boast; on the contrary, they are prone to lament and even to feel guilty. And the old discussion among academic psychologists on the difference between 'pure' and 'applied' research, and which should receive priority, still continues.

Explanations given by the psychologists themselves for this dissatisfaction about the application of social sciences can be summarized under two headings. The first one could be labelled 'the two cultures hypothesis'. Values and needs motivating the researcher are said to be strongly different from values and needs experienced in the field by managers, planners and policy-making people. Many comments exist on this gap: negative results have no value to the practitioner but represent useful information for the researcher; time is needed for good research when reality cannot wait, etcetera. A second explanation is found in the difficult role assigned to the social scientist who is asked to say what is the 'right' way to behave. Either he has to accept the role of a 'social superman', or to express candidly his doubts and problems about psychological and social issues, his need to experiment and check, thus risking the loss of some of his influence, specially when dealing with social, ethical and accepted behavioural norms.

When put that way, the application of social sciences looks hopeless and, even worse, the stage is set for the development of conflict. From my own experience of fifteen years voluntarily devoted to 'applied research', I am convinced that this analysis lacks a sound foundation and that the general issue of the applicability of social sciences is wrongly phrased. Therefore, I shall try to show that (1) social sciences, far from being non-applied, are too easily, and too loosely applied; (2) their application follows the well-known rules governing change agents — which means that social scientists themselves do not apply their own knowledge and (3) the real problem is to know what, as social scientists, we learn from the application of social sciences. In other words, is the application of social sciences a mere application of research results developed elsewhere, or a research activity in itself? To put it more bluntly, is there such a thing as applied research in social sciences?

Social sciences are too easily applied

Not long ago, every French occupational psychologist meeting for the first time with a manager would see him (before coming to the main objective of their meeting) open his drawer, bring out a translation of Herzberg's *Work and the Nature of Man* and ask, 'Have you read Herzberg?' Obviously the manager had, and liked it — especially the idea that you can motivate workers with something other than money.

New ideas which are easy to grasp and which answer the important problems of the day are quickly understood and applied; in fact, the simpler they are, the more attractive they look. New techniques are no less tempting. In both cases, the attraction of novelty is rarely moderated by checking proofs or scrutinizing available evidence. Indeed, T-groups, sensitivity training, programmed learning, quality circles, job enrichment, autonomous groups, uncoercive education, behavioural therapy — all were more easily accepted than power looms in the textile industry and robotization in automobile plants. Users of new theories and new techniques do not bother about generalizability, intercultural differences or statistical significance. They usually take a theory for granted as soon as it is available in print. And new techniques are accepted as being efficient because they are used elsewhere. Even worse, psychological tools, once adopted, resist evidence from well-founded refutation. From this point of view, the history of tests used in industry is an interesting one. In spite of Ghiselli's (1966) well-documented survey on their weak and erratic validities, these tests continued to be used for selection procedures, as test printers' sales figures can bear witness. Later, when statistical progress and data-processing enabled psychologists to take account of a variety of sophistications (like sampling errors, size of sample as well as sample criteria, and lack of reliability), meta-analysis showed congnitive tests to have substantial validity for most occupational activities: thus, somewhat unscrupulous practitioners were proved right! (Schmidt et al., 1981)

In a more general way, one cannot but feel impressed when watching how new concepts introduced by social scientists in the last half-century gained acceptance and are now widely used in all kinds of settings. Even though psychoanalysis as a therapy is still strongly questioned, the importance of the unconscious, the psychological meaning of slips of the tongue and forgotten behaviour are commonly accepted; social climate, socio-technical systems, needs hierarchy, brainstorming and group creativity belong to the lay vocabulary — while social scientists are unanimous in contesting group superiority in creativity, in condemning as unproven Maslow's hierarchical model as well as Herzberg's two-factors theory of satisfaction, and in admitting that they do not know exactly what is meant by 'social climate'.

This is why, far from lamenting the poor use made of the social sciences, we should stand as sentries at the door of our ideas and techniques and warn the users on the risks of applying them without proper care and adequate skill. Let me quote a recent example where the negotiation between my research team and potential users dealt precisely with the unexpected consequences of new techniques. Two years ago, the French agency in charge of vocational and educational information among secondary school students asked us to build a self-corrected general evaluation test so as to help fifteen-year-old adolescents in evaluating their aptitudes and interests. Given time and money, we felt able to build such a test, and even to put it on a computer for easy accessibility and administration. However, we did not discuss the feasibility of the project or its cost. We tried to attract the attention of the agency staff to its unknown consequences: what happens when test results are given to an adolescent without a psychologist available to help him (or her) understand the data and cope with them? Therefore, we proposed (and eventually developed) a research on how the self-concept changes when a subject receives test results (Lévy-Leboyer, 1984). This is a case when applying social sciences also meant helping the potential user to evaluate the consequences and the risks associated with a new technique and reduce the practitioner's spontaneous enthusiasm for computer-assisted testing.

Technically feasible applications are not always sound applications. To use Miller's (1969) words (while not agreeing with his position), social science knowledge, and its apparently easily used tools, should not be 'given away' freely with the implicit assumption that they will always contribute to human welfare. We should be more concerned about the misuse of our theories and techniques than about their non-use.

Social sciences as change agents
It is true that social sciences often gain acceptance too easily. At the same time it is also true that specific research results are not applied or, to say the same thing more frankly, are applied less than some of us wish them to be. I will try here to describe several examples where a team of psychologists, researchers in a university department, were called in as external consultants and asked to obtain answers to specific problems. These problems were all within the field of social psychology, in work or environmental settings. I hope to show through these examples that

technical advice can be easily accepted but that role and value changes can and do block the application of social science results, even if these results appear to be of little importance at first sight.

My first example is a case of a very easy and efficient application. Some years ago, the French agency dealing with alcoholism (*Haut Comité d'Etudes et d'Information sur l'Alcoolisme*) came to us with a very specific question. A large part of its budget was used on giving information on the dangers of alcoholism, mainly through television. Its advertising organization (perhaps having read Janis, 1967), suggested that fear-arousing information should be avoided. The agency staff felt uncertain about this policy and wanted to check with social scientists. We were able to perform a thorough survey of the literature and, afterwards, a field experiment (see Lévy-Leboyer and Moser, 1977a; 1977b). The research results were clear-cut and convinced the sponsors of the need to modify their advertising policy: attitudes to both alcohol and drinking habits were capable of being changed only when youngsters were exposed to fear-arousing information. This confirmed our hypothesis, as Janis showed that fear-arousing information is counterproductive only when there is no alternative to the fear-arousing event. In the following month, the contents of the television sequences were entirely redesigned in line with the conclusions of our research. This is a case where a specific question, already framed within a body of psychological knowledge, was given a clear answer, directly understood by the 'client' and immediately applied in their decision-making.

The second example is at the other end of the easy–difficult dimension. Five years ago, my research team became interested in vandalism. We wanted to study the kind of behaviour for which it was difficult to see an obvious motivation. This time, we were not contacted by a public agency. On the contrary, looking for experimental fields, we contacted various administrations (education, transport, urban administrations etc.) where vandalism is known to exist. Among them, the Post Office Ministry which spends a lot of money repairing vandalized telephone booths showed interest and, after some negotiation, agreed to sponsor a field research on the vandals' motivation. We started by examining the available statistics on telephone vandalism and tried to build up a picture of the variance and possible variance factors of telephone booth vandalism. While doing this, we discovered two facts: first, there was a great deal of ambiguity in the definition of vandalism. In the statistics it was usually added to the normal wear and tear of equipment, as well as to breaking of equipment in order to steal money. Secondly, our problem and the Post Office's problems were basically different: we wanted to understand the vandals' motivation as a good example of motivation to destroy without any obvious reward; they wanted to find ways to protect phones against destruction whatever its motives.

The research project developed with difficulty because of this mis-understanding. Through the statistics on vandalism, we discovered that the larger the number of users of the telphone booth, the higher were its chances of being vandalized. This appeared to be an observation without psychological meaning. However, discussion with Post Office technicians led to a better understanding of the situation. When the coin-receiving box is full, the phone can no longer function. In the very busy booths, and in spite of regularly planned money collections, this happens quite often. Could the frustration of not being able to make a phone call be an explanation for aggressiveness towards the telephone? It would take too long to describe here our systematic observations of behaviour when the telephone is out of order (see Moser, 1984). Results can be summarized in two sentences: first, people who bang the phone and violently hit its various parts are ordinary angry customers, not the young unsocial delinquents. Secondly, the frustration due to not being able to make a call, plus the fact that banging the telephone may indeed restore its use, explains a large percentage of this vandalism.

We then proposed a research action. Various solutions aimed at giving the customer more control over the situation were discussed in a working session with researchers and staff from the Public Telephone Department. It was decided to redesign the poster placed in the booth so as to give clear information on alternatives in case of a non-func-tioning telephone. A map of the street was included, showing where to find another phone, and how to go to the nearest post office, with instructions on how to get the lost money back.

This poster was placed in a carefully chosen sample of booths where the phone was put out of order for a whole day. We used the same observation grid as previously. Results were convincing: people read the poster, spent less time in the booth and stopped hitting the telephone. Instead they looked for another telephone booth. The research con-clusions were presented during a final working session, to the satis-faction of the participants and written up in a report for further use. Eventually an article was accepted in a scientific journal (Moser and Lévy-Leboyer, forthcoming). But no application whatsoever followed. Why? Most probably because the adoption of a new policy in the infor-mation given to the customer would have implied a deep change in atti-tudes concerning the relationship between the post office administration and their customers. They were on the 'right' side; they were officials who offered a service to their compatriots. They were looking for negative factors like lunatic, socially deviant behaviour and people guilty of malignant aggressiveness towards public property. Our analysis clearly reversed the roles. Here was a decent customer, a housewife maybe coming from the market, a businessman on a journey, wanting to make a phone call. Placed in front of inadequate equipment and left with no possibility either of complaining or of carrying out his or her intention of communicating by phone, they had a right to be angry. It is interesting to compare this research with the alcoholism project. In the first case, we acted only as technical advisers; on the contrary in the telephone case, we acted as change agents. We could not foresee at the beginning of the research work that it would develop that way and therefore no proper action was taken to prepare our clients for a different role. This seems to be the reason why our findings were not used.

A third example illustrates a problem which lies between the two preceding cases. It is a case where technical skill was asked for and used but where we had to show that behaviour determinants are too complex to be expressed in simple rules easy to apply. The starting point appears to be very similar to the one we met when looking at the alcoholism problem. The head manager of a plant belonging to one of the French automobile corporations wished to get a better use of some heavy investment. Therefore he wished to establish a schedule which would cover 100 per cent of the time, i.e. night and day, week days and weekends. This project was distrusted by the *Comité d'entreprise* (Works Committee) which hesitated because it did not know what the workers' attitudes would be. Such full-time use of equipment does exist in other work settings, such as hospitals, highway tolls, etc, but no worker belonging to that plant had ever experienced an 'abnormal timetable' such as working three days (Friday, Saturday, Sunday) and not the rest of the week. Actually, nobody knew what the workers' reactions might be. This would not have been important if only one or two possibilities existed for the new timetables. The reality was different. The personnel department of the plant was able to propose fifty schemes, according to the length of each working day, the different shifts, the number of Saturdays and Sundays being work days, the allocation of rest days, etc. Each scheme fulfilled the aim of the plant manager — i.e. full use of the equipment — but one had to be chosen and properly organized. Besides, the personnel department needed to know for which scheme enough volunteers would be found on the plant, in order, if possible, not to hire new manpower.

What kind of information was required? First, which timetables would attract enough volunteers? Second, who was attracted by what? i.e. rules to predict which type of timetable would be popular among different categories of workers, such as those living near or far away; bachelors or married; with babies or schoolchildren, or grown-up children; with a working or non-working wife.

Before we came, both the manager and the unions, through their newsletters, tried to elicit some reactions, without any results — except a workers' motion saying that they would agree with a modification of their present timetables only if made on a voluntary basis. We agreed to organize a survey, because it represented an exceptional opportunity to test the expectancy-valence model of decision-making. Our plan was to build an interview guideline exploring carefully all the consequences of various unusual working time schedules and the valence of these consequences. The scheme was explained to the staff first, to the Works Committee afterwards. Conditions protecting anonymity were strictly defined; plans were established in order to get a list of respondents, chosen by computer so as to have a sample representative by age, seniority, qualification and home/work distance. The results of 254 interviews gave us a wealth of data to test the expectancy-value model (Lévy-Leboyer, 1983) as well as a clear idea of the timetables acceptable to a sufficient number of workers, and those which would never be acceptable.

This information was given to the plant staff during a one-day working session where not only the results but also the experimental procedure were examined and discussed. Application followed immediately and successfully. This means that the plant management were able to choose a time schedule which fitted both their needs and the workers' expected preferences. They offered this new timetable to potential volunteers and got more volunteers than needed. Therefore, one can say the validation of our predictions resulted from the application itself. This was not the case with the first example, where application also followed the presentation of research results.

It is interesting to mention that our results did not yield a set of rules linking demographic characteristics (age, civil status, qualification, residence) and time schedules preferences. As we expected, every worker surveyed had a personal environment justifying an individual set of consequences and a subjective evaluation of their valences, not explained by the objective characteristics of what can be called life-space. No rule could be provided for the plant staff to predict the evolution of preferences among manpower. As we warned our clients before starting that clear demographic rules would probably not exist, we felt that our study achieved its end. Still convinced that workers' preferences have to be governed by the objective characteristics of their life situation, they reprocessed our data, with no success. But at a final meeting between researchers and staff, it was clear that, on this point, we were seen as having failed to establish basic or universal rules of guidance.

Can we say that in this case the results produced by the social scientists were applied? Yes and no. Yes, in so far as we gave technical information which was used to good effect. No, in so far as we were unable to convince the staff that preferences and choices related to work conditions are not automatic consequences of the objective characteristics of individuals. We drew the client's attention to the following four significant circumstances:

1. The importance of the workers' initial stance about their freedom of choice
2. The fact that, at the beginning of the survey, a one-day strike was organized by the workers to show their determination
3. The peculiar conditions of this short strike with work interrupted everywhere except in the office where psychologists were conducting the interviews
4. The fact that the workers invited to interviews kept coming strictly on time.

In spite of this evidence the staff conception of workers' motivation remained very limited, with no room for the general idea of individual hierarchies of value. This is obviously an example where being an efficient change agent would have taken more time and needed a different approach.

I have another example I want to describe and comment on. In this case no immediate application could be foreseen, taking into account the very nature of the results. The question dealt with noise annoyance. Understanding of its meaning is important for two different reasons. First, when people living or working somewhere express strongly their annoyance about uncontrollable noise, there is a socio-environmental problem. The community has to take a position and, if necessary, to take proper action. Secondly, measuring noise is very difficult because noise is not a pure sound and is therefore physically complex, because it varies from one minute to another, and because it may be very different at two places not far from one another. Regulations cannot easily be expressed in terms of limited noise, and limited annoyance would be a good substitute. Moreover, several 'units' of noise exist, with weighting of the different components of noise, in time and in frequencies. Which one is the best? Maybe the one which correlates best with annoyance. Understanding the meaning of noise annoyance could then open new possibilities in regulations and in methodology. However, the problem raised by noise annoyance evaluation is not simple. The scatter and variance of annoyance expressed in the same place or in the same workshop is very high; and there are always, everywhere, some people complaining strongly as well as some people not at all annoyed by noise. Therefore, acoustics experts hope that psychologists would be able to find psychological traits to explain the variance of expressed annoyance.

Such a question can be summarized in one short sentence but we needed a whole page to explain its meaning and, on the way, one loses the idea for a possible application. We can try to analyse the alternatives. Let us suppose that we can identify psychological factors determining a sensitiveness to noise, although this does not seem to be possible. How could such a discovery be applied? Should planners test citizens and give those who are not-sensitive noisy dwellings? Should the sensitive be allocated to quiet houses, or submitted to some kind of behaviour therapy? All these possible applications are absurd. Suppose, on the contrary, that noise annoyance is partly linked (which seems to be the case) to an evaluation of the general quality of the environment, and to comparisons between expected and actual noise, and between previous and present experience of noise. This would explain some of the variance but not help the use of noise annoyance statistics by policy-makers. Application in that case means helping to find other sources of information, such as the 'objective' effects of noise (on behaviour, health, sleep, etc.) to evaluate the harm caused by noise. This is an interesting situation for the researcher. Usually it is said that null hypo-thesis is of no interest to the practitioner. This is not true here. If no psychological traits can contribute to the variance of noise annoyance, this information is valuable for the policy-makers, maybe even more than would be the proof of a significant contribution, since this would raise ethical problems in application.

To summarize, technical pieces of information, answering very specific questions without any need to reformulate them, are easily accepted and used. But the situation is very different when the social science contribution means a change in policy, or in basic attitudes within the client group or organization. Defence mechanisms are activated and take several possible forms, from totally ignoring the available evidence to questioning its scientific quality or objectivity, or else, reorganizing the whole situation so that the problem itself loses its topicality. This analysis is not inconsistent with our first proposition (social sciences are too easily applied). When a 'social innovation' is available and fits with the organization culture, it will be too quickly and easily accepted and used. This is why we learn about a culture or a social system by looking at the innovations it accepts or rejects.

Applying psychology or applied psychology?
What has been said in the preceding pages about the difficulties met by change agents could be observed as well for other fields of knowledge when technical or scientifical progress threatens an existing network of power influence and upsets a well-established division of roles. How-ever, the issues raised by the application of social sciences have a peculiarity which could be due to the assumed gap between laboratory findings and field applications. When we question the utilization of the knowledge built up by the social sciences, we implicitly suppose that there are two quite distinct activities, one which is devoted to developing this knowledge, and which takes place in academic environ-

ments and in laboratories, i.e. in 'clean', well-controlled and unprejudiced settings. The second is devoted only to applying what has been found elsewhere. This dichotomy between scientific innovation and passive application could be rooted in the desire of the social sciences to prove that they belong to the scientific community, so as to gain the prestige associated with 'pure' science and non-profit activity. Supporters of this view are often found in academic circles (universities and public research agencies) where being seen as truly 'scientific' gives access to institutional support and money. It therefore pays to claim that one has nothing to do with usefulness, efficiency or short-term economic value.

For all those whose objective is not to apply previously acquired knowledge, but to try and be useful with the conceptual and technical skills they are able to master, the reality is quite different (Lévy-Leboyer, 1978). There are three reasons for this.

First, there is no routine for social science application, not only because every problem is unique and cannot be solved by a rule of thumb, but rather because there are no general rules, only 'contingency' observations. Let's be more specific using a well-known example. Psychologists believed for a long time that some people had a gift for authority and behaved in a way which aroused obedience, whatever the situation and the societal environment. Numerous researches, developed in actual organizations and not in artificial situations built inside the laboratory, showed that reality is more complex. Actual efficient leader behaviour is found to vary with the situational characteristics and especially with the task content, the leader's power and the organizational structure. In the same way, environmental pressure may or may not be a cause of stress, according to cultural traditions and family values. Worker participation increases, decreases, or does not affect performance according to workers' values and expectations, etc. This is why no practitioner in social sciences can describe a 'good' way to practise leadership, a 'good' organizational structure, and an invariably efficient way to communicate.

Second, the situations we have to cope with in real life are always complex. We have, long ago, given up the hope of reducing the existing order to obtain simpler elements which could be studied independently, or to which previously acquired theoretical knowledge could be applied. Why is this so? Because all the elements of the social situation are linked together in a 'systemic' way. Which means that there is a network of complex relationships between all the components making up the situation, to a point that every social situation has to be captured as a whole and not as an addition of isolated elements. It is impossible, for example, to predict a worker's potential only on the basis of test scores: we must also have information on his experience, academic achievement, family background, and so on. When faced with a child who cannot learn how to read, it is not enough to find out about his skills in reading requisites, we must also know if he wishes to read, what are his relationships with adults, and what in his social class it means to read fluently.

Third, as laboratory experiments are developed to a short time schedule, they cannot take into account human plasticity. When social scientists are free to observe real situations in a scientific way, the level of plasticity they are able to discover is always amazing. The mere fact of acting a role has long-term effects on any individual; self-concepts develop through feedback obtained from others in social situations; learned helplessness deeply affects future behaviour.

These three features of social science application — uniqueness of the situation, systemic quality of its components, human plasticity — help us to understand why social scientists working on applied problems feel more and more that social sciences do develop original theoretical models, concepts and techniques through the experience of application itself. For a long time, social reality looked too complex for us to process the data we could gather in field experiments. Since computer technology has increased tremendously the amount of data we are able to deal with, applied social sciences represent a domain in which we should expect new developments to be born out of 'utilization'. These developments overtake the innovation potential of laboratory research and make the mere issue of research utilization obsolete.

References

Ghiselli, E. E. (1966) *The Validity of Occupational Aptitude Tests.* New York: John Wiley.

Janis, I. L. (1967) 'Effects of Fear-arousal on Attitude Change: Recent Developments in Theory and Experimental Research', in L. Berkowitz (ed.), *Advances in Experimental Psychology,* Vol. 3. London: Academic Press .

Lévy-Leboyer, C. (1983) *Le choix des horaires.* Paris: Éditions du CNRS.

Lévy-Leboyer, C. (1978) 'Psychologie appliquée ou application de la psychologie?', *Revue Internationale de Psychologie Appliquée,* 28 (2): 81–6.

Lévy-Leboyer, C. (1984) 'Maturité vocationnelle, self-concept et tests I — Attitudes et projets', *Revue de Psychologie Appliquée,* 34 (3): 215–28; and 'II — Resultats aux tests et self-concept', *Revue de Psychologie Appliquée,* 34 (4) 305–322.

Lévy-Leboyer, C. and G. Moser (1977a) 'La peur est-elle un bon moyen pour modifier les attitudes et les comportements?', *Année Psychologique,* 77: 225–38.

Lévy-Leboyer, C. and G. Moser (1977b) 'La peur comme moyen de dissuasion: le cas de l'alcoolisme,' *Revue de l'alcoolisme,* 23(2): 1–31.

Miller, G. A. (1969) 'Psychology as a Means of Promoting Human Welfare', *American Psychologist,* 24: 1063–75.

Moser, G. (1984) 'Everyday Vandalism', Ch. 10 in C. Lévy-Leboyer (ed.), *Vandalism, Behavior and Motivations.* Amsterdam, North-Holland.

Moser, G. and C. Lévy-Leboyer (forthcoming) 'Inadequate Environment and Situation Control', *Environment and Behavior.*

Schmidt, F. L., J. E. Hunter and K. Pearlman (1981) 'Task Differences as Moderators of Aptitude Test Validity in Selection: a Red Herring', *Journal of Applied Psychology,* 66: 166–85.

3

Three projects involving prediction

Leslie T. Wilkins

Forecasting methods provide for the decision-maker a means whereby the future may be robbed of some of its surprises. Examples of three projects from widely differing areas of application are discussed in this chapter. All descriptions of research projects are incomplete and to some degree, therefore, inaccurate. That is not to say that all research workers practise deception in their papers, rather that the incompleteness and inaccuracies occur because the writers wish their reports to be understood.

Though I have agreed to the suggestion that I should prepare a manuscript reporting the case history of some 'successful' social research projects with which I have been associated, I am aware that by the very fact of authoring this work it may seem that my role was more influential than, in effect, it was.

The inter-connectedness of prior events and ideas

Most projects which have outcomes assessed as 'successful' may seem to deal with quite specific and self-contained problems. Hence it would seem reasonable to assume that they had a definite beginning and ending. Certainly there is a kind of *a* beginning when the necessary funds become available and the work can commence. But while that may be the beginning of the spending of money (and financial reward for the scientist) it is almost certain that it is not the beginning of the relevant ideas, concepts and theories. Money would not have been available for any projects which had no basis of reference. Perhaps these antecedents are usually more important than the events which appear to be *the* beginning?

I have chosen three examples which are strongly related in terms of method and also by historical events. However, the subject matter of the projects, the means whereby the problems came to be recognized and the political features of each are strikingly different.

The organization of each had few elements in common, and the costs range from a little over £1,000 (with allowances for inflation and differences of dates of operation, say £5,000), to over a million dollars.

The cheapest project, and the one for which the degree of success can be precisely spelled out in the saving of government expenditure, was concerned with the projection of the demand by ex-servicemen who had served in the British Armed Forces in the 1939–45 war (Wilkins, 1948). The second project comprised several sectors, including an epidemiological study of deafness in the population of Britain and an estimate of the potential demand for hearing aids should these be provided through the proposed National Health Legislation (Wilkins, 1949).

For the third example we turn to the United States and report on the projects which resulted in the development of *Guidelines* for parole boards and judges. 'Guidelines' systems have been put into effect not only in the federal penal system but also in a number of states where the purpose is to constrain discretion (and hence reduce disparity) in the determination of parole and in the sentencing decisions of judges (Wilkins, 1981).

Serendipity and luck

The adage 'nothing succeeds like success' is not in accord with my experience. Even projects which could only be classified as outright failures have contributed to the development of work which was outstandingly successful. On at least one occasion (see Slater, 1947) I was extremely fortunate: the preceding failure was not mine but that of a much-respected research colleague.

In addition to the impact of prior work, pure chance has also played a large part in successful research. This is particularly so for the third example. Though it was the most costly and has, without doubt, had far more impact on social affairs than the other examples, it would not have begun but for a series of events which were unplanned and unconnected with the research. The research which led to the development of the 'Guidelines' movement might be said to have been an accidental birth. Perhaps good, successful research needs an environment where the unplanned can happen.[1]

Successful demand forecast saves money

Some little time after the end of the 1939–45 war, preparations were being made by the Treasury for the minting and distribution of campaign stars and medals. The armed services took the view that all entitled persons should receive their awards. Thus, the numbers of each produced should match the number of entitlements. This would mean that about 20 million medals would have to be struck — a major task for the Royal Mint. These would require distribution to over 4 million entitled persons. The magnitude of the distribution task alone required the procuring, setting up and staffing (in North Wales) of a special office.

An interesting problem for the Treasury officers was to obtain a reasonable estimate of the proportion of entitled persons who would want their awards. If this was less than 50 per cent it would not be necessary to set up the special offices. Chance events alone decided the reference of this problem to the government Wartime Survey Unit. Research was carried out, the global demand estimate was given as 35 per cent (with a probable error of 5 per cent).[2]

General approach to
forecasting demand for medals

Before estimating likely future activity it is necessary to have a reasonably detailed description of the nature of that activity. In the case of campaign stars and medals the essential elements of the proposed procedure were relatively simple.

Many ex-service personnel had returned to different addresses from that last recorded on their service records. It was proposed, therefore, that cards should be made available at all post offices throughout the country and those entitled to medals should complete one showing their service number, name and current address. A large national advertising campaign would draw the attention of entitled persons to the availability of the cards and of the need to use one to notify their address. This was a similar procedure to that adopted with regard to additional clothing coupons (ration entitlement), and the take-up of these was believed to be over 99 per cent. Thus, it was possible to assume that all entitled persons would know of the availability of the awards. No person is more than a mile or so from a post office and a personal visit was not necessary, anyone could pick up the required card.

Notes on method of research

It was postulated that an effective demand would be entered (a card would be collected and posted) if the individual 'really wanted' to obtain the awards. A small sample of about 1,000 ex-service personnel would be sufficient to provide a general estimate with a sampling error of about 5 per cent. Sampling error was, however, likely to be less of a problem than other errors in the estimation process. The method adopted had to make assumptions. It seemed obvious that a numerical scale of 'attitude towards medals' was needed. A random sample of entitled persons' last known addresses was reasonably easy to obtain, and the persons concerned who were still living there could be interviewed by trained interviewers of the Wartime Survey Unit. A sample of those who had moved might also be traced and similarly interviewed. Given a scale of 'attitude' it should be possible to distribute the sample accordingly. Those with low scores would be unlikely to bother to get the form or, if they did, they would probably forget to post it. Those with high scores would almost certainly follow the procedures and obtain their awards. The question remained of how much 'attitude' was required to overcome how much 'inertia', and, of course, how to construct the 'attitude' scale.

The statistical literature had reported several scaling techniques, one of which had considerable mathematical appeal because of its claim to produce a 'uni-dimensional' feature. But it was this technique which had failed to provide good discrimination for Slater on a similar problem.

Rather than a few questions which were carefully selected to provide a uni-dimensional scale, it was thought to be better to seek and use simple dichotomous responses to a large number of questions. Accordingly, I drew upon an analogue from communication theory: redundancy can improve communication in a 'noisy channel'. Therefore, we should draw up a number of questions all of which may vaguely be thought to be correlated with the postulated 'attitude to medals'. (There is also the analogy with the measurement of 'G' in intelligence test construction which was popular at that time.) A scale based on the assumption that the 'centroid factor' was the required attitude score was successful in distributing the sampled informants along an 'attitude' scale.

A small field-test enabled a cutting point to be identified along this scale. But it was not quite as simple as that.

Interviewer bias had been noted as a problem in many studies which focused on attitudes. It seemed unsafe, therefore, to rely on aggregated data, but to examine the performance of each field interviewer. A simple analysis of the attitude scores of informants by sex and age of interviewer showed a striking correlation between the age of female interviewers and the mean attitude score of their population samples. Men seemed less than usually concerned about receiving their war medals when they were interviewed by young women. The age of male interviewers was uncorrelated with mean attitude score (6.25). For women interviewers, however, the mean informant attitude score for the two youngest (female interviewer) groups was 5.9 and 5.7 and rose (monotonically) to 8.0 for the eldest group.

The project and the accuracy of the estimation of the demand has been noted. The fact that it was possible to put a precise figure on the savings resulting from a research was unusual and afforded valuable publicity for the methods. Much of consequence was to follow later from the parliamentary attention which the project received.

The demand for hearing aids

The second case-history concerns a project which also involved the estimation of demand, but used different methods. The need for this research related to the proposed National Health Service legislation. Would it be possible (i.e. financially acceptable) to provide hearing aids under the Act for those who could benefit from their use? With the medals demand, estimation of the number of persons entitled was known, but how many persons were deaf? How many of those who were, could benefit from the use of the aids then available?

The first problem was to define deafness. While there is a medical definition in terms of hearing loss over various frequencies, this does not necessarily equate with the social definition or the subjective definition of the patient. Demand for hearing aids might be associated with any of the possible definitions. However, unless a sufferer was aware of the defect and sought medical opinion the medical/clinical definition would be irrelevant.

The incidence and prevalence of deafness
The first task of the survey was to establish a figure for the proportion of the public (over eighteen years of age) who were suffering from hearing loss in the population of England, Scotland and Wales. This would identify the 'qualified' population. In the medals project a gross estimate demand for categories of awards was the only requirement; individuals or their characteristics were of no concern. In the deafness project, we had a wider interest, and perhaps a more complex task. Two estimates of demand were required: (1) the applications likely to be received at clinics which would provide aids when such was indicated, and (2) the number of aids that should be produced if a decision was taken to include the provision of aids within the compass of the National Health Act then in progress through Parliament.

Experience of previously successful forecasting projects (including the 'medals' case) suggested that direct verbal statements of sampled members of the public should not be regarded as providing any reasonable guide to their likely future action. Any hypothetical question is suspect! However, verbal data were the only kind of data available to us by which we could assess the deafness category. Such data had to be collected and then subjected to tests. If the data survived severe tests, then further analysis might be justified.

Simple tests sufficed to check the internal reliability of the informants' statements. In the main these relied upon cross-tabulation of information supplied at different times during the interview and were concerned with a number of different topics.

The within maxima and within minima estimates derived from different bases were remarkably close to each other. This provided ground for confidence. Accordingly, the government decided to include the provision of hearing aids within the scope of the National Health Service.

As later events have proved, technological factors had a considerable impact upon the design of hearing aids. The size of components has been reduced beyond that imagined in 1948; the power consumption has been reduced to a mere fraction with consequent reduction in weight and cost of batteries; and the quality of the reproduction in terms of sound/noise levels, comfort of wearing and the like have immeasurably improved. The product for which demand estimates were made (the Medresco) was a very different product from the hearing aid of today.

Distant connections of research

The third project, concerned with sentencing disparity, has had strong scientific and political connections with both the medals and the deafness projects. Chance also applied its heavy hand. But before we consider some of the features of this example, perhaps some proof of its 'success' is required. Of course, much depends upon the criterion of 'success'. Improvements in determination of the time offenders should stay in prison is, in national terms, a small matter. To some, if offenders were merely detained for longer, that would be all the improvement desired. Whatever the moral issues involved in the disposition of persons found guilty, most would agree that the idea of justice implies fairness, and fairness implies a lack of disparity in sentencing.

This project addressed the issues of disparity and fairness. It had, and is still having a considerable impact both on academic criminal justice in the United States and in the practice in that country of the majority of state parole boards, as well as in the federal courts and the courts of more than a dozen states.[3]

The turn to crime

From time to time governments have economy drives and carry out investigations into the work of the civil service. An economy drive in Britain led indirectly to the project to estimate the demand for campaign stars and medals. The government Wartime Survey Unit was being investigated and this provided an opportunity to propose that the demand should be estimated by the use of sampling methods. A later economy drive led to an interview between Sir George Benson, chairman of the Public Accounts Committee, and members of the Survey Unit, including myself. At the time of the interview it was not known that in addition to being chairman of the Public Accounts Committee, Sir George was also chairman of the Howard League for Penal Reform, and had served time in prison for being a conscientious objector. Hearing about the medals and the hearing aids projects led him to ask whether we knew anything about 'prediction in criminology' — though 'prediction' was not a term used in the discussion and, indeed, was not a term we would employ to describe the estimation methods which had been used in any of the prior projects. Sir George had, apparently, made an association between our work and a report of a project carried out at Harvard in which Sheldon and Eleanor Glueck claimed to be able to 'predict' the likely return to crime of persons discharged from a reformatory (Glueck, 1930). He asked whether or not it was our view that the same methods would work as well in England. This question could not be answered immediately, but a meeting was arranged after the work had been studied. He understood our report on the Gluecks' work to mean that (1) 'prediction of recidivism' would work in England, and (2) we could do a better job than had been done in the USA!

Many tortuous (probably also nefarious!) manoeuvres followed the initial discussions. This is not the appropriate place to note these, but suffice it to say that it was Sir George Benson who enlisted the co-operation of Dr Hermann Mannheim and produced the 'shot-gun marriage' which resulted in the work, *Prediction Methods in Relation to Borstal Training* (Mannheim and Wilkins, 1955).

This work was to have considerable influence. From both the academic and practitioner viewpoint and in terms of the impact it was to have on future research it was certainly a major 'success'. Yet in Britain it did not get anywhere. It did not have an influence on policy because the research remained isolated from the value choices of policy. Decision-makers thought that if they only had sufficient and accurate information, they would know what to decide. The 'prediction' research provided the information which, initially, policy-makers thought was precisely what was required. When that information became available, however, they realized that it was not adequate. Prediction methods provided a figure which was a reliable and powerful estimate of the individual offender's risk of recidivism. But the identification of the worst risks or the better risks did not indicate how the decisions should take this into account. But, of course, research was commissioned by policy-makers, and policy-making could not be delegated to research workers. In England, the two worlds never came together. Such a combined effort had to await an appropriate time and the confluence of many factors (again among them, pure chance), and a climate of judicial thought which could respond to statistical ideas. In the United States such a climate arose first among members of the federal parole board.

A short history of the parole 'Guidelines' projects
The methods employed in the research studies leading to the establishment of 'Guidelines' for parole decisions (which developed into methods of sentencing policy control) had strong connections with the early 'prediction' work at Harvard, still earlier work in Massachusetts and Illinois, and the British Social Survey. It was the latter, however, which raised the idea of a 'decision theoretic' basis and related this to the use of the statistical discriminant function. This decision reference,

in turn, had somewhat uncertain roots in quite remote and early projects, but, of course, specific events triggered the actual commencement of the project. However, when the project began there was no thought of inventing anything like 'Guidelines'. The idea of using a mathematical model, not only to 'mirror' the decisions, but as a means for stating a policy of parole decision-making came in the course of the second phase of the research.

While the specific series of triggering events were unusual, it is unlikely that they were completely atypical. Perhaps the 'critical path' may seem rather like a crazy paving leading from origin to successful implementation. But it may be prognostic of a successful outcome of research if those involved in it experience, from time to time, a sense of bewilderment by the turnings in the path research seems to take.

The specific nature of the project will, it is hoped, be interesting, but its specific elements are less relevant than the general points which are illustrated in the story.

I have tried to make this report as factually accurate as possible, but much is derived from recall unaided by papers or tapes. After the project had received funding, detailed records were kept and meetings were taped. But to begin at that stage would, perhaps, omit one of the main features of the history and probably a major interest. Getting started, particularly getting access to money for a research, is usually seen by research workers as very important.

The trigger of irrelevant interests and status conflict

In retrospect, it is most obvious that the states of the art in two fields — namely, parole and computer information retrieval systems — were necessary ingredients of the climate in which the project could begin. More important was the fact that United States (federal) parole board members were operating in an environment of increasingly hostile publicity. While an observer from above would see this, neither feature at the time claimed any attention.

Dr Don Gottfredson and I were each, in our own way, interested in computer developments, and no doubt the chairman of the parole board was, for his part, aware of the criticisms of parole decision procedures both in the press and in articles and books. How these two situations were to form a creative 'mix' was a chemistry of chance. The incident which provided this 'mix' seemed at the time to be irrelevant.

It happened thus.

A senior member of the staff of the Department of Justice who was concerned with provision of funds to approved research projects was organizing some aspects of the annual congress of the American Correctional Association. He apparently thought that an additional paper was required on 'a research topic'. John Conrad was that person.

He had, over several years, been professionally associated with both Don Gottfredson and myself. He was also aware that we had often worked together on research projects; sometimes Gottfredson being the 'principal investigator' (i.e. doing the management) and sometimes myself, depending upon the role our respective institutions could play in the research undertaken. Conrad knew us well enough to telephone and ask us to work up a paper on any topic we might wish to air. (He probably did not actually speak to both of us, but the idea of a joint paper was his.)

At that time Gottfredson had in his possession a large collection of data on parole releases with follow-up indicating whether they had committed further crimes. He was interested to obtain the use of a computer to facilitate analyses — computers at that time being very expensive and software limited. Lockheed had a 'property' known as DIALOG — a Boolian intercept search software package which they were interested to market. A potential market was seen among those to be present at the American Correctional Association Congress to be held in Boston in the autumn. A deal was struck. Lockheed would place Gottfredson's data on their computer, and they would supply the necessary equipment to provide a demonstration of DIALOG at the congress. We would present a paper based on analysis of Gottfredson's data on recidivism, using the on-line interactive potential of the Lockheed system. The demonstration (though relying on a simple telephone link over 3,000 miles), worked. A few members of the audience remained after the presentation and took more careful note of the facilities provided by the Lockheed system. Among those persons was George Reid, then chairman of the United States Parole Board (now termed Parole Commission). His interest was, perhaps, sharpened by his awareness of the recent criticism of his board's decision-making. In any event, at that time he formed the opinion that 'the computer might help'. It should also be noted that the Federal Bureau of Investigation had recently obtained a computer and that department's status had been enhanced by just that fact. Computers were new in Washington departments of government and few could assess the relevance of the equipment. If the Parole Board could claim no more than to 'have' one, criticism might be muted; it would show that they were up-to-date.

Criminal justice and all matters relating to the control of crime or dealings with offenders were high on the list of political priorities. It was a good time to put in a request for increases in manpower, and a better time to seek new equipment. For whatever reason, chairman Reid set about seeking a computer for the use of the Parole Board and this meant that his request passed to Conrad's desk. Conrad was not averse to the idea of providing support for improved decision-making by the board, but it was not clear to him how the board might benefit from the physical location in their department of an on-line system of data retrieval and analysis. He agreed to meet the costs of the supply of a computer, provided that research was conducted to ensure that its potential was realized; he was prepared to make available the necessary funds for the research.

First question — wrong question!

Lockheed, having demonstrated their DIALOG system using actual parole data, were, of course, at a considerable advantage over other possible contenders for the supply of a computer to the board. Furthermore, Gottfredson and myself were also at an advantage in that we had already done a considerable amount of work on re-conviction rates of released offenders and had been able to demonstrate, with Lockheed, the facilities of retrieval and classification which the Lockheed software provided. Perhaps it was not surprising that Don Gottfredson and myself were awarded research funds to carry out a research study of 'Parole Decision-making' with permission to install on a trial basis the DIALOG system in the board's Washington offices. Observations of the situations generated by the computerized data-base and its availability to the board's officers were to provide the data by which the change was to be assessed. Board members or other officers were shown how to obtain data and to select categories for display and analysis. The research staff acted as technical consultants to the board and its staff in seeking to exploit the computer system to 'improve' the decisions. The kinds of decisions made, the time taken in making them and the subjective attitudes of decision-makers provided data.

In the research proposal which provided the basis for funding, we had stated that we could not guarantee any useful results from our participation. We were prepared to commit ourselves only to an initial phase, though we expected that, should this work out well, we would be permitted to continue with research. (This was in accord with recommendations we had made regarding strategies of funding social research when in a prior study we had revealed much waste. See Wilkins and Gottfredson, 1969.)

Our observations in this phase quickly demonstrated for us that problems concerning decisions cannot be simplifiable to problems of information. The board members, in common with most decision-makers, were quite wrong in their initial, deeply-held belief that they could make much better decisions if only they had more and better information which was amenable to analysis. Without too much prompting from the research staff, the board members and other staff officers soon discovered for themselves that no matter how quickly accessible, classifiable, relevant or analysable the data provided by the new system, their decision problems remained. As disillusion set in and it became clear to the senior decision-makers that direct interaction between themselves and the computer was not helpful, there was a short period when it was thought that this might be because they were too busy to exploit the facilities adequately. The computer at the elbow of top-level decision-makers had not worked out. So, perhaps it was thought, a specialist could act as a go-between? The decision-makers could pose questions which the expert could 'put to the computer' and return with 'answers'. The senior research assistant of our team was allocated to this role and was taken on to the board's payroll. This method of utilizing the computer through an intermediary did not work out much better than the earlier phase. The 'intermediary', however, proved most useful and was retained on the staff of the board.

Phase one had been costly and seemingly a failure. In retrospect it can, I think, be conclusively shown to have been a necessary phase. Until the problem could be restated, and the revised statement became acceptable to the client, there was no point in seeking answers. Phase one enabled more appropriate questions to be posed and members of the board did not have to accept these on trust; they had experienced for themselves the basis for our position. For the research team we now had hard evidence that we were not dealing with a problem of information but a problem of decision-making; a quite different problem requiring the stating of different questions.

Client/technician vs role exchange team approach

The change in the statement of the research problems from a focus upon the provision of 'information systems' to a study of decision policy meant a change in the status of the research staff. No longer would it be possible for Gottfredson and myself to claim that we were merely assisting the policy-makers through provision of appropriate technology to deal with *their* problems; nor that our work was 'value-free'! We could no longer do research *for* the board, but it must be *with* the board. Fortunately, we had anticipated this kind of position. In the proposal for the first phase we had indicated that because we were breaking completely new ground we could not fill in any details in the form of a research contract: the only method of funding was through the medium of a grant. We undertook that if at any time it became clear to us that it was unprofitable to continue we could 'walk out' from our role as consultants to the board, advise the Department of Justice agency accordingly and return unspent funds. While we had the right (on our unquestioned assessment) to 'walk out', the board, obviously, had the right also to cease to continue working with us.

Both the board and the research team wanted to make all possible administrative provisions to ensure that the project did not terminate because of misunderstandings or other insufficient reasons. Thus, it was thought that, should a dispute arise, both parties might seek arbitration. It seemed likely that persons who would qualify as arbitrators in such an event could be named before any need to consult them arose. Why not, then, include one or two such persons as members of a steering and policy committee? The board nominated Professor Herbert Solomon, Dean of Statistics at Stanford University. The research team could think of no other, thus, while chosen as potential arbitrator, Professor Solomon was elected chairman of the committee.

Having touched on the subject of the steering committee, we should note one or two other matters of significance in its composition. In addition to the board, the project directors and the chairman, the funding agency provided an ex-officio member. Of more interest was the provision of two places for 'observer state representatives'. These were chairmen of parole boards in states not involved in the research. The original rationale for their inclusion was that if the research proved useful, it would be likely to commend itself to other parole boards, and if two states had representatives who worked with the project as it applied to the Federal Board, they would be informed and projects in their states might 'leap-frog' some stages. In the event, they fulfilled a different and perhaps more important role. They were involved, in their respective states, in the business of parole decisions similar to those of the United States board, but their decisions were not under direct scrutiny by research staff. Perhaps their role, as they came to see it, was to ensure that the Federal Board provided a full account and accurate description — as they themselves put it, they 'kept the board honest' by their presence. The committee worked extremely well. There were only two occasions when it seemed likely that the research would founder: once when the research team feared that it would have to report that a scientific approach was not possible because certain data were 'not available', and once when it was essential that the research team present evidence which required the board to reverse its stated basic philosophy of decision-making. It is obvious that both crises were survived. The former, it must be assumed, at considerable personal cost to the chairman of the board. The latter was more a fear among the research staff; in the event the chairman not only accepted the findings but capitalized on them. But we will touch upon these two situations again after the necessary discussion of the revised statement of the basis of the project.

Reconstructing the basic problem
1. Discovering decision processes. Before the digression about the administrative arrangements, we had noted that the problems of decision-making were not problems of the available information. Clearly there was a relationship between the information available and

the decision made in the case, but what was it? Perhaps before we could assist the board further we needed to have a better understanding of the processes of information search and use.

Many research studies have sought to find out what information is used and how decisions are made by the simple approach of asking decision-makers. This cannot work. A person cannot think about how the decision is being made and at the same time carry out the decision process itself. There is no way whereby we can divide our mind into two (or more) parts and make one part observe what the other part is up to! After the decision has been made we may think back on the process, but this process is subject to all the problems of recall. Observation of decision-makers at work may help, but only part of the process is observable. For example, the information called for can be noted, but we would not know whether the information was considered.

2. Studying the decisions. Simulation procedures can, as it were, render the decision-making procedures in 'slow motion', and enable observations to be made which are not otherwise feasible. Another approach is to attempt to arrive at the same end result as that of the usual human decision process, but to do so by means of an equation or model. All of these methods were employed in the parole decision study.

The simulation and the model work gave very similar results. Verbal reporting of the procedures believed to be followed which derived from introspection of the decison-makers, however, provided a quite different explanation. The board explained their decisions as 'granting or refusing the petition' (a dichotomous choice). Initially this was accepted as the function, but the mathematical model suggested that the decision was not whether to grant or refuse — it was not even of a dichotomous type! The best fitting was obtained if we assumed that the board was 'setting time' — that is, they were deciding for how long the offender should serve in prison: a kind of sentence review.

3. Human factors and ethical concerns. When the results were discussed with board members (as was each stage of the findings) they were able to recognize that a major consideration in granting a petition was 'whether he had done enough time'. Acceptance of the 'time setting' explanation facilitated better models and closer fitting to the board's decisions.

It should not be assumed that all parole boards were working to a similar model. Indeed, subsequent research found that for at least one Southern state neither a dichotomy nor a time estimate provided the best statistical fitting to the decision. There was a branching system which could be likened to a steeplechase — to 'win' (i.e. to be paroled) the petitioner had to jump all the obstacles. Any one 'negative' could result in the petition being denied.

It must be stressed that there is no suggestion that the 'best' fitting statistical model reflects the mental processes of the decision-makers. The claim which can be made may be stated thus: if it were required to replace the existing decision-makers by a computer, then a type of program of the kind which provided an optimal 'fit' would, other things being equal, be preferable to other methods. However, other things may not be equal, and there may be features of the optimal fit model which are objectionable.

It does not follow that such objectionable features are also present in the subjective decision process.[5]

When the board (and for that matter, too, the research staff) accepted the idea that their parole decisions were 'a matter of time', rather than of granting or refusing petitions, the work on the main project had almost to begin again with the correct specification of the problem. The revised statement of the research problem had some overtones of policy — the board was not expected to carry out a sentencing function because, some argued, that was the function of judges. But we must skip these issues in this report.

4. Policy as an equation? It may suffice to say that the phrasing of the research task was revised in the light of the early studies, and that the simulation research was particularly convincing. The next major step was to produce the 'best' fitting model, that is, the model which could most closely replace the current decisions of the board. This was not because it was assumed that the current practice was to be preserved, but rather that we might, with the board and the committees, study the model(s) and ascertain whether any patterns observed in the mathematical representation might be usefully adopted as 'policy' statements. One of the criticisms of the Parole Board at the time was that it had no parole policy. The board claimed that its policy was that each case was dealt with individually on its merits. This led to criticism of arbitrary and capricious decisions.[6]

The 'best' model required three dimensions. The first might be identified as the seriousness of the crime for which the offender had been found guilty in the current case. The second was recognized as the 'predictive' factor. The third was related to behaviour in prison. However, the variance explained was greatest for the first, still considerable for the second, but quite small for the third (probably because other means were available to deal with serious prison crimes). It seemed desirable, therefore, to drop the third dimension. A two-dimensional model is fairly easy for lay people to understand, but a three-dimensional model would not, perhaps, be so useful. There are also problems of 'scoring' the more complex models and, perhaps, the more sophisticated models can produce difficulties if the basic data are not of high reliability.

Thus, a two-dimensional model was presented to the board. There was some surprise that about 80 percent of their decisions could be quite well predicted by the use of the equations which were set up in a square table or matrix. The chairman rightly remarked that the model looked somewhat like a mileage chart! Precisely what the dynamics of the situation were it is not now possible to recall. However, at some point, the chairman of the board remarked that the 'matrix' seemed to him to be acceptable as a specification of board policy. The board gave most weight to its assessment of the seriousness of the current crime and also looked carefully at the prior record of offences and used these as a guide to culpability and as indicators of the probability of recidivism. At this point, the model, which began as a kind of 'descriptive' model, became 'prescriptive'.

While the original model has been modified, its general features remain the same as the original. Not that subsequent changes have been trivial; rather the model has proved flexible and powerful enough to accommodate change.

Some other problems
The history of the development of sentencing and parole guidelines was not all plain sailing, nor were many of the difficulties met capable of specification in scientific or technical terms. Indeed, most problems were not technical, though technical issues may have served as the vehicle for expression of what were essentially human relations problems. A few notes on the more important of these may be of interest.

1. Decisions not to make decisions! At one time in the parole decision project the research staff thought that they might have to recommend to the funding agency that the project be abandoned. The success of the project turned, of course, upon data available from the board and other administrative agencies concerned with offenders. The board had made available all data on all cases where they had made a decision. (After all, we were studying parole decision-making.) However, it only emerged after a major section of the project had been completed that there were other cases where the board had made no decision. These cases did not receive 'hearings' and hence no 'parole' decision was taken — they were left to 'take their course'. No data on these cases had been made available to the research staff, indeed the board did not have any significant data. There was only one source for these data, and in the past this source had refused any kind of co-operation in any research. The research viewpoint was that a 'decision not to decide' was as relevant as any other decision. The board was somewhat surprised when the research staff indicated that they could not continue without data on the whole 'population of concern'. The chairman asked that he be given a little time to see if he could obtain the necessary data. Let three facts only be recorded and the connection left to the imagination. The data were obtained; the chairman was removed from the chair; the release of the data involved the Nixon administration, and the persons concerned were Attorney-General Mitchell, FBI Chief, Edgar Hoover and A. N. Other.

2. *Building and spending goodwill.* Prior to the meeting at which the research staff presented the finding that it was possible to use a two-dimensional model with results very similar to those of the board's actual recent decisions, there had been much apprehension. How was this finding likely to be received? How would this fit with the board's insistence that it had no policy except that each case was dealt with on its merits? Would this be the end of the project. In the event, the meeting provided the most constructive turning point in the research. In later, similar projects concerned with sentencing (where judges were in a similar relationship with the research staff as the Parole Board), similar 'crises' were experienced. It was well noted by an observer that it was fortunate that much goodwill is built up in the early stages, because at this kind of meeting much of it is spent.

There were, of course, other crises. The work — in its scientific aspects — has suffered most from its success. It became more and more widely known and other state parole boards began to seek similar models to facilitate their decisions. With this popularity there developed more interest on the part of legislatures and professional bodies such as prosecutors and defence attornies. Soon some entrepreneurs saw opportunities for themselves in suggesting that the original model needed modification. They could claim to be able to develop such a modified ('better') product and began marketing these claims. Evaluation studies have shown that while the United States Parole Commission methods have worked well, particularly in the reduction of disparity, this has not been the case with some other (modified) systems, though some modifications have been effective. At the time of writing, the sentencing system in use in the state of Minnesota (though different from that described) was broadly based on sound research and is also quite successful. Success or failure seems to be closely related to two features, (1) quality research which is rigorous rather than elegant, and (2) close relationships (power-sharing) between research and policy interests.

Lessons from the three case histories
1. Research methods
Perhaps the most general warning sounded by the research studies is that it should never be assumed that people can predict their own likely future behaviour. None the less, this does not mean that future behaviour cannot be predicted provided that a satisfactory model can be

linked with adequate statistical analysis. Similarly, introspection is an unreliable source of information as to thought processes.

Secondly, it is clear that useful data can be generated by noting and simulating relevant activities by subjects and by relating these data to verbal statements concerning the issues under investigation.

Thirdly, and perhaps most importantly, those events which may be attributed to serendipity are extremely valuable. It is, of course, not possible to create and control such events, but it is possible to have research environments where these kinds of situations are observed and capitalized upon, and other research environments where the stimulus of these events would be lost. Much depends upon the style of management, and perhaps also on the personality of the director of the research institution.

2. Research policy and management

For those concerned with the higher levels of management in industry and government, the medals study illustrates that it is those who are most likely to benefit from the results of research who are often the least likely to recognize where it could be applied. This is not because they are incompetent managers or administrators, but because they are not aware of the methodology of research. How could they be?

The parole 'Guidelines' project would have foundered in its early stages if the original statement of the problem had not been completely changed. Such change of direction of a project is possible only where the research staff and the administrators are in close, continuous communication. A research contract which spelled out the 'research product' to be 'delivered' could have inhibited the changing specifications of the research task as the problem became better understood.

If research workers are to play their part in the development of industry and government there must be improved channels of communication between research methodologists and those in charge of policy. Furthermore, the communication and responsibility must be a shared function where the scientist takes some responsibility for the outcome of his recommendations and the policy-makers recognize the pursuit of scientific inquiry (even social research inquiry) as an institution in its own right.

Notes

1. Merton (1957) comments: 'so develops the new type of scientific worker. To work he must be employed by a bureaucracy with laboratory resources ... and this bureaucracy exerts a constant pressure upon the official to be methodological, prudent, disciplined'... This implies that behaviour must be predictable. In these kinds of environments, chance events are 'bad'.

2. The demand, in fact, turned out to be 34.7 percent. (see *Hansard*, Vol. 466 [132] 21 June 1949).

3. It is difficult to select references to demonstrate the significance of the research and its applications. Leaving aside the academic impact, it may be briefly noted that at the time of writing methods derived from the project are, in the United States, the basis of the work of a recently constituted Sentencing Commission. These methods are essentially the same as those which the Federal Parole Commission adopted upon completion of the project and has used ever since. In England, an advisory committee of the Home Office (Advisory Council on the Penal System (1978) *Sentences of Imprisonment*. London: HMSO) studied the methods but concluded that: 'Sentencing guidelines would have a more direct impact upon sentencing than our proposals, and we doubt that such a sophisticated formulation would be acceptable in the English context.'

4. This person, Peter Hoffman, will appear frequently in the later history of the research in which he became a central figure. He has also continued to develop guidelines and has been significantly concerned with the drafting of legislation to the setting up of a Sentencing Commission as noted earlier.

5. For a short discussion of the problem of 'useful' but 'objectionable' information and a report on the current practice of the board with notes on reasons for modification of the original predictive scale, see Hoffman, 1983.

6. See, for example, Frankel, 1972.

References

Frankel, M. (1972) *Criminal Sentences: Law without Order*. New York: Hill and Wang.

Gluek, S. and E. (1930) *500 Criminal Careers*. New York: Knopf.

Hoffman, P. (1983) 'Screening for Risk: a Revised Salient Factor Score', *Journal of Criminal Justice*, 11: 539–47

Mannheim, M. and L. T. Wilkins (1955) *Prediction Methods in Relation to Borstal Training*. London: HMSO.

Merton, R. K. (1957) *Social Theory and Social Structure*. Glencoe, Ill.: Free Press.

Slater, P. (1947) *The Demand for the Civil Defence Medal*, Government Social Survey Report. London: HMSO.

Wilkins, L. T. (1948) *The Demand for Campaign Stars and Medals*, Government Social Survey Report. London: HMSO.

Wilkins, L. T. (1949) *Survey of the Prevalence of Deafness in the Population of England, Scotland and Wales*, Government Social Survey Report. London: HMSO.

Wilkins, L. T. (1981) *The Principles of Guidelines for Sentencing*. National Institute of Justice, Department of Justice, US Government Printing Office (1981 341-233/1816), Washington, DC.

Wilkins, L. T. and D. Gottfredson (1969) *Research, Demonstration and Social Action*, Department of Health, Education and Welfare Project. Davis, Ca.: NCCD.

4

The misapplication of social science at Unesco

Peter Lengyel

In 1946, the first General Conference of Unesco, meeting in Paris under the presidency of Léon Blum, took what must be regarded as an historic step. At the urging principally of the American delegation it decided to set up an autonomous social science department and programme for the fledgling organization as one of the five substantive fields for which it was to possess a specific mandate. Such a decision was far from obvious at the time, nor did it go unopposed, for the French, along with a few other founder-members, were in favour of a more traditional solution linking what they preferred (and still prefer) to call *'les sciences humaines'* with the humanities in which they believed them to be inextricably embedded. That the social sciences were nevertheless awarded independent status, thus legitimizing them as disciplines with distinct identities and trajectories, giving them a good address within the United Nations grouping, was both symbolically and practically most important. It held out the prospect that they might develop an international momentum of their own, based on the widening recognition of their capacities and utility, even if it could not from the outset be perceived just how they would fare as the universe of membership first rose to some 100 by 1960 and then to over 160 in the 1980s.

Two things, however, were clearly enough perceived by members of the Social Science Committee of the Preparatory Commission on the programme of Unesco in the report it submitted to the 1946 Paris General Conference. The first was that the social sciences are heavily culture-bound and infused with the ideologies of those communities which give rise to their different varieties. The second was the danger of their 'devastating misuse by demagogues and dictators alike' and the consequent need for an agency like Unesco to help prevent their 'distortion and abuse for narrowly partisan ends.'[1] If only these two basic insights had been kept clearly in focus over the next four decades and a programme evolved which steered deftly between the Scylla of cultural bias and the Charybdis of misapplication, then the record of the international social scientific endeavour might not be as disappointing as it has turned out to be. For the recognition of cultural bias should have cautioned against the ready acceptance of disciplines and approaches as these emerged out of (mainly Western) academic traditions while encouraging the critical assessment of core techniques or conceptualizations to measure their applicability in various settings. The danger of 'devastating misuse', on the other hand, should have tempered the passion to apply social sciences to any number of 'problems' or situations which they are not necessarily well equipped to analyse clearly, let alone to resolve. Moreover, it should have alerted professionals to the fact that, especially in an inter-governmental organization, it is more important to set out with precision what the basic tools of social science can, in any given state of the art, be expected to do, and what is beyond their capacities as a demonstration of scientific probity rather than accepting all assignments of a broadly socio-economic character as suitable for handling. For the difference between the application of social science domestically and internationally is this: domestically, the inbuilt cultural bias is congruent with the local value system and the empirical evidence marshalled is specific and meaningful, while international 'application' generally implies a transfer of cultural bias and the use of comparative evidence, often of questionable validity. Thus, international social scientific work is often characterized by abstract generalization and marred by obscuring superficiality which discredits it and throws unnecessary doubt on those who produce it, sound enough though many of them may be when confronted with a more familiar and limited exercise on their home ground.

I have analysed in historical perspective how the Unesco endeavour as a whole came to grief in my book, *International Social Science: the Unesco Experience* (New Brunswick, N.J.: Transaction Books, 1986,) to show both the vicissitudes at the institutional base and the behaviour of the surrounding professional constituency and clientele. Here, I propose to concentrate upon considerations relating to the application and use of the social sciences.

From the very start, the Social Science Department at Unesco contained a key Division of Applied Social Science. Application was interpreted as the illumination, by the general activation of the 'best' scientific apparatus, of certain broad themes, some originally grouped under a project known as 'Study of Tensions Crucial to Peace'. These themes included nationalism and internationalism, population questions, racism and the social impact of technological progress. During the 1950s, attention crystallized especially around racism, urbanization, migration, industrialization and the emerging perplexities of technical assistance. They were all likely to appeal in many quarters and thus to obtain support when they were put forward in the biennial programmes and budgets. At no stage, however, was it specified just how they were to be broached, and with what end in view. For racism, matters were comparatively simple. The object was to display scientific evidence in a campaign of public enlightenment through the popularized packaging of findings, and the promulgation of expert statements to counter Nazi and other propaganda poison.[2] Here was a classic recruitment of social science into directed advocacy which soon exacted its political price. In 1956, South Africa, a founder-member of Unesco, withdrew from an organization which was issuing messages incompatible with its official policy. The incident did not serve to deflect Unesco away from possibly dangerous terrain, quite properly so since anti-racism formed part of its ideological mandate. But what about other themes? No a priori objective or position was implicit in them. Unesco had no mandate to promote or oppose industrialization, urbanization or migration. It might therefore have been valid to examine just how and with what ends in view, an inter-governmental organization proposed to apply social science to such a set of complex and continuing processes.

For it was already clear enough that the organization could conduct no research itself, commanded insufficient resources (and could not commit those it had reliably over periods in excess of two years) to commission original work of wide scope, and possessed only such observational capacities as could be drawn from member states. The options open were consequently narrow. One of them would have been to seek to improve the capacities of governments to monitor and analyse selected socio-economic phenomena and trends. The choice adopted, however, consisted essentially of assembling and packaging concepts and findings from academic sources primarily for the sup-posed benefit of advanced scholarship and in the cause of international intellectual co-operation, which was surely part of Unesco's basic mandate. Whether it was entirely to the advantage of the social sciences in the world at large, and at the inter-governmental level in particular, is retrospectively open to doubt.

A good example of results is the book *Industrialization and Society* (edited by B.F. Hozelitz and Wilbert E. Moore, 1963) probably one of the most comprehensive and authoritative of Unesco's social scientific publications, and also ironically one of the last on a theme on which a great deal of documentation had preceded it. It contains fourteen scholarly essays covering various facets, a summary of substantive find-ings and four appendices, three of which are not strictly on the subject announced by the title. The essays do not enter into details concerning the origin of evidence or the research behind the arguments, nor does the book set out how, in what framework and to what purpose the processes in question are to be broached technically in different settings. What might be a minimum data-base? Which of many interrelated vari-ables should be monitored and by what means? Can findings be made comparable or transferred legitimately from country to country? Yet these are some of the questions to be addressed if it is seriously proposed to arouse the interest of governments in the use of social science and application to specific areas. Furthermore, in 1963, when *Industrialization and Society* appeared, another problem became ripe for clarification: was Unesco the appropriate base from which to co-ordinate or promote a major intellectual thrust in social science, and if so, of what type? The United Nations group of inter-governmental organizations is often referred to as a 'system' which is precisely what it is not, for it possesses neither a central locus of control nor adequate co-ordinating mechanisms at functional levels. The resulting poly-centrism, each agency being instructed by its own sovereign general assembly, general conference or board of member states, has proved particularly deleterious to social science since it has led to great dispersion, overlap, duplication and dilution. Social science, overwhelmingly in its applied forms, is practised throughout the group: at the UN itself (chiefly demography and statistics), at the World Health Organization, the International Labour Organization or the Food and Agricultural Organization (in ways related to their functional mandates), at the UN Institute for Training and Research, the UN University, the UN Research Institute for Social Development, the regional Economic Commissions or as field projects, or components thereof, all over the world. The most complete socio-economic data files are those of the World Bank, which also issues the most authoritative reports on world trends.

In such a situation Unesco might reasonably have opted for a specialized role, concentrating upon support for and development of the epistemological and professional bases of social science leaving applications largely to others, yet it continued to dabble in a variety of applications without establishing either exclusivity or an impressive reputation in any one of them. And as the years rolled on, the absence of all-round vision of Unesco's mission in the social sciences caused them to become step-children in that very corner of the UN group in which they were supposed to have a secure home.

This happened because, again in the early 1960s, a great expansion occurred throughout the inter-governmental nexus fuelled by the availability of massive funding for operational activities in the field, that is to say, essentially within the 'Third World'. At Unesco, the demand expressed through the priorities set by governments as recipients of aid was particularly directed towards educational and scientific services. Social science projects, even if proposed, were seldom high on the priority listings, which meant that the programme shrank, first relative to the others, then absolutely as it was punished for its failure to appeal. René Maheu, the organization's director-general from 1962 to 1974, had scant sympathy for the social sciences and would have liked to abolish them as an autonomous programme altogether. Prevented from doing so he chose instead to reduce them as far as possible to a purely auxiliary role, as supports for Unesco's educational, natural scientific, cultural and mass communications concerns. What was not clarified at a time when the social science boom in the world at large was at its zenith — or indeed since — was Unesco's failure to make any serious pitch to convince governments that these sciences could effectively be applied and that predictable benefits might be drawn from the appropriate use of the quasi-technology they have to offer. Many of the newer member states badly needed to be persuaded that such, to them often unfamiliar, knowledge bases could, in fact, be of practical help, notably in their developmental initiatives, and that they were not merely subjects of arcane academic interest or fashionable, exotic fads cultivated by a few specialists eager to emulate the 'advanced' countries. They got little encouragement to see things with that slant from Unesco.

The backlash made itself felt about a decade later. By the mid-1970s no pattern of accepted international practice or transfer based on experience in different groups of countries at varying levels of development and sophistication had emerged. On the contrary, the continued imposition of theoretical paradigms and unreconstructed methodology from the industrialized North, of whatever underlying ideological hue, led the South to call for the 'indigenization' of the social sciences. Even if that is still not much more than a reactive slogan it is a significant index of failure. For if discriminating efforts had been made to establish orders of priority and adaptive praxis by working upwards from the quality and scope of the primary data-bases,[3] by testing and adjusting scientific instruments and by attending to the necessary infrastructure step by careful step, 'indigenization' might well have occurred gradually and spontaneously. The mistake was to persist with action from the other end, trying to transplant social science wholesale and thereby inevitably exposing its cultural fragility, a feature quite realistically noted by those who had drafted the first Unesco programme in 1946.

The institutional situation at the international level is, of course, to a considerable extent the reflection of the political will and perspectives of member states. And here again the social sciences are at a great disadvantage. In matters of health, of education, labour, finance, often also in those of science and culture, there are natural interlocutors at national levels in the form of ministries, or at least of central bodies like museums or libraries. Not so in the social sciences, which means that contacts tend to be directly with selected academic bodies, certain centres or even teams. In some cases — the socialist Academies of Science, for example — the choice of partners is restricted and obvious, but in many it is rather wide and fortuitous. This invests particular responsibilities in the professional structures to inform and shape the international enterprise. Not much by way of national policies exist in this domain, the only area of universal governmental concern being statistics, pre-empted by the UN at which the network linking national statistical offices is solidly centred. The specialized agencies, and notably Unesco, on the other hand, are surrounded by constellations of non-governmental organizations with consultative status, the inputs of which are supposed to represent the best professional advice in the process of programming. For the social sciences there are fifteen major non-governmental organizations, mostly disciplinary associations, all but one federated under the International Social Science Council. They are collectively both an interest lobby and a privileged clientele receiving subsidies and occasional contractual assignments. In return they are regularly invited to contribute to the structuration of the programme and to come up with proposals. Further professional influence can flow through national channels, by appropriate expert representation on delegations to important conferences and in other ways.

By and large, the profession has been notably negligent and incoherent in grasping the opportunities opened up by access to the unique international base at Unesco. Disciplinary provincialism, academic blinkers, small-scale thinking and, above all, absence of thorough analysis of what it might be most appropriate for an inter-governmental organization to pursue so as to enlist the support of governments, all contributed to weakening the professional input. The state-centric bias of inter-governmental organizations being inherent, social scientists should have been among the first to recognize it as a constraining parameter and not try to swim against the current by introducing into these forums ideas which are often profoundly unsettling to many governments. Certainly, state sponsorship tends to favour a rather narrow line of conventionally applied work, often necessarily apologetic of the status quo or at least blandly non-committal. That explains why much of it emanating from international organizations is so superficial. But the cure does not seem to lie in trying to slip a critically 'scientific' — as opposed to frankly political — case past the defences of orthodoxy, for this inevitably means bending science to a cause, however worthy it may be, which is precisely part of the danger of misuse against which such a strong warning was issued back in 1946. The weight of what is propounded from an inter-governmental base in the name of social sciences should instead favour a process of leverage by which the accreditation of sound scientific procedures, based on the manipulation of high-quality empirical data, acts back on governments to persuade them to promote the capacities of the available quasi-technology to inform their own decision-making and monitoring systems. In other words, matters should be broached from the scientific, not the social end.

The pardonable impulse of governments is to take some problem as it seems to manifest itself on the ground — be it crime, pollution, land-use, demands for wider human rights or the foreign exchange shortage — and to refer it to 'experts' in order to obtain an appropriately structured approach or even suggested solutions. Clearly, this tends to strain the capacities of professionals who are hard put to it to come up with sound 'answers' to questions often badly formulated or but marginally amenable to scientific treatment at all. Nevertheless, in national contexts, expertise can enrich the domestic debate and sharpen the focus on specific issues. This valuable function of social scientific input is, however, greatly inhibited at the international level where it is very rarely possible to deal with specific cases or to address identified decision-makers or power centres. The adoption of the broadly meliorative advocacy function, which has an honourable history in many countries, by inter-governmental agencies thus obscures an essential difference in the mechanisms of influence. Domestically, advocacy seeks to inform policy directly and specifically, and is often successful in doing so. Internationally, whatever impact may be achieved by advocacy is so diffuse and general that, paradoxically enough, it easily degenerates into a sort of ritualized conventional wisdom at one extreme while stifling open debate at the other. To explain how this happens is not easy and can only be sketchily attempted here. At the outset, consensus must be sought on what is to be tackled at all. Some subjects may be taboo and simply cannot be raised in international forums so long as they remain so: this was the case with birth control for many years. Next, perspectives adopted must appeal to a great majority of member states, or at least not arouse strong opposition from some. This is the case with the drive towards modernization and development: nobody is going to court opprobrium by suggesting, even gently, that it may not always and everywhere be entirely desirable. Through such selectivity a skew in initial attitudes is introduced which eliminates countervailing currents of opinion and fixes the direction of advocacy along prescribed lines. What is then expected of social science is to buttress the case along these lines leading to selective and repetitive illustration rather than to a search after causal relationships and behavioural regularities.

Directed advocacy is common enough in other contexts, whether in the service of public or private interests. But, at least in vigilant democratic countries, there are usually critics to point to its limitations and biases and to propose alternative approaches. Not so at the inter-governmental level, where directed advocacy is both self-serving and hegemonic. Thus, a good deal of energy has been devoted in different parts of the UN network to examining the role of multinational corporations in the world economy. Can one even imagine raising the problem of corrupt governments in these same circles with a view, for example, to weighing the alleged exploitation of multinational corporations against the depredations of corrupt governments on a cost-benefit basis? Hardly, yet the question deserves elucidation by the application of social scientific tools.

Among Unesco activities most sharply attacked by the United States and other countries which have recently become openly critical of the agency, certain portions of the social science programme (notably those dealing with human rights and those betraying an overtly state-centric approach to development) figure only too prominently. Directed advocacy and tendentious selectivity have thus demonstrably been carried too far: the social sciences now carry blame not only for being otiose but also for bias. It is a very serious setback for which, it must be said, the profession bears heavy responsibility. For, among inter-governmental organizations, Unesco is surely the one where professional constituencies carry most weight. Perhaps it is no exaggeration to say that many governments have been financing Unesco partly in the unspoken hope that professional brains trusts, thus encouraged, might perform minor miracles where others, less expert and far-sighted, had failed. If such hopes existed they must now be dashed so far as social scientists are concerned. For the profession has shown scant caution. Originally assembled mainly for purposes of intellectual co-operation, the professional structures surrounding Unesco still consist mainly of international disciplinary associations of academic economists, sociologists, political scientists, etc. There is some contradiction in expecting those who are not, on the whole, very close to problems as they are actually experienced nor particularly trained in handling them practically to apply the social sciences effectively. Yet this professional constituency eagerly accepted whatever was proposed, seeking contracts, advisorships and subsidies for restricted circles which only marginally and occasionally extended to those actually applying the quasi-technology of social science in industry, the media, education, therapy, management and a host of other avenues. Thus, the mismatch between increasing emphasis on applications (clearly expressed by Maheu's successor to the director-generalship, Amadou-Mahtar M'Bow, when he set up a quite sizeable Sector of Social Sciences and their Applications in 1975 with a number of divisions to attend to problem areas like the environment, development, youth and human rights) and continuing reliance largely on academic collaborators went unnoticed. The only sphere in which the quasi-technology was given some play — that of modelling and simulation — was also the most neglected and misunderstood within the organization.

Yet when it came to making the inevitable cutbacks resulting from the decisions of the United States, the United Kingdom and Singapore to withdraw from Unesco (thus depriving it of some 30 per cent of its budget), this relatively new sector once again became the prime target for drastic reductions. Several of its divisions were allowed simply to fade away while the functions of others were transferred out of it. A possible fusion with the Sector of Natural Sciences, sometimes mooted and not entirely unpromising as a solution, has not been carried through. Thus, by early 1986, the Social Science Sector had become a rump barely able to sustain routine activities pursued since the 1940s, its programme a mere patchwork of coincidentally surviving projects and its staff well below the critical minimum necessary to execute an enterprise at an international level. Since the surrounding non-governmental network has suffered a little less in financial terms, a tendency has emerged to share out tasks between the Secretariat and the International Social Science Council, in particular, on ad hoc bases which run counter to the original ideas of complementarity, feed-in and feed-back between them. This could ultimately lead to an unhealthy symbiosis in which the division of labour and responsibility for results is so diluted that effective control is lost and what remains of Unesco's involvement in the social sciences merely reflects a series of convenient arrangements between subsidized but largely captive external associations and the skeleton structures remaining within the organization's secretariat.

It is impossible to say whether, once Unesco emerges from its current crisis (if it emerges), the social science programme will be re-cast so as to provide some opening for more operationally applied capacities. Certainly, what I call the quasi-technology — the tools, instruments and techniques, if preferred — does not add up to a vast arsenal. But it does comprise ways of apprehending, shaping, monitoring and controlling phenomena and the course of events in many areas by polling, sample surveying, testing, typologizing, systems analysis, counselling, economic calculations and so on. Furthermore, the quasi-technology draws attention to the required data-bases and tends to sidestep ideology and directed advocacy by separating out measurable, quantifiable cores from the rest, thereby also transcending endless and finally pointless debates on disciplinary scope and frontiers which have done much harm by transmitting typically academic disputes into circles where their futility is only too readily apparent.

Perhaps an argument in favour of purification through technocracy sounds a trifle desperate. I would decidedly not advance it as relevant to the social sciences where these are maturely grounded in the established cultural mainstream and where they play important roles in socio-economic dialectics. But the transfer of value-loaded bodies of knowledge in partly disembodied and distorted forms from mature centres to callow peripheries via inter-governmental organizations has caused so much confusion and been so misconstrued that retreat into technicity appears to be a necessary corrective, at least for a time. How to integrate the social sciences for citizenship training, as elements of general education or of culture every society must work out for itself: formal transmission through international agencies can be of assistance only within a locally developed framework. The quasi-technology, on the contrary, could be handled internationally with a degree of confidence in so far as it is much more modest in its pretentions, success and failure, adaptation and inadaptation being also easier to evaluate. If social scientists wish to recapture some of the credibility they have lost through ambitious opportunism and failure to deliver impressive results, a season away from the pulpit, soberly honing tools at the workbench may well do their reputation a power of good.

Notes

1. These phrases are quoted from page 3 of Document Unesco/Prep. Com./Soc. Sci./Com. dated 4 June 1946.

2. Three series of what were originally separate booklets appeared between 1951 and 1970: 'Race and Society', 'The Race Question and Modern Thought' and 'The Race Question in Modern Science'. All the booklets appeared in English and French and some were translated into certain of nineteen languages.

3. In 1983 there were still four countries which had never even conducted a census: Ethiopia, Chad, Zaire and Laos. See J. Brenez and William Seltzer (1983) 'La collecte des informations démographiques dans les pays du Tiers Monde', *Revue Tiers Monde*, 94 (April–June): 246.

5

A research programme on the utilization of the social sciences

Ansgar Weymann, Ludwig Ellermann, Matthias Wingens

This chapter deals with two different aspects of research on the utilization of social sciences. First, it gives some information concerning a research programme set up by the German National Science Foundation (*Deutsche Forschungsgemeinschaft*) entitled 'Utilization of Social Sciences' (*Verwendung sozialwissenschaftlicher Forschungsergebnisse*). Secondly, it reports on some of the major findings of an empirical research project which is part of the programme just mentioned. This project investigates the utilization of social sciences in labour market policy in the Federal Republic of Germany since 1967.

The research programme
'Utilization of Social Sciences'
The German National Science Foundation (DFG) has several ways of financing projects. Besides offering individual grants to applicants it establishes a restricted number of large-scale programmes called Focused Research Programmes (*Schwerpunktprogramme*). These Focused Research Programmes reflect the long-term policy of the DFG. Such a programme is funded usually for a period of between five and ten years.

Focused Research Programmes assemble teams of scientific research fellows with the same academic interests in a given problem area, but with different approaches, and a diversity of university facilities and backgrounds. There is open competition for membership in the programme and this produces a variety of participants from several universities in Germany and even abroad.

The programme 'Utilization of Social Sciences' is one of less than a dozen Focused Research Programmes in the social sciences. It was initiated by Heinz Hartmann (University of Munster) and Ulrich Beck (University of Bamberg), both professors of sociology. More than twenty projects have been financed since the programme was launched. The number of fellows in this programme varies between thirty and forty.

What is the purpose of the 'Utilization of Social Science' programme? A preliminary answer is given by the decree of the National Science Foundation's senate:

> There is evidence that Social Science has influenced policy and society extensively in the last fifteen years. At the same time it cannot be claimed that systematic research on utilization is pursued. Therefore we do not always know which findings are selected and implemented by users, and which factors determine the utilization in various institutions (like government departments, trade unions or companies).
>
> Research on utilization can produce some insight into the 'usefulness of findings' from the point of view of scientists and it can allow the 'correction of prejudices' on the part of users. Furthermore, it may define potentialities and boundaries of applied social science in general. [The President, National Science Foundation, grant no. 322 144, 1981, p.3]

The National Science Foundation's decree gives more detailed arguments why a utilization research programme should be launched. It refers to a growing interest with utilization documented by journals, books, national and international conferences, and it describes the present situation of social sciences in the Federal Republic. The document argues that after a tremendous expansion in staff and students the social sciences are now suffering from stagnation and in some disciplines even an overall reduction. This is contrasted with the use of evaluation and implementation research in education, public administration, welfare and labour market policies. These efforts were made mainly by the 'Great Coalition' between Christian Democrats and Social Democrats (1967–8) and during the first years of the 'Social-Liberal Coalition' (from 1969 on) but have decreased since that time. The document tries to explain the reason for recent changes. One argument is that too much was promised by social scientists, and too much was expected by users. The above-cited 'insights into usefulness' of findings by producers and the quoted 'correction of prejudgements by users' points to the fact that users nowadays tend to be sceptical concerning 'applicability', and that producers tend to withdraw from 'applied science' to the ivory tower of intellectualism. Another argument is that users established a number of large 'inhouse research units' which make university research superfluous in many fields. A third argument is that university graduates in sociology, social-psychology and education meet with extremely bad labour market conditions and this situation is used as an argument for further cuts in university budgets in these disciplines.

In summary, the academic social sciences have to respond to a severe challenge. The problem of non-utilization after a period of intensive utilization is, in Germany at least, first of all a problem for sociology, and for university research. Consequently this discipline is the core of the programme, but many other disciplines have joined in the meantime, for instance social-psychology, education, psychology, political sciences and history. Even economics and law are not excluded.

In its investigations the programme does not give equal attention to all aspects of utilization. It focuses on the process of using research in a variety of organizations. On the other hand it is not concerned with the conditions of producing applicable findings or with bargaining and mediating between producers and users. It is not restricted to specific forms of findings or knowledge. In this way survey statistics, results of empirical work and theoretical explanations are included, as are anthropological and current social theories (e.g. post-industrialism) which contribute to and influence public debate. This broad scope ensures that neither 'applied social science', conducted mainly in various research institutes outside universities, nor academic, 'intellectual' social science work predominant in universities, is excluded. It does not discriminate between 'commissioned research' and so called 'basic research'.

The researchers use several theoretical models and the programme encourages them to strive for improvement. Some projects use a *'market-model'* based on exchange theory. Others suppose that there is no market of goods called 'findings'. They argue that supply, demand and profit are not useful concepts. Instead they conceive social science research as a process of continuing *'enlightenment'*. Using this model, researchers investigate the impact of social sciences on public debate of political issues, or on a change of values and norms (culture). A third model gives attention to the present extensive influence of government and administration on social science research policy by commissioning research and by setting up in-house research units (this is also partially true for business). A fourth model regards utilization under the aspect of *conflicting interests* between producers and users. This group gives much attention to class structure, stratification, political movements and campaigns.

The policy of the programme is to accumulate a large body of data and to reformulate and integrate theoretical approaches. A special scientific problem in this respect is to work out a more precise definition of the concepts 'finding' and 'knowledge' in the social sciences. Furthermore, it is important to redefine the analytical concept of 'utilization'.

In terms of policy-making there are several objectives. As a first step, the programme attempts to stimulate a rational, empirically-grounded public debate on utilization. This is meant to overcome the tendency for arid conflicts on 'principles'. The constant see-saw between overestimating the usefulness of social sciences on the one hand and its condemnation on the other must be replaced by an objective assessment. Social research itself has to provide the data. As a second step, research on utilization could be a valuable instrument for reducing the

split-off between 'applied social sciences' on the one hand, and 'intellectual, academic social science', on the other. Thirdly, the programme
aims to stimulate a deliberate and, if possible, organized policy towards
a general and long-term improvement of utilization of the social
sciences.

Before concluding this section I shall give the reader some idea of the
scope of the various projects of the programme. They include the
following:

1. Utilization of social sciences concerning juvenile delinquency, the reform
   of juvenile courts, juvenile criminal law and the laws regulating the
   execution of sentences.
2. The influence of social sciences on adult education institutions maintained by trade unions.
3. The comparative impact of social sciences and other disciplines on the
   prevention and treatment of drug abuse.
4. The role of social sciences in the elaboration of regulations for compulsory vocational training by the Federal Institute for Vocational Training
   (Bundesinstitut für Berufsbildung).
5. The utilization of social sciences in establishing experimental high
   schools.
6. Evaluation research on the installation of new mass media (for instance,
   cable and satellite television).
7. Experimental reorganization of labour in factories (work design, semi-
   autonomous groups and participative decision-making).
8. The extent to which the German Alpine Club makes use of social
   sciences in its educational programmes.
9. Investigation of the differences in utilization between research commissioned by public bodies and private organizations.

Project on social science utilization in labour market policy and recurrent vocational training
The problem

One of the more important fields in which utilization took place was the
labour market and education policy. Mainly under the perspective of
manpower planning, the adult education system was substantially
reorganized. As a consequence of labour market forecasting, this part of
the educational system was enlarged and concentrated on vocational
training. Vocational training includes retraining on the job, training for a
new job including recognized qualifications or training for higher
professional skills within an existing occupation. Meanwhile, the scope
of courses offered is extended to the 'treatment' of specific groups like
juvenile unemployed, integration of 'foreign guest workers', reinte-
gration of ex-convicts, etc. Adult education at first was only part of the
labour market policy but more recently has become part of the general
social welfare and social security policy.

The development of the labour market and education policy is an interesting field for an investigation of research utilization, because the legislation in that field requests and even explicitly prescribes the use of social science research. Among several statutes concerning labour market policy and vocational training, the most important is the Employment Creation Act *(Arbeitsforderungsgesetz;* AFG), which was passed by the Bundestag in 1969. This legislation regulates, among other things, the establishment of the Institute for Labour Market and Occupational Research *(Institut fur Arbeitsmarkt und Berufsforschung;* IAB). The task of this institute is to provide continuously the necessary scientific findings, for example forecasting for carrying out labour market policy. The setting up of IAB was immediately followed by the establishment of the Federal Institute for Vocational Training *(Bundes-institut fur Berufsbildung;* BiBB) which, in addition to research, is also responsible for teaching curricula and standards of qualifications.

The establishment of these two research and development institutes was accompanied by the installation of several consulting bodies. Futhermore, the Ministry of Labour and Social Order (BMAS) and the Ministry of Science and Education (BMBW) commissioned a large number of social research projects.

Findings from these sources serve two purposes. First, they may be used ex ante in decision-making and secondly they were used to support governmental arguments in public debates ex post.

Design of the project
The research attempts to find answers to the following questions:
1. Do ministers, unions and employers use social sciences?
2. Which findings do they use and which are ignored?
3. Are there differences in utilization between the various users?
4. Can a change in utilization be observed over the period from 1967 (preparation of the Employment Creation Act, AFG) to 1982?

The design of the research project uses three steps of data collection:
1. By means of a quantitative, computer-assisted content analysis it investigates the annual reports of ministries, unions and employers.
2. The same method is applied to proceedings of the Bundestag and its committees.
3. Finally, interviews are carried out with important personalities from government, unions and employing bodies. The information obtained under 1. and 2. is fed back and followed up by asking under what circumstances research utilization was facilitated or obstructed.

Some preliminary findings
This chapter reports the first step of the analysis. All findings are supported at conventional levels of statistical significance.

1. Specifying sources. In the annual reports investigated we identified a large number of references to social sciences ($n = 761$). But only in approximately 10 percent of all cases is the source of findings specifically mentioned. Ninety percent of these accurately cited sources were non-university social science research units.

2. Differences between users. The extent of utilization varies substantially between different users. Of the total number of identified research references the following percentages apply: Ministry of Labour and Social Order (BMAS) 45 percent; German Trade Union Federation (DGB) 21 percent; Ministry of Education and Sciences (BMBW) 18 percent; Employers Federation (BDA) 16 percent.

3. Fields of utilized research knowledge. The findings referred to in the records belong to a vast variety of research fields. The most important fields are the following: research on skills and qualifications (14 percent); analyses of the welfare state policy and problems (15 percent); investigations into the educational system (10 percent). All other fields are of minor importance.

4. Different styles of referring to social sciences. Only a small proportion of the social sciences used was classified as general theory (3 percent), empirical research results (4 percent) or mass statistics (4 percent. More often users refer to global descriptions like 'post-industrial society' (13 percent). However, the bulk of knowledge (76 percent) is confined to the specific social problems, and, as we saw in the previous paragraph, sources are only rarely cited.

5. Changes since 1967. Since 1969 when the Employment Creation Act (AFG) was passed, several amendments were added by the Bundestag. We scrutinized especially four amendments and found that the utilization of social sciences changed greatly from period to period. The total utilization of social sciences shows the following profile: 48 percent in 1967-9; 9 percent in 1974-5; 29 percent in 1977-9 and 14 percent in 1982-3. As can be seen from these figures, the impact of social sciences never regained the strength it enjoyed in the sixties. The second peak in distribution is due to severe cuts in welfare budgets at the end of the seventies. This reflects a struggle between the various ends and means of welfare state policies.

6. The structure of arguments. Although the reality of social science findings generally assumes a high degree of complexity, the arguments of users fail to reflect this. For instance, it is said that for every fact there is assumed to be a simple cause, and every political end can be achieved by appropriate means.

This kind of simplistic argument is used quite often to combine labour market and education policies, including attempts to reduce or elimate unemployment.

7. *Prescriptive and predictive utilizations.* The majority of all references to social science findings is—not surprisingly—descriptive (69 percent). But findings are very often incorporated in prescriptive (25 percent) and predictive (6 percent) contexts. At this point it is interesting to note that the Ministry of Labour and Social Order makes use significantly more often of predictive argument, while the Ministry of Education and Science tends towards *prescriptive* arguments. The employers prefer primarily a descriptive use of findings.

To illustrate the reported findings some quotations can be presented:

Descriptive. Referring to our survey, 23 percent of the unemployed are interested in a second vocational skill, 13 percent strive to complete acquisition of their first skill, 7 percent wish to achieve the school degree they failed to achieve at before. [INFRATEST-Institute, cited by Ministry of Labour and Social Order, 1978]

Prescriptive. [Professor] Lutz ... speaks of 'training on the job' being quite insufficient, for qualifications acquired this way have only a restricted use or no value on the labour market outside the company. From that finding the conclusion must be drawn that educational politics have to counteract those tendencies by instituting a variety of continuing schemes of education like ... [Institute for Sociological Research, ISF, cited by Ministry of Education and Science, 1978]

Summary and conclusions
Summary
1. The total number of references to social science was 761.
2. Only in about 10 percent of all cases was the source specified.
3. Users differ greatly in the extent to which they make use of social sciences.
4. Utilization changes significantly over time.
5. Utilization depends on the social and political issues involved.
6. Utilization is biased and prefers or ignores specific research fields and research approaches.
7. The structure of arguments is quite simplistic whenever social sciences are used.
8. Without following any particular logic, utilization is sometimes embedded in prescriptive or predictive contexts.

Conclusions
The passing of the Employment Creation Act (AFG) came about during a 'reform period' of German politics. In order to indicate the strong

belief in the utilization of social sciences at that time and that it sprang from the desire to base political measures on rational decision, I shall cite from the Ministry of Labour and Social Order, 1967:

> Continuing research carried out in the fields of occupations, labour market and education will henceforward clear up the basic processes and effects of technological, economical and social developments. Cyclical fluctuations including seasonal and structural changes in the labour market, qualitative and quantitative changes in occupations will be investigated. This research will be the foundation for all political measures carried out with the intention of maintaining stability and progress.

Such well-intended but impractical statements are quite typical of the sixties. They refer to the enlightenment ideal of rationality.

Another finding further amplifies the close connection between policy and science. In preparing the AFG Act the steering committee of the Parliament (AfAS) organized three hearings. Social scientists contributed 26 percent of all the evidence brought to the committee. The other participants came from unions, employers and from several groups with vested interests. If we take a closer look at the group of invited scientists we discover the important fact that only 20 percent of the social scientists came from universities, the remainder come from independent or business/union-supported research units. The conclusion is that there was a substantial social science utilization but mainly derived from non-university institutes.

Several amendments followed the original Employment Creation Act — legislation and more hearings were arranged. However, the number of invited social scientists gradually decreased while the participation of employers and especially unions increased. From the point of view of academia this observation may provoke the conclusion of an overall decreasing utilization of social sciences during the seventies. But such a conclusion is precipitate. First of all, a continuous influence of the Ministry of Labour's in-house social scientists was guaranteed through delegates of the Federal Office of Labour (*Bundesanstalt für Arbeit; BfA*) which is attached to the Ministry. Important here was the influence of the Institute for Labour Market and Occupational Research and of the Federal Institute for Vocational Training, whose establishment we noted earlier. Also there were other, indirect ways of making use of social sciences. Both unions and employers maintain their own large social science research institutes which provide the necessary social science background information for their delegates.

Therefore, non-utilization is first of all a problem for academic social sciences at the universities. This is well in line with the fact that the explicit citing of sources we found in the *material in 90 percent of all cases refers to non-university research units.* To pose it the other way round: we cannot conclude that the utilization of social sciences is minimal. Looking at the present situation we can say that any traditional bipolar model of exchange between 'producers' and 'users' of social science research is misleading. Changes in the forms and process of utilization are due to the large number of non-academic research units maintained by government, employers and unions. Producers and users are often identical in organizational terms. Another aspect of the connection between science and users is the expansion of commissioned university research and of research requested from private institutes. Their findings sometimes remain unpublished as a result of specific provisions in the research contracts. Finally, we should mention the existence of informal advisory councils in which scientific knowledge is continuously transferred and is used directly in decision-making. Taking all these arguments together we are inclined to the third of the previously mentioned models of utilization. The 'administration' model of utilization is the most useful one in our specific field. This model draws attention to the extensive influence of government and government-related bodies on social science policy through specially commissioned research and through the use of in-house research units.

I will end with a final consideration. This chapter has given an outline of the present situation and the preceding twenty years of utilization of social science. But one cannot simply extrapolate the analysed development to the future. Therefore, the forecast that utilization of social sciences in labour market and education policy will be completely restricted to non-university institutes might be wrong. There are some indicators suggesting a different outlook.

The large non-university research units tend to become bureau-cratized. This is the result of sheer size, civil servant mentality and political control. In a sense they produce 'fast and accurately' more and more of the same material, but lack flexibility and innovation. Realizing this problem the authorities are again becoming more interested in independent and university research which is intended to provide alternative solutions for urgent social problems. This, for example, was stressed by the former Minister of Education and Science, and by the present State Secretary of the Ministry. Both participated in a panel discussion held during the annual meeting of the German Sociological Association in Dortmund in 1984. To this suggestion social scientists may reply with the question, how many of the proposed alternatives will be used effectively? But there is yet another question concerning social science itself: what alternatives are the social sciences able to offer? The future of utilization depends on the accumulation of applicable knowledge, as well as on the goodwill of users.

Note

This chapter was written at the Netherlands Institute for Advanced Study (NIAS). We would like to thank Eckehard Konig (Hannover) for polishing the English.

6

Social science and social policy: who uses whom?

Robert H. Haveman

The social science research enterprise is large and absorbs substantial resources. In the US in 1980, federal government expenditure for social science research stood at over $1,000 million, having grown from a level of $150 million in 1964. It is a worthy activity to inquire into the impact of this research on society in general, and on the making of public policy in particular. However, this 'utilization question' masks another, equally interesting interaction between society or policy-making and the social sciences: to what extent do social science and its practitioners respond to trends in social thinking, to new developments in public policy, or to new sources of potential funding ?

In this brief paper, I attempt to shed some light on this question by tracing the impact of a major change in policy in the US — the War on Poverty-Great Society initiative in 1964 — on the direction and nature of the social sciences in the subsequent period.

The War on Poverty and the demand for social research: the coalescence in 1965
The early 1960s in the US, it will be recalled, was the era of 'McNamar-aism' in the federal government. Robert McNamara was President Kennedy's Secretary of Defense. He came to that position from the Presidency of the Ford Motor Company, where he had become con-vinced that applying modern management and 'systems analysis' tech-niques to public choices could make contributions to public sector efficiency. Relying heavily on military analysts from the RAND Cor-poration in California — a government-supported research and analytic 'think-tank' — McNamara created an Office of Assistant Secretary for Planning and Evaluation which became a mini-RAND-type think-tank within the department itself.

The history of that office and its contributions have been often described. For our purpose, it was important for one primary reason — its presence and the notoriety which accompanied it signalled a new approach to doing business in government. Systematic evaluations of the impacts of various policy options were to be made, and these evaluations were to guide the choices of decision-makers.

The influence of the McNamara approach culminated in the mandating of a new planning-programming-budgeting system (PPBS) by President Johnson in an executive order to all federal agencies in 1965. It required them to undertake the application of benefit-cost analysis, cost-effectiveness analysis, and programme evaluation techniques to their programme decisions.

The date on which the executive order was signed was just one year after the signing of the Economic Opportunity Act initiating the War on Poverty and establishing the Office of Economic Opportunity (OEO) as part of the White House. OEO was established to plan and propose strategies for mounting a governmental attack on the poverty problem. Through a process not well understood but, in retrospect, not surprising, the leading designers of the War on Poverty were RAND-type analysts, devoted to PPBS principles. The staff appointed by them to OEO was heavily populated by recruits from McNamara's Defense Department. If systematic analysis could guide defence-related decisions, and if a conscious planning-programming-budgeting approach would improve the effectiveness of government decisions in all areas, surely such an approach would be essential in planning for and mounting a War on Poverty.

From the very inception of planning for the War on Poverty, then, the assumption that research and evaluation should guide decisions has been a central tenet. Indeed, even during the earliest days of OEO, the planning, research and analysis (PR and E) office in the agency played an important, if not dominant, role in guiding policy decisions in the agency. And, central to the activities of that office was the belief that making policy to assist low-income people required answers to such questions as the following:

1. How is poverty to be defined, and given an appropriate definition? How many poor people are there? And, if the poor can be counted, what are their characteristics?
2. What factors have caused poverty, and which have led to its persistence over time? Is there a vicious circle of poverty which must somehow be broken? Is there a culture of poverty? To what extent does poverty have a racial basis?
3. What are the possible options for reducing poverty, and what is the likely effectiveness of each? Is manpower training, education, community action, rural development or direct cash transfers the superior approach to combating poverty?

Questions such as these, it should be noted, are basically social scientific in character. They are questions on which the social science research community should be able to shed light.

In addition to asking such questions, both OEO and a wide variety of other federal agencies which sensed an opportunity to tie their programmes to the anti-poverty mission began to support social science research on poverty-related issues. An Institute for Research on Poverty (IRP) was established at the University of Wisconsin-Madison with the purpose of conducting research on *'the nature, causes, and cures of poverty'*. The staff of the institute was to comprise many disciplines, including economics, sociology, psychology, law and related fields. Further, to underline the uncertain nature of this research domain, the institute staff would itself decide the kinds of problems to be researched, although at the same time IRP would be responsive to the research suggestions and requests of OEO.

Issues involving 'the nature, causes and cures of poverty' span a wide range. Indeed, portions of traditional sub-fields in economics, sociology and psychology could immediately be included in this definition. The fields of income distribution in economics and social stratification in sociology and social psychology are two examples.

In addition, research grants and contracts were awarded to numerous individual social scientists and social research organizations on a wide

TABLE 1

Federal poverty research and research-related activities ($ millions, current)

	Research	Demonstrations for policy development	Programme evaluation	Statistics	Total
1965	—	—	—	—	2.5
1968[b]	a	a	a	a	6.4
1971[b]	a	a	a	a	23.0
1976[c]	60	55	16	10	143.0
1977[d]	89.6	a	a	a	a

[a] Breakdown is unavailable.

[b] Data for 1968 and 1971 are external expenditures for research by the PR and E Office of OEO.

[c] Data for 1976 are from a tabulation of data assembled in Abramson, 1978.

[d] Data for 1977 are from fourteen federal agencies. The definition of poverty research is 'research activities that could be defined as systematic, intensive study directed toward the greater knowledge or understanding of individuals or groups with low incomes, or of public policies and programs concerned with individuals or groups with low incomes' Covello, 1979. The $89.6 million figure includes most of the research expenditures shown for 1976. To the extent that data from only fourteen agencies are included, it is an underestimate of the total level of federal support for poverty research narrowly defined.

variety of poverty-related questions. It is difficult to estimate the volume of federal government support for poverty research with any accuracy. Yet, by piecing together information from a variety of sources a rough picture of the growth of this support can be pieced together. It is presented in Table 1.

Based on these and related statistics, it seems reasonable to conclude that federal R&D (research) spending sponsored by War on Poverty programmes grew from less than $5 million per year prior to 1965 to approximately $200 million per year by 1980. Total federal R&D spending on poverty-related issues — a broader definition of federal proverty-related research and development spending — stood at about $1 billion in 1980 with 'research' comprising about one-third of this total. These figures compare with about $22 billion per year of total federal R&D expenditures. This growth was the greatest in the period 1965–76, which were the years of the Johnson (1963–8), Nixon (1968–72) and Nixon-Ford (1972–6) administrations. While Nixon's policy was viewed as far less supportive of social policy initiatives than that of his predecessor, in fact, there was little in the way of reduced outlays on War on Poverty programmes. Moreover, research and development spending was relied on throughout the Nixon years as a substitute for initiating new spending programmes. Moreover, the large social experiments in income maintenance, health insurance and housing assistance begun prior to 1972 ripened during the Nixon

TABLE 2

Federal poverty and poverty-related research, spending, as a proportion of some research and social welfare expenditure aggregates, 1976

	Federal poverty research	Federal poverty-related research
In 1976	*$60 million*	*$251 million*
As % of total national R & D spending	0.15	0.64
As % of total national research spending	0.41	1.72
As % of total national research spending on social sciences	7.23	30.12
As % of total federal research spending	0.76	3.17
As % of total public social welfare spending	0.05	0.20
As % of total social welfare spending on the poor	0.10	0.43

administration. Some reduction in the growth of poverty research
support came with the Carter administration (1976–80), which reductions presaged the outright retrenchment and collapse of support after
1980.

Table 2 presents the relationship of two estimates of federal poverty
research support — the narrowly defined 'poverty research' category
and the broader 'poverty-related research' category — to other research
and social welfare spending aggregates for 1976. While the narrow
definition of federal poverty research spending — that by federal anti-
poverty agencies — suggests that poverty research spending is about 7
percent of total national social science research spending, such spending
is less than 0.5 percent of the total national research budget. The
broader definition of federal poverty-related research spending — that
by all federal programmes related to the poverty problem — indicates
that poverty-related research accounts for about 30 percent of total
social science research spending in 1976 and about 2 percent of
national research spending. The bottom two rows suggest that federal
poverty (or poverty-related) research expenditures are trivial proportions of public social welfare spending or of public social welfare
expenditures going to people whose income fell below the poverty line
before receiving government income transfers. The broad definition of
federal poverty research spending was less than one-half of one percent
of public expenditures on the pre-transfer poor population by the late
1970s.

The response of the social science community to the demand for poverty research

The post-1965 period saw a burst of policy measures enacted by the
federal government on behalf of the poor. It also saw an unprecedented
level of research spending by War on Poverty programmes, and by
programmes related to the poverty problem which were quick to seize
on the poverty issue as a rationale for expansion.

A natural question regarding this flurry of political action and
research spending concerns its impact on the output of the social
science disciplines. Is there substance to Henry Aaron's (1978) assertion?[1]

> The subjects on which analysts do research are influenced by prevailing
> political interests and preconceptions. One need not be cynical to recog-
> nize that research agendas are influenced by the flow of money from
> government and foundations, which in turn try to use research budgets at
> least in part to improve decisions on current issues of public policy.
> [p.157]

To what extent, then, has the content and nature of the research
output of the social sciences been altered by the concern with anti-

poverty issues? How extensive was the increased emphasis on poverty-related research and has it persisted?

These questions are difficult to answer. Our approach has been to study the research output of the social science disciplines over time, in an attempt to identify the change in the level of poverty-related work within the disciplines before and after the War on Poverty. The disciplines included in our inquiry are economics, political science and sociology. These are the major fields of social research on which federal support for research on 'the nature, causes, and cures of poverty' has been focused.

In assessing the quantitative role of poverty-related research within these disciplines, we have taken three approaches. First, we focus on the five leading journals in each discipline and analyse the extent of poverty-related research in each over time. This provides an indicator of the extent to which poverty-related research has, over time, penetrated the highest and most prestigious outlets within each discipline. Second, to gain an indicator of breadth, we have tabulated the poverty-related content of articles in a fixed set of economics journals existing in 1980 over the same time period.

TABLE 3
Poverty-related research in five leading economics, sociology and political science journals, 1960–80

	Number of poverty-related articles	Poverty-related articles as % of total	Poverty-related pages as % of total
Economics			
1962–4	3	0.4	0.5
1971–3	59	6.4	6.5
1978–80	40	3.6	3.8
Political Science			
1962–4	2	0.4	0.5
1971–3	11	2.0	1.9
1978–80	10	2.0	1.7
Sociology			
1962–4	15	2.6	2.4
1971–3	41	6.2	8.8
1978–80	48	7.5	7.8

Table 3 summarizes the extent of poverty-related research in the five leading journals in economics, political science and sociology, from the early 1960s to 1980. The selection of the journals is, of course, judgemental, but the final choice was made only after consulting scholars in each of the disciplines.

The journals selected, by discipline, are:

Economics
   American Economic Review
   Econometrica
   Journal of Political Economy
   Quarterly Journal of Economics
   Review of Economics and Statistics
Political Science
   American Political Science Review
   American Journal of Political Science
   Journal of Politics
   Political Science Quarterly
   Western Political Quarterly
Sociology
   American Journal of Sociology
   American Sociological Review
   Social Forces
   Sociology and Sociological Research
   Sociological Quarterly

Consider, first, the economics journals. Prior to 1965, very little poverty-related research was published in these leading journals; in the 1971–3 period (taken to be representative of the period after the declaration of the War on Poverty), a large increase in poverty-related research is observed. Up to 6.5 percent of the articles and pages published in these leading journals focused on the problem of poverty. By the late 1970s, a significant tailing off of research output to between 3.5 and 4.0 percent of journal content is recorded. Four of the five journals showed a rapid decrease in the intensity of their poverty-related publishing from the early to the late 1970s; only *Econometrica* — whose tie to policy-related concerns is probably the least of all the journals — showed a persistent increase over the entire period.

While the overall pattern in political science is similar to that in economics, the increase from before to after the declaration of the War on Poverty is not nearly so large. However, the increase which did occur appears more persistent. In the 1962–4 period, poverty articles as a percent of the total stood at 0.4 in both economics and political science. While the percentage rose to more than 5 in economics, it peaked at 2 in political science.

Like economics and political science, the pattern of rapid increase in the representation of poverty research from before to after the declaration of the War on Poverty is also clearly seen in the five sociology journals. However, in sociology, the 1962–4 base level of poverty research is substantially higher than in these other two disciplines —

about 2.5 percent of articles and pages, as compared to 0.5 percent. Moreover, the level of poverty research in the peak 1971–3 period is greater in the sociology journals than in those of the other two disciplines — 6 percent in terms of articles and 9 percent in terms of pages, compared to about 6 percent in economics and 2 percent in political science. The persistence of interest in poverty research in sociology is clearly greater than in the other two disciplines. In the most recent period, over 7.5 percent of material in these sociology journals was devoted to poverty research, compared to less than 2 percent in political science and 3.5–4 percent in economics.

All of the disciplines, then, displayed a rapid increase in poverty research from the 1962–4 period to the 1971–3 period. This interest was sustained and persistent in both political science and sociology, though at a substantially higher level in the latter discipline. In economics, the substantial spurt of interest in poverty research in the post-1965 period had tapered off by 1980.

The data presented in Table 3 are for the leading journals in each of the three primary social science disciplines. Given the general difficulty of publishing material on highly topical issues in the leading scholarly journals, it could be claimed that the pattern shown in the tables is not representative of the discipline as a whole.

As a check on this pattern in one of the disciplines — economics — we made an effort to obtain a more global assessment of the incidence of poverty-related research over time.[2]

TABLE 4
Poverty-related research in ten 1963-listed economics journals, 1963–80

	Total number of articles published	Number of poverty-related articles	Poverty-related articles as % of total
1963	457	20	4.3
1968	323	27	8.4
1973	444	31	7.0
1980	391	30	7.7

To obtain this more comprehensive view, we have taken the ten journals (other than those analysed in Table 3) whose contents were indexed and abstracted in the 1963 *Journal of Economic Abstracts* and which were either general economics journals in English published in the United States, or international journals in English in special fields closely related to the poverty problem.[3] Holding constant this population of journals, we have tabulated the absolute number of poverty-related articles and the percentage of the total number of articles in these journals which were poverty-related (see Table 4). In this 1963 base set of journals, then, the incidence of poverty-related articles is about 3–4 percentage points higher than for the five leading economics journals, throughout the period. The pattern of increase in the incidence of poverty-related articles is similar across both sets of journals, increasing substantially from before to after the War on Poverty was announced. However, the persistence of poverty-related research appears to be greater in the ten journals than in the five leading journals. Indeed, after dropping from over 8 percent of the total in 1968 to 7 percent in 1973, the incidence (and the absolute number) of poverty-related articles in the ten journals had again increased by 1980.

The social science community:
intellectual leader or follower?

Whether measured by indicators of inputs — federal research and R&D spending — or outputs, it is clear that the War on Poverty has had a substantial impact on the social science disciplines. Federal R&D spending by War on Poverty programmes grew from a few millions of dollars at the inception of the War on Poverty to about $200 million by 1980 (Table 1). The poverty research (as opposed to R&D) component of this spending grew from, say, $1 million in 1965 to about $75 million in 1980. While these amounts are small relative to aggregate federal research spending, they came to equal about 10 percent of all federal social science research spending by 1980. Indeed, the increase of federal poverty research spending over the 1965–80 period accounts for over 15 percent of the growth in total social science research spending over this period. A broader definition of research on poverty issues — what we have called poverty-related research — stood at about 40 percent of total federal social science research by 1980, and equalled about one-half of the growth in federal social science resmarch spending over the 1965-80 period.

The output indicators tell much the same story. Irrespective of discipline, poverty-related research has come to occupy an increased share of journal space. This is true in both the leading journals of each discipline, and (at least in economics) in all of the relevant journals. From 1962–3 to 1980, poverty-related research increased from about 0.5 percent to about 4 percent of the space in the leading economics journals, from 0.5 percent to 2 percent of the space in the leading political science journals, and from 2 to about 8 percent of the space in the leading sociology journals. In economics, the incidence of poverty-related research is even greater in journals other than the five leading ones. About 8 percent of articles in non-leading journals were poverty-related in 1980, up from about 4 percent in 1965. This pattern, of course, prompts the speculation that the research outputs stimulated by current policy interests and supported by public money reflecting these interests are not at the frontier of the field. Research may be stimulated, and research directions altered, but are the social science disciplines advanced — either in substance or in method? Alternatively, the leading journals in the social science disciplines may avoid publishing research on topics of current interest, to limit potential claims of topicality at the expense of quality. Perhaps truth lies in both speculations.[4]

Finally, it is interesting to note that the proportion of journal output in these disciplines in 1980 corresponds rather closely to the 10 percent of all federal social science research spending which was accounted for by poverty research in 1980. Whether measured by input or by output, then, poverty research has come to occupy an important place in the social sciences disciplines. It would be hard to deny that the 'flow of money from government' has not influenced 'research agendas'. Aaron's claim would appear to have substance. Surely, the answer to the question of who uses whom is the one that an economist would expect: by its very nature, both parties to a free exchange benefit from it. The question of utilization, then, runs both ways.

Notes

1. Aaron (1978) went on to assert the following regarding the impact on the social sciences of this policy-making and research support:

> Much of this research was the direct result of the legislation itself, which required that a stipulated fraction of appropriations be spent on research and evaluation. Much was undertaken independently by hordes of academics issuing forth from graduate schools motivated not only by the ethics of scholarship but also by the desire to publish rather than perish. The products of this effort consisted of evaluation reports prepared under government contracts, journal articles prepared by academic scholars — often under government grants or contracts — books, magazine and newspaper articles, and an enormous amount of conversation about the new programs, how they worked and whether they were effective, all couched in a language that literally did not exist in prior decades and that those untrained in the social sciences could not understand. Even those who did not understand the language tried to speak it or write it. [p.170]

2. For several reasons, this more global calculation is difficult. First, while the five leading journals constitute a fixed pool from which to observe the incidence of poverty-related research over time, there is no such fixed pool for the discipline as a whole. Over time, journals are both initiated and phased out. Indeed, over the 1960–80 period there has been a veritable explosion in the number of journals in economics. Moreover, the set of journals included in the major bibliographic sources in the discipline has changed over time, with a general tendency toward increased coverage. Second, once one moves from the leading journals in a discipline to a wider selection of journals, the boundaries of the discipline become less clear. Finally, as the set of journals becomes more inclusive, the sheer number of articles on which a

judgement needs to be made regarding inclusion or non-inclusion as poverty research grows rapidly.

3. The *Journal of Economic Abstracts* is the predecessor to the *Journal of Economic Literature*. The ten journals included are:

American Journal of Economics and Sociology
Industrial and Labor Relations Review
Industrial Relations
Journal of the American Statistical Association
Journal of Law and Economics
Land Economics
Monthly Labor Review
National Tax Journal
Southern Economic Journal
Western Economic Review.

4. In a forthcoming book (Haveman, forthcoming), I conclude that the public poverty-related research support provided after 1965 had an impact on both the knowledge content and the method of the social science disciplines. In terms of gains in knowledge, I examine the research fields of (1) measuring economic well-being, poverty and inequality, (2) estimating the economic and social impacts of income support policies, (3) estimating the determinants of status attainment, and (4) research developments on the effects of education spending and reform, the extent and impacts of discrimination, and the potentials of labour market instruments. Methodological gains related to the War on Poverty initiative were found to be substantial in the areas of (1) evaluation research and policy analysis, (2) social experimentation, (3) econometric procedures for dealing with selectivity, and (4) microdata simulation modeling.

References

Aaron, Henry (1978) *Politics and the Professors: The Great Society in Perspective.* Washington, DC: Brookings Institution.

Abramson, Mark A. (1978) *The Funding of Social Knowledge Production and Application: A Survey of Federal Agencies.* Washington, DC: National Academy of Sciences.

Covello, Vincent A. (1979) 'Poverty Research in the United States: A Review of Federal Programs and Research Organizations', in National Academy of Sciences, *Evaluating Federal Support of Poverty Research.* Washington, DC: National Academy of Sciences.

Haveman, Robert (forthcoming) *Poverty Policy and Poverty Research, 1965–1980.* Madison: University of Wisconsin Press.

7

The ethics of research in a public enterprise

A.J. Berry, T. Capps, D. Cooper,
T. Hopper and E.A. Lowe

This chapter tells of a research project which was undertaken by a team
of academics in the publicly-owned UK coal industry from 1982 to
1984. At the end of that period the industry was subjected to a severe
industrial relations dispute. The details of the dispute are still a matter
of public debate and analysis. The central issue of the strike was the
planned reduction in production capacity. The management of the
National Coal Board (NCB) considered that the associated reduction in
manpower could be achieved by a programme of voluntary redundancy.
The National Union of Mineworkers sought to prevent this loss of jobs
and, following an announcement that the Cortonwood coalmine was to
be closed, called their members out on strike. In some parts of the coal
industry large numbers of workers chose to remain at work, arguing that
the union had not balloted its members prior to calling the strike. At the
start of the strike some 70 percent of the workers were out; more than a
year later the strike was ended with more than half of the workers at
work. It is important to note that the dispute was particularly bitter both
between coalminers, police, management and the government. The
dispute left a legacy of fractured communities and aborted trust which
will last for several generations.

The purposes of the authors in conducting the research project were
to develop understanding of how the management system of control and
accountability is perceived from the various viewpoints of involved
'actors', of contributing to the development of management theory and
of contributing to the effectiveness of the focal organization in its social
context. In order to conduct research within an organization it is
necessary to obtain the consent and support of at least some of its
members. The negotiation of access is problematic and occasionally
limiting of both the focus of a research study and the publication of the
findings as a contribution to academic development. Research findings
are not value neutral and often challenge the conceptions of the very
members who gave consent for the research to be conducted.

The specific issue raised here is that of the nature of obligation and responsibilities arising in the conduct of academic research in conditions of acute and lengthy industrial conflict. The team chose to make some of their insights publicly available rather than limiting them to the organization. This choice foreclosed further research and led to the exclusion of the research team from further involvement in the research topics both by the organization's managers, by others hired as consultants by the managers and by a professional body which became involved in publication of some of the researchers' analysis.

Section 1 of this chapter describes the conflict which arose when the researchers sought to make a contribution to the public debate about the future of the industry in the midst of a severe industrial dispute.

Section 2 gives an account of the genesis, conduct and conclusions of the research project within the organization.

Section 3 considers the implications for social science research which can be drawn from this project and publication.

1. The decision to write and publish
This section describes the conflict which arose when the researchers sought to use the insights of research to make a contribution to the public debate about the future of the coal industry in the midst of a severe industrial dispute. The central point made by the researchers was that the accounting measures of profit and loss as presented in the National Coal Board's accounts were an inadequate basis for the public justification for plant closure decisions; that such decisions should consider future marginal costs and revenues and transfer prices for the supply of coal to other UK nationalized industries. The arguments for and against the decision to publish the paper are discussed. The response of the NCB was to foreclose further research and to refuse to engage in a review of the researchers' arguments and those of other academics. The NCB established a private inquiry into its accounting practices which excluded the researchers. The publishers of the journal *Accountancy* (the Institute of Chartered Accountants in England and Wales) also set up an inquiry which excluded the research team.

Some eight months after the start of the dispute two members of the research team were approached by other academic colleagues on the topic of the closures of 'uneconomic' mines. The decision to close productive capacity was being publicly debated on the notion that unprofitable meant uneconomic.[1] Further, there were numerous public statements being made about the size of the 'subsidy' paid by the government to the NCB.

The approach and these debates forced the research team to reconsider its role. The key question for us was whether we should respond to the approach which had been made to us. Since it would have been impossible to conduct an academic discussion in camera, such a step would entail a public debate. The arguments against responding were that any public statement by us would be seen as either support for the position of the NCB or as support for the National Union of Mineworkers, that our research had been quite explicitly kept away from the closure decisions and processes, that responding would probably mean the end of research co-operation from the managers, that publication would embarrass the sponsors of the earlier research, that access for other researchers might be prejudiced. Finally, the relation between accounting and economic costs for decision-making was one of the hoary classics of undergraduate education. The arguments for responding were that the dispute was extraordinarily damaging and costly, the fact of unpleasant conflict is not an excuse for standing on the sidelines, and that the endemic public confusion of accounting concepts such as profitability with economic concepts of future social costs and benefits meant that we had a responsibility to offer what insights we had. Further, it was an opportunity to show that the technical accounting matters were not trivial and that accounting was not a neutral technical activity. We believed that accounting reports were being used in a partisan manner and this should be the stuff of public debate.[2] Broadly, we decided, after lengthy debate, that our responsibility as scholars went beyond our immediate interests as researchers, and, more sharply, that we were prepared to forego the chance of working alongside the NCB managers in any future work upon the development of their accounting and control procedures.

The response of the research team was to prepare a draft paper on the relationship between the financial accounts of the Coal Board and an economic analysis of the closure of coal mines. Following discussions of this draft among members of the research team we agreed that this paper would be based upon published data only, as we had no wish to make use of any data which could be regarded as privileged or arising directly from the research. The central argument in the paper was that the accounting definition and measurement of 'profit' is an inadequate basis for decision-making. We used the publicly available data for the Cortonwood coalmine to illustrate some of the detailed points. What was at issue was the fact that we challenged the public belief that 'unprofitable' meant 'uneconomic' and by implication that public justification of pit closure decisions based upon this unfortunate belief was less than reliable. Five main points were made:

1. Given the interdependence within the NCB, and within the energy sector (e.g. oil, gas, electricity) and with other nationalized industries (railways and steel-making), there are major problems in determining a fair and reasonable revenue figure for sales proceeds in economic and financial terms for the NCB as a whole and individual collieries in particular.

2. The NCB accounts are prepared on an absorption basis (broadly,

all costs are allocated to units of production). It is exceedingly difficult to appraise the relative contribution of a pit (let alone a production face within a pit) as such information is not collated on an ongoing basis. Emphasis is instead concentrated on profit/tonne and unit costs. Given that many costs appear to be fixed, volume is therefore encouraged at a time of overproduction.

3. Not all costs included in the NCB standard account statement (called the F23), for presenting colliery profit and loss are related to current pit operation (e.g. early retirement costs and area and HQ overheads are omitted).

4. Depreciation is included, but more as a book-keeping convention than because it is a relevant cost for decision purposes. A capital change would be more relevant, if extremely objective.

5. Most importantly, the standard account statement (F23) is an historic account. Such accounts are unreliable for predicting future expected profits, especially given the uncertain geology and lengthy development work in deep mining.

The final version of the paper was prepared by two members of the team and submitted to the journal '*Accountancy*', chosen because it was a professional journal which was not overtly political. The paper was submitted in the normal way, except that it was written about the central issue in the middle of an increasingly bitter dispute, marked by escalating violence and the continuation of hard positions by government, management and unions alike. The editorial staff of the journal, very properly, saw the likely impact of this paper and, having negotiated a revised text (which included a more provocative title) with the two team members, released a date-embargoed version to the press. They also sent a copy to the National Coal Board for their comment. The team regrets that a copy was not sent to the NCB directly, but the paper was intended for a wider audience, and we had no wish to implicate the earlier sponsors with our views.

As the team understood the matter, the NCB staff preferred that the paper should not be published but they had no wish to censure the argument. Furthermore, the NCB had complained that there were errors of fact in the paper. The authors took the view that they had a responsibility to ensure that any 'errors' were considered. So the team agreed to withhold publication until after a discussion with the NCB finance staff at Board HQ. However, the date-embargoed copy of the version of the paper attracted considerable press and television news coverage, some of which focused on whether the NCB had attempted to suppress the piece together with the question of whether the accounts were a sensible basis for making colliery closure decisions. Indeed, the original version of the article was the subject of parliamentary discussions and led to Margaret Thatcher, the Prime Minister, stating on 6 December 1984:

> If the Hon. Gentleman regards the matter of coal merely as one of accounting — and thinks that it can all be done with mirrors — he will be happy if we eliminate the £1.3 billion a year subsidy to the NCB. This is not a matter of accounting but a matter of fact.[3]

It is ironic that the less publicized but crucial parts of the argument in the paper were that, firstly, the transfer pricing between the Central Electricity Generating Board (which is a public enterprise that buys nearly 70 percent of the coal produced by the NCB) and the NCB and, secondly, the treatment of redundancy payments did indeed make the the subsidy a mere contrivance (or a matter of mirrors).

The meeting to discuss the paper
The meeting of the NCB finance staff and the project team took place at the NCB HQ in a strained atmosphere. After the events surrounding the release of the initial draft had been clarified, the NCB gave us their view of the 'errors' and misunderstandings in the piece. Of special relevance were the calculations of marginal costs associated with the Cortonwood Colliery, the proposed closure of which had been the flashpoint of the dispute. The team had drawn its data from published sources and estimates and was pleased to accept the data from the NCB, to which we had not had access, and incorporated this new data into the paper. The NCB forcibly stated that closure decisions were based upon an analysis of markets, potential revenues, potential costs together with the likely effects of additional capital investment; a procedure which went well beyond the confines of financial accounts. The team accepted this and observed that such an understanding had been indicated in the paper. However, the team had been unable to study the process of closure decisions by the original agreement with the area managers. The team members also rebutted any suggestion that they had used any confidential data in the preparation of the paper. We understood that the evidence which we presented on that occasion was accepted by the NCB. We also held to our view that the financial measures of profit and loss were the currency of public debate and justification of closures, and that this indeed was the central thrust of the paper (although this focus had not been emphasized by the press).

A non-executive director of the NCB who was also present at this meeting suggested that the rights of academics to publish were subordinate to wider issues, although he was not forthcoming as to the nature of these wider issues. We were unclear whether this was a ploy agreed by the NCB management to see whether we could be frightened off or whether it was merely the whim of the individual. Rightly or wrongly the members of the team perceived this intervention as a hint of censorship and bullying, which highlighted the dilemma of the team but strengthened its resolve to publish.

The revision of the paper

The central argument in the paper was left unchanged; otherwise the team put considerable effort into making the text of the paper somewhat less abrasive and more exact. The team was careful to amend the statements about the marginal costs of the Cortonwood Colliery to include the new data which the NCB had provided. More detailed attention was given to the issue of relevant prices of unsaleable coal and the transfer price of coal products from the NCB to the Central Electricity Generating Board (which takes 70 percent of output). The key to this issue of transfer pricing was the problem of establishing a notional world market price for coal landed in the UK, when there was no such commodity relevant for a sensible comparative analysis.

Copies of the revised paper were sent to the editor of the journal *Accountancy* and to the NCB. The team agreed that the journal could prepare a press release. The NCB was upset to find that the team had not fundamentally revised the argument. The press picked up the story and in general gave a reasonable report of the views of the team and of those of the NCB.

When the paper was finally published, the journal also carried a comment by the NCB's board member for finance. In this comment he restated that the NCB used a complex procedure to consider closure of productive capacity, a view which we had acknowledged in the paper. The question of the confusion of accounting measures of profit and loss with broader economic considerations of benefits and costs was not addressed by the NCB. Other parts of the comment set out to discredit the authors by claiming that we had used privileged information in order to produce the paper in spite of the fact that we had made clear to the NCB that all of the data used in the paper were drawn from published sources and had understood that the NCB had accepted this point.

An NCB inquiry. In the comment to our paper, the NCB announced that it was to set up an investigation of its own:

> In view of the widespread publicity these matters have attracted, we believe that the accountancy profession, the people in the Coal industry and the general public deserve a detailed commentary upon all the issues raised. The Board have, therefore, invited eminent and independent accountants to work with us in preparing a report. (Harrison, 1985)

The membership of this group included an academic accountant and three other senior members of the accounting profession, presumably as consultants. In response to our request to this new group for a meeting we were asked to provide, 'from our files', chapter and verse for the argument that public justification for closures is debated upon notions of profit and loss. Not only did we supply references to the statements of the Prime Minister about the closure of loss-making pits, but we also referred them to *Hansard*, Select Commitee Reports and various reports in the NCB's publication *Coal News.*

Some ten months later the research team was invited to meet these consultants but the consultants were unwilling or unable to state the terms of reference for their inquiry, nor were they prepared to discuss their methods or their findings or understandings. The consultants were to report to the NCB and had no discretion to publish their findings. A report was finally published (Custis et al., 1985) by the NCB.

The publishers' inquiry. A second consequence of the publication of the paper was that the publishers of the journal, the Institute of Chartered Accountants in England and Wales (ICAEW), set up an inquiry with no public terms of reference to examine the events surrounding the publication of the paper in the journal. Apparently, they were worried about how an article with political implications could have been published in a professional journal. As the team of researchers understand the matter, this inquiry was partly conducted by the NCB board member for finance, he being a member of the council of the ICAEW. This seemed less than the pursuit of a true and fair view, especially as the team had reason to know that his recall of the events surrounding publication was rather limited. One of the research team, who is a fellow of the ICAEW, was refused the chance to give a view to this inquiry or indeed to be appraised of the terms of reference. A report had been circulated to the ICAEW council members; only at the insistence of a rather independent member of the council was a note added to the effect that the research team had not been consulted. This process of exclusion of half of the available evidence (i.e. the experience and factual knowledge of the research team) seems to have been a kind of closure of mind of a professional body, apparently more concerned to support a person rather than gain full knowledge.

Other consequences of publication are harder to identify, particularly since the team is not now actively involved with the NCB. Certainly, the contents of the article have been used by other commentators in their analyses of NCB and for future energy strategies for the UK. The ramifications of the consultants' report with regard to NCB accounting practices is also unknown but it seems that the arguments in *Accountancy* and other published articles, including that of the Monopolies and Merger Commission, have been interpreted as criticisms of extant practices. From the weight of evidence and argument advanced it is probable that the principal changes of attitude and behaviour should be located within the government ministries responsible for energy and finance as well as within the NCB itself.

2. The genesis of a research project

This section gives an account of the genesis, conduct and conclusions of the research project in the National Coal Board. The processes described provide an insight into the complex relationships between researchers and managers, the degree of misunderstandings and the extent to which they failed to meet each others' perceptions of the essential purposes and processes in the studies. The uses of the results of this research were limited by the nature of these misunderstandings. In no simple sense was this the fault of one or other party to the project.

One of the criticisms of accounting research is that a great deal of it has been more concerned with theorizing (e.g. the debate on inflation accounting) than with the worlds of professional and managerial practice. To respond to this criticism a meeting was arranged between the Sheffield committee of the Institute of Cost and Management Accountants (ICMA) and the accounting group in the University of Sheffield. This initiative led to the creation of a research group whose work is the subject of this paper.

The researchers were seeking to create a research project involving close collaborative work with management in an interpretive and action framework. There was thus a conscious wish to develop a relationship with this part of the NCB in order to explore the possibility of conducting research. Approval was granted without difficulty but involved certain constraints, which we agreed to accept. These were that we would confine our investigations to the management team in the area, that is we would not have any contact with any of the trade unions or with the headquarters of the National Coal Board on the specific subject matters in the research. Also we agreed not to study decisions and procedures relating to the closure of collieries. Apart from these provisos we were given generous access to the managers and to relevant documentation. It was also agreed that the management would be enabled to comment on any publication arising directly out of the research. At that time the Monopolies and Mergers Commission (MMC) was conducting an investigation of the NCB. The research team was provided with access to some of the relevant documents prepared originally for the MMC.

At no time did the host organization provide any money, although it provided considerable time for discussion, interviewing, etc. There was no question of any payment for the time of the research team, this being already covered by the nature of the academic appointments.

Research strategy

At the inception of the project it was our view that a particularly fruitful way of exploring management control practices would be to adopt a 'grounded theory' approach, (Glaser and Strauss, 1967). The researchers were infused with theory having recently completed a monograph on new approaches to management control, (Lowe and Machin, 1983). We also wished to create an action research mode in order that we could, through the project, make a contribution to the development of accounting and control procedures within the host organization. The research strategy was then to gain some credibility by coming to understand the actual accounting and control processes in one of the NCB areas.

Primary data collection methods were from documents and records and through a series of interviews with a variety of members of the management teams at the area office and at the individual pits together with discussions with members of the area accounting staff. Later we augmented this data through interviews with accountants, planners, marketing and industrial relations personnel at regional and national levels. These interviews were based on an interview protocol. The team tried to have three members present at all interviews in order to ensure adequate coverage, to follow interesting leads and to enable notes to be compared in order to produce a sufficiently accurate record of the responses of the interviewee.

The result of this stage of the research was the preparation of a report to the management of the area. The report was a descriptive analysis of the control procedures of that area. To the extent that the report appeared to be a confirmation of the understandings of the managers, the researchers were confident that the methods which had been used were appropriate to the research objectives. This report was written in a non-technical style. There were a number of important issues deeply embedded in the report. Among them the themes of the management of ambiguity and uncertainty, the degree of shared meanings accorded to the accounting and control procedures and the decoupled nature of the organization[4] were significant issues (Berry et al., 1985a).

The response of the management team was one of muted interest with some expressions of disappointment that the report had not been more critical. Perhaps this was a disguised way of telling the team that they had not provided solutions to some of the difficulties or concerns among the area staff. The report was focused upon management control from perspectives of accounting and organization theory together with discussion from broader financial and economic considerations. This caused some surprise. However, the team had demonstrated its ability to understand the issues in the organization, had gained some level of credibility and was permitted to continue further research. Indeed, the chief accountant of the area was prepared to present the paper jointly with the research team at two conferences and to discuss the value of practitioners liaising with academics in research work.

The second phase

The thrust of the second phase of the project, which was funded through the Open Door Scheme of the Economic and Social Research Council,[5] was a detailed review of the processes of accounting and accountability both at the area level and at several of the coalmines. The project also included an assessment of the degree to which financial thinking had permeated the production units, i.e. collieries.

The primary task of this phase of the research was to describe the process of accountability from the coal-face management to as high up the organization as possible.

Use of the second report

The report, based on the second phase, was of considerable interest to the accounting staff. Reactions of the management team were more muted. Perhaps this was because there were no specific recommendations for action.[6] Rather, there was a series of issues to which the managers were directed as part of a possible path to the development of organizational control procedures. At a meeting between the research team and the area managers, the managers indicated that the findings were accurate but they were seeking immediate prescriptions. The area director curtailed discussion by stating that there was no alternative to existing methods. The researchers asked for, and were granted, permission to discuss the report with individual managers. Unhappily, the onset of the industrial dispute frustrated these discussions.

The report was deposited with the Economic and Social Research Council. It found a further use in that the research team was invited to present the report to the members of two of the senior management courses at the NCB Staff College.

As far as the team was able to discover, the report had no direct effect upon the practices of the area. From previous research studies and by reputation, the area was limited, by its remit from the HQ, to production matters with a rather nugatory approach to any economic considerations. In that sense the area management was unable to have an effect upon its procedures to include more attention to the economic implications of its actions. However, the report did seem to parallel some of the observations being made by a consulting firm about the use and value of devolving a business unit approach further down the hierarchy.

The methods of the researchers, in their wish to manage a project which involved the managers in all of its stages, were somewhat at odds with the prevailing styles of line managers. To some extent the results of this stage of the project were a challenge to the conceptions which the managers had of their roles, authority and powers. The evidence that the carrying out of the accountability process was based upon some technical deficiencies and that such processes served ends other than, and in addition to, those formally acknowledged was not admissible. Similarly, developmental methods at odds with the traditional styles of management were discomforting.

The third phase
The research team was becoming interested in extending its studies into the whole organization of the NCB. Several themes were emerging as priorities, among them a comparative study of control and accounting in coal industries in other countries and a study of the social and political context of the industries. We were interested in describing the manner in which governments had sought to control these coal industries; the team was preparing to develop a history of the relationship of the NCB and the UK Government in the period prior to nationalization and since nationalization. Following upon the publication of the paper described above, this strand of research was abandoned.

3. The implications for social science research
One central problem which arises in this saga is the question of owner-ship of the research process and that of the research findings or that of the insights generated by the researchers. The specific remit of the research was that nothing would be published without prior feedback to the managers and that no confidential data would be disclosed. The problem arose here not in the process of the actual research but in the fact that the organization in focus had been catapulted into a conten-tious process of change and subsequently into a severe industrial dispute. While it is true that the findings of the research were partially rejected (see earlier discussion) the paper which gave rise to the fracas was a parallel activity of a group of well-informed academics who knew enough to construct an argument from public rather than private sources.

   The research team takes the standpoint that in this case its responsi-bility as academics overrode considerations of courtesy to the managers of the NCB. In no way did the team breach the undertakings which it gave to the managers but team members are aware that the publication of a critical paper by a group which did have considerable insight into the NCB financial procedures could be taken as more authoritative than the mere quality of the arguments. It was our view that the very serious and difficult nature of the industry's problems meant that we must attempt to influence the debate, in public, which it was hoped would

lead to a broadly acceptable and intelligible resolution of those problems. The values of the researchers were such that they made the choice
to publish. This decision generated the fantasy that the researchers were
all left–wingers, politically inspired — but this was untrue. Three of the
authors are broadly in sympathy with the Labour Party, one is a member
of the Liberal Party and the fifth has no interest in politics at all. None of
the team had ever been faced with the conflicts of responsibilty in
research so sharply. While this may be rich testament to the protected
world of academics, it is also witness to the polarized nature of political
and academic debate in the UK, for it was observable that the contribution of the findings and ideas from social science were unacceptable
to either the government or to the managers of the National Coal Board.

We discovered some of the limitations of the pursuit of research in
conditions of conflict. It was clear to us that the conflictual nature of the
industry meant that the output of the research process could not in any
practical manner be seen as value-free. We also discovered that it was
deemed unhelpful to challenge or to focus upon those values as obstacles to development. While a number of managers agreed with the
descriptions and insights of the research, it was also clear that the
managers were unwilling to consider any process of change which could
be generated from the research.

The responsibilities to the academic community had been met
through the publication of the first and second reports and it is much to
the credit of the managers of the focal area of the NCB that they
consented to the publication of these papers. Some further dissemination of the research was possible through discussions at the NCB staff
college. It is important to note, however, that the primary difficulty
arose from the decision of the researchers to focus upon a matter which
had been explicitly excluded from the original research.

The methodology, essentially a grounded theory approach, together
with the constraints within which the research was conducted, led to a
partial understanding of the processes of management control in the
NCB area. This partial understanding may be more influenced by a
replication of managerial ideologies than the authors could determine.
This unintended consequence of the research is witness to the difficulties associated with the grounded theory approach of ensuring that
observations are adequate with respect to the phenomena to be studied.
While to some extent academic colleagues have used the research
reported in Berry et al. (1985a) as an exemplar of the grounded theory
approach to management control, one useful outcome of this research is
a new insight for the researchers of the limitations of their methodology.

There is one central issue remaining in this story of the uses and
abuses of social science research. That issue is the overt power wielded
to deny the potential application of the insights of the research and the

power used by the managers to deny a variety of alternative frameworks for the analysis of management decisions, together with the power of the organization to foreclose further research and the power of the council of a professional institute to exclude from themselves data which would materially contribute to their inquiry. In all of these cases the consequence of the exercise of power was to limit the application of research ideas in a general sense. The unobtrusive power (Hardy, 1985) exercised by the UK government to limit the analysis and focus of the NCB management's decisions on closures to the legal boundary of the NCB was a key element in the definition of the public debate. The evidence for this is the lack of any published government statement of the wider costs and benefits of the proposed changes to the coal industry. Of course, the research team was not powerless, nor was it the passive victim of other people's power. Members of the research team empowered themselves to engage in the research project within the terms of reference agreed and to modify their own behaviour in order to contribute to a public debate in the middle of an acute industrial conflict.

Notes

1. The NCB defines 'uneconomic' at its legal boundary. This means that its measure must be profit/loss as it has no publicly known means of measuring profitability of pits (there being no developed sets of balance sheets with measures of capital employed for each of the collieries). It is conceivable that the NCB calculates the net present value of the future cash flows associated with the proposal to close a colliery; it is difficult to comment on this point because nothing of this nature is published. Of course, any such calculation would only include cash flows at the boundary of the NCB and would exclude any externalities: that is, any costs borne by the social security departments or losses borne by domestic suppliers would be ignored.

2. Glyn (1984) had offered the argument that the financial accounts of the NCB were not completely helpful in closure decisions as they did not include costs incurred external to the NCB; e.g. the costs of unemployment benefit. Equally Robinson's (1984) analysis of the NCB showed that a separation of some of the NCB's costs into 'sunk' and 'avoidable' would markedly change the decisions about the appropriate capacity to be kept in production. It is inconceivable that the economists of the NCB staff were unable to perform the analysis which Glyn, Robinson and the research team had made. It is, of course, possible that assumptions about the length of time which the unemployment benefits would be paid would differ but the central issue here is the fact that the costs and benefits of closure of capacity must include those external to the NCB.

3. There is a well-worn argument that the current UK government wishes to reduce the cash flow to the NCB without any consideration of the consequences for the social security budgets. The appointment of the new chairman, Mr McGregor, was predicted upon the notion that he would lead the NCB into a programme to increase technical efficiency, increase investment in the high output collieries and reduce any government subsidies by a closure programme. However, by an odd quirk

of domestic politics the UK government had increased the subsidy to the NCB in 1981 in order to prevent the NCB from proceeding with the closure of some twenty collieries. (It was thought that the government was so unpopular that it did not wish to provoke a politically damaging dispute.) It is important to note that the Secretary of State for Social Security did not engage in a debate about the effects of government actions in general and the NCB in particular upon unemployment payments, health, etc.

4. This notion of the research organization having an uncoupled control structure is similar to the idea of organizations as loosely coupled systems, meaning that in addition to an attachment between two or more parts of an organization each also maintains its own identity and separateness (cf. Weick, 1979).

5. For further details of the Open Door Scheme see Chapter 8.

6. The wording of the Open Door Scheme of the Economic and Social Research Council which provided the funding could be interpreted as a consultancy approach and raised false expectations.

References

Berry A. J., T. Capps, D. Cooper, P. Ferguson, T. Hopper and E. A. Lowe (1985a) 'Management Control in an Area of the NCB. Rationales of Accounting Practices in a Public Enterprise', *Accounting Organisations and Society*, 10 (1): 3–28.

Berry, A. J., T. Capps, D. Cooper, P. Ferguson, T. Hopper and E. A. Lowe (1985b) 'NCB Accounts — A Mine of Mis-information?', *Accountancy*, January.

Capps et al. (1984) *Report to the ESRC.*

Custis, P. J., D. Morpeth, E. Stamp and D. P. Tweedie (1985) 'Report of an Independent Committee of Inquiry on Certain Accounting Matters Relating to the Affairs of the National Coal Board'. London: NCB.

Glaser, B. G. and A. Strauss (1967) *The Discovery of Grounded Theory.* New York: Aldine.

Glyn, A. (1984) 'The Economic Case Against Pit Closures'. Sheffield: NUM.

Hardy, C. (1985) 'The Nature of Unobtrusive Power', *Journal of Management Studies.*

Harrison, B. (1985) 'Pitfalls of Academic Accounting', *Accountancy*, January.

Lowe, E. A. and J. L. Machin (1983) *New Perspectives in Management Control.* London: Macmillan.

Robinson, W. (1984) 'How Large a Coal Industry?', *Economic Outlook*, 9 (3).

Weick, D (1979) *The Social Psychology of Organizing.* Reading, Mass: Addison-Wesley.

8

Research as action: an experiment in utilizing the social sciences

John Gill

This chapter reports three years' research into the pilot phase of the Social Science Research Council's[1] Open Door scheme, a scheme designed to facilitate social science research utilization. First, some general issues of social science utilization are examined, followed by the background to the creation of the Council's Open Door scheme to help meet these difficulties. Then, findings from research into the pilot phase of the scheme from 1977 to 1980 are discussed, including its future operation and potential for influencing managerial activity in its widest sense.

The managerial academic interface

The term 'social science research' has negative connotations for managers and, indeed, for many sections of our society. This was brought home to me, for example, when I was advised by an experienced industrial copywriter, whose job was to produce marketing brochures for managerial customers, that both the words 'social scientist' and 'research' were better replaced if a favourable impact was desirable. When managers free-associate with the term 'social science research' they generally think of long time-scales; esoteric, non-applicable, highly theoretical findings; and loss of control over data which may be threatening to the status quo and widely accepted managerial ideologies. By contrast, managers have been greatly influenced by the large number of attractively packaged commercial social science approaches to leadership, problem solving and organizational change. Paradoxically, the academic social science community regards most of these as inadequately tested, diagnostically weak and based on partial, out-of-date theory. In consequence, it is not surprising that users often experience disillusionment after considerable financial investment, and social science applications come to be jokingly regarded as a 'flavour of the month' approach determined according to particular managerial fads and fancies (Tranfield et al., 1975). This poses the dilemma for the applied academic social scientist of reconciling the twin objectives of the

99

application of knowledge and methodological caution. Cherns (1970) makes this point when he matches managerial problems to research institutions in terms of the research methods they use, and comes to the conclusion that the more generalizable the research findings, and hence their greater general utility, the weaker the possibility that they will get into practice. Managers complain that the language of the social sciences is expressed in jargon designed deliberately to make simple ideas difficult to understand, although, as has been pointed out elsewhere, managers do not seem to have the same difficulty with the languages of economics, marketing or finance (Heller, 1976). It might well be that accusations of jargon, while partially true, are simply one of a number of managerial defences which underlie basic concerns about social science research. One of these concerns, to which we shall return later, may well be that such research is potentially very threatening to core issues of managerial ideology and values in ways which financial, economic and marketing data are not; this is perhaps further confirmed by the greater managerial control of the packaged social science approach mentioned earlier. If this speculation is so, then the ways in which social science researchers work with managers, and the degree of control which the latter have over the research, may well, in the future, be very significant in reducing the antipathy which exists and which is well put by Rowan. According to Rowan (1974), a sophisticated manager asked to comment on the work of traditional social science researchers would probably say:

> 'I don't like the way you claim to be objective when your objectivity is somewhat phoney and only succeeds in generalizing your work to the point of irrelevance and triviality. Nor do I like the way in which you claim to be neutral and kid yourself you are not involved when in fact you greatly care how the results come out. At the same time, if you really could be cold and neutral, I wouldn't like that either because you are in reality part of the data and that position is a symptom of a fundamental psychological defect common amongst would-be scientists.'

This brings us to the role of the academic researcher. Ultimately, the rewards of successful research for academic initiators of research proposals to funding bodies are career advancement in academic institutions and further grant support. Accordingly, it is not surprising that most researchers choose their language and methods to impress their peer group, not only when requesting funds for research proposals, but also in papers presenting findings from the work. As a crude generalization, it is probably the case that research methods for new projects are primarily chosen by researchers according to the known preferences of various funding bodies and the academic community, rather than suiting methods to the problem under investigation. As

Argyris (1970) points out, there are similarities between mechanistic systems and the system created during 'rigorous' research. The researcher presents his problem and clearly defines his objectives; he controls the subject and carries out an expert diagnosis; action from the work is minimal and the subject is largely unaffected. The academic is chiefly concerned with publishing findings from his work. Not only is this an indirect way to influence change, it is probably made less capable of assimilation by unintelligible writing as a deliberate strategy. Modest support has been found for what Scott Armstrong (1980) calls the 'Dr Fox phenomenon'; that is, that management scientists gain academic prestige by unintelligible writing. A positive correlation was found between the prestige of ten management journals and their 'fog indices' (reading difficulty). Furthermore, thirty-two faculty members were asked to rate the prestige of four passages from management journals. The content of the passages was held constant while readability was varied. The passages that were more difficult to read were rated higher in research competence (Scott Armstrong, 1980; Remus, 1977).

Similarly, Ansoff (1977) speculated on three reasons why the results of management science do not sell and came to the conclusion, first, that, as in any commercial marketing situation, there is no incentive for the client to learn the seller's language. This places the burden of learning on the scientist and, regrettably, it seems that neither social nor management scientists have risen to the occasion. As we have seen, instead of learning users' language, they have deliberately developed an unintelligible jargon of their own. However, learning the language is not enough. To be saleable the product must be practical, attractive, interesting and valid within the customer's culture.

Research methods and utilization
On the above analysis, there are then considerable differences to be reconciled between the managerial and academic cultures if academic research is to be utilized and both parties, academics and users, are to benefit. Cherns (1968) points out the differences between user needs, motivations and values and those of researchers, and offers solutions based on a research strategy which has become known as action research

> a vehicle for concept-swapping and for changing and redesigning organizations. It involves identifying the goals of an organization, analysing its operations, and introducing change by means of fully monitored and evaluated experiments. (Cherns, 1973)

The action research process is illustrated diagrammatically in Figure 1 and is contrasted with 'pure' research and consultancy in Table 1.

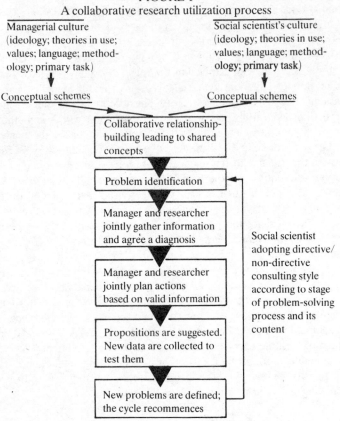

FIGURE 1
A collaborative research utilization process

| Managerial culture (ideology; theories in use; values; language; methodology; primary task) | Social scientist's culture (ideology; theories in use; values; language; methodology; primary task) |

Conceptual schemes   Conceptual schemes

Collaborative relationship-building leading to shared concepts

Problem identification

Manager and researcher jointly gather information and agree a diagnosis

Manager and researcher jointly plan actions based on valid information

Propositions are suggested. New data are collected to test them

New problems are defined; the cycle recommences

Social scientist adopting directive/non-directive consulting style according to stage of problem-solving process and its content

Action research has a large literature (Gill, 1978). Today a considerable amount of research work is done in this tradition, particularly by the Tavistock Institute and its disciples, but the fact remains that such work is peripheral to mainstream social science research (Brown, 1967).[2] The main attack on action research is contained in a plea for the separation of social science from practice by analogy with the natural science division of labour between scientist and engineer. This has become institutionalized to the extent that many funding bodies are, to say the least, lukewarm about research proposals in the action research tradition. They are likely to suggest that the researcher is at best confused and insufficiently specific or trying to obtain public funds for consultancy. As Fineman (1981) states in an attack on social science research funding practice:

> Research councils will usually ask for *specific* aims of the research and for *specific* details of how the data are to be collected, and the nature

TABLE 1
'Action' research, consultancy and 'pure' research

Stages	'Action' research	Consultancy	'Pure' research
Entry	Client or researcher presents problem. Mutually agreed goals.	Client presents problems and defines goals.	Researcher presents problem and defines goals.
Contracting	Business and psychological contracting Mutual control.	Business contract. Consultant controls client.	Researcher controls client as expert. Keeps client happy. Minimal contracting.
Diagnosis	Joint diagnosis Client data/researcher's concepts.	Consultant diagnosis. Often minimal. Sells package.	Researcher carries out expert diagnosis. Client provides data.
Action	Feedback, dissonance. Joint action plan. Client action with support. Published.	Consultant prescribes action. Not published.	Report often designed to impress client with how much he has learned and how competent he is. Published.
Evaluation	New problems emerge. Recycled generalizations emerge.	Rarely undertaken by neutrals.	Rarely undertaken.
Withdrawal	Client self-supporting.	Client dependent.	Client dependent.

and form of the expected results ... the spectre of the physical research paradigm looms pressing the researcher to distill, firm and sharpen his inquiry. (Fineman, 1981)

One of the most comprehensive critiques of current organizational research is provided by Argyris (1970) and Argyris and Schon (1974). It is argued that the traditional research model in organizational behaviour has proved inadequate to its task and has unintended consequences. It is predicted that rigorous research designs in experimental or field settings will tend to place clients in positions similar to those that organizations create for their employees on the shop floor. Clients in this situation adapt by becoming dependent or by rejecting a positive, collaborative role, or by withdrawing in some way and providing minimally useful data.

Argyris describes what he terms organic research as modifying the established concepts of rigorous methodology. The rigour of the research is not changed by the approach, rather the degree to which clients are involved by researchers in those activities in order that they are prepared to give and get valid and useful information, and that with such information they may make an informed and free choice from alternative courses of action. Argyris maintains further that unless researchers resist the temptation, under client pressure, to tell them what to do, the researcher will lose his own free choice and be controlled by the anxieties of his clients. Free client choice is important, for it is suggested that it leads to internal client commitment to the goals of the research which is then more likely to be utilized.

Argyris stresses the value of open relationships and trust between client and researcher and the evaluation of the researcher's own behaviour as an essential part of the data. In these terms, research is not only a means of generating content knowledge, which may or may not be used, it is also a process for tackling problems faced directly by users.

Some research since Argyris wrote, by van de Vall and his colleagues, has examined 120 applied social research projects in the Netherlands (van de Vall et al., 1976). In general, their findings are supportive of Argyris (see also Chapter 14).

The more we examine research methodology the more we need to examine the way the researcher is implicated in his own investigations and particularly so in field research. What are the social relationships between the researcher and user, for example, and how do these affect outcomes? There are very few studies which describe the work of inter-disciplinary research and action teams and none of these includes the client's reactions.

It was, therefore, particularly interesting to us to be asked to monitor the pilot stage of the then Social Science Research Council's Open Door scheme which, among other objectives, was designed to explore these issues.

The origins and objectives of
the Open Door scheme
The Open Door scheme had its origins in the work of the Consumer Relations Sub-Committee of the then Social Science Research Council's (SSRC) Management and Industrial Relations Committee. The sub-committee drew on the range of work concerned with research utilization which was developing in the 1960s and early 1970s in several countries and disciplines.

By far the most radical initiative of the Consumer Relations Sub-Committee was to recommend the introduction of what became known as the council's Open Door scheme. The scheme was conceived as a counter to the institutionalized way in which research is largely funded by the research councils, namely by academic researchers requesting support for proposals conceived and initiated by them. The utility of such research being indirectly communicated to the generality of managers, trade unionists, other potential users and the research councils through publication and final reports. Two main principles guided the introduction of the scheme. First, that consumers of research should be involved at the stage when the research objectives and design were being formulated if they were to become committed to the research objectives and so have an interest in utilizing the research output. Secondly, that it was desirable that the rather narrow range of beneficiaries of management and industrial relations research through the council's committees should, if possible, be widened to include other groups which had not previously had easy access to research funds.

A number of benefits was expected from such a scheme. A closer relationship would be developed between the SSRC and potential users of social science research; new opportunities, which would probably not otherwise have been provided, would be presented to researchers to test research concepts, including ways of influencing users. It was also anticipated that such research would contribute both to the solution of practical idiosyncratic problems and to the body of general social science knowledge. Finally, it was also expected that such a scheme would provide greater understanding within SSRC of the problems and choices faced by a Management and Industrial Relations Committee which was endeavouring to tackle problem-centred research and issues of research utilization.

This last point needs some elaboration as being a core issue for the future operation of the scheme and another illustration of the pure and applied split referred to earlier. The first chairman of the Social Science Research Council had described how the role of a management and industrial relations committee was envisaged by its founders in 1965. It was to be one of several 'counter committees ... which would be concerned with fields of application rather than disciplines'.[3] Clearly such a committee only flourishes by being experimental and innovative and this philosophy rests uneasily in a body with particular administrative conventions and policies and a preponderance of 'discipline' committees. The distinctive features of a counter committee are to seek guidance from constituents other than the academic; to form judgements about issues for which other committees may be ill-equipped; and to take a more active interest in on-going projects than simply judging research results on an academic's final report. Clearly, the Open Door scheme was designed to help meet some of these objectives but in doing so it was to polarize the tensions between discipline and counter committees contained within the same administrative framework.

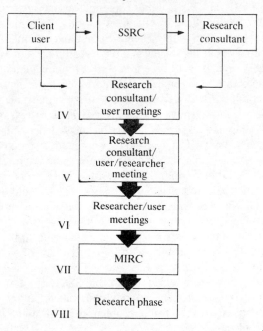

FIGURE 2
The SSRC's Open Door scheme

The design of the Open Door scheme (see Figure 2)

It was decided that the scheme should be widely promoted as an opportunity for managers, trade unionists or any established group to propose topics on one or two pieces of paper for social science research arising from practical, work-related problems. Such proposals would be scrutinized by the SSRC office to see that they fell broadly within the management and industrial relations area and proposers would then be put in touch with experienced researchers in the management and industrial relations field; these researchers becoming known as 'research consultants'. Research consultants would then advise clients on the research feasibility of their proposals and, in consultation with proposers, attempt to match the project with a suitable researcher. Once the researcher was introduced to and accepted by the proposer, the research consultant would withdraw and the researcher would formulate a research proposal in consultation with the proposers and submit it through the normal research grant scheme procedure. That is to say, the research grant application would be processed by the Management and Industrial Relations Committee (and other committees of the SSRC if the research area was considered to be relevant to them) which, in the usual way, would take the advice of referees in reaching a decision. The scheme was finally introduced in March 1977, on an experimental basis for three years, after considerable delay occasioned by council's reservations about the scheme. Chiefly, these focused on the costs of running and servicing the scheme; the amount of research funds likely to be generated; and a concern to maintain the standards of the research grant scheme in the face of applied, user-generated research. Concerns were also expressed about research consultants suggesting researchers from their own institutions and this was debarred.

Monitoring the Open Door scheme

As has been discussed earlier, knowledge of the utilization process and particularly researcher/user interactions is limited. It was, therefore, of particular interest to researchers to be able to gain direct access to the relationships between users, research consultants and researchers engaged in the pilot stage of the Open Door scheme. Our objective in the research was two-fold; to help the SSRC to improve specific aspects of the Open Door scheme and, simultaneously, to investigate the inter-actions of the parties to the scheme as they occurred in the hope that this might enable us to understand and conceptualize the action research process in general.[4] This opportunity was, of course, unusual. It is naturally difficult to gain access to the interactions of researchers and consultants with their clients as such events are by their very nature highly personalized. Such studies as exist are, therefore, mostly personal reportage by clients, consultants and actions researchers introspecting about, and trying to conceptualize, their own consulting experiences after the event (Hughes, 1977), or particular cases of interventions where the authors used an action research or consulting framework (Young, 1975). Initially, we were asked by the SSRC to monitor the early phases of the scheme (i.e. Stages I to V, Figure 2), and later the total scheme including the research phase. Accordingly, we were interested in previous work on the role of the consultant (action researcher) and on consultant/client relationships. There are two over-lapping sources of information on these matters. A number of writers have examined the consultant role and, often by analogy with leadership theory, the multiple approaches or styles the consultant used. This work has been extended by others in an examination of the style appropriate to different stages of the consulting process and the nature of the consultant/client relationship.

The consultant role. Systematic research studies of the nature of the work of consultants and their role are unusual (Steel, 1975; Sinha, 1979), although a number of academics who spend time in active consultancy have reflected on the consulting process and attempted to conceptualize it (Sofer, 1961; Klein, 1976; Sadler and Barry, 1970; Tranfield, 1978). Beckhard (1974), in particular, considers assumptions about expectations, power and results held initially by both clients and consultants. Indeed, power is an issue considered by a number of authors (Schein, 1969) and was to become a major focus of the Open Door research.

Consultant/user relationships. In a research-based study, Kolb and Frohman (1970) introduce a multi-stage model of the consulting process. The model centres on two issues which are interrelated. One concerns the relationship between consultant and user. Who influences whom? How open will the user and consultant be with each other? The second concerns the nature of the work. How is the problem defined? What solutions are considered? The stages in the model are described as 'scouting', 'entry', 'diagnosis', 'planning', 'action', 'evaluation' and 'termination', and for each stage the authors suggest several key issues. Since we were initially concerned with the early stages of the Open Door scheme we were particularly interested in the 'entry' stage of the model.

Glidewell (1959) defines the entry problem in terms of the goodness of fit between the consultant and user social system with respect to three variables: the perception of need; the perception of prospective equity of role, resource and reward distribution; and the perception of prospective appropriateness of feeling exchange, with special concerns about dependency and counter-dependency.

Frohman (1968) similarly lists ten areas in which agreement over expectations is important in order to develop an effective working relationship.

Kolb and Frohman (1970) believe that the most important issue in the consulting process is power, i.e. gaining the influence to work effectively with the user. They believe that the most effective power base is 'the informal influence that flows from collaborative problem definition and solution'.

One empirical example of the detrimental effects of a consultant's over-concern with power is Sethi's (1968) study of effective and ineffective organizational consultants. He found that ineffective change agents were more concerned with their personal goals, and with their political position within the organization, than were the effective change agents, who were more concerned about task accomplishment.

This work has been exptended by Kolb and Boyatsis (1970) who have empirically validated the hypothesis that moderate levels of achievement, affiliation and power motivation in the consultant and user are optimal for effective help to take place.

Objectives and methods of research
into the Open Door scheme

The success of the Open Door scheme then, would seem to depend on the extent to which the user is committed to the redefined proposal and to the researcher; the proposal meeting SSRC research grant criteria; user, SSRC and researchers meeting their goals; and congruency between Open Door scheme procedures and the overall goals of the scheme. We, therefore, decided to gather information to test the following propositions:

1. The greater the problem definition varies from that originally put forward by the user, the less the user will be committed to it unless the relationship between research consultant and user has been mutually satisfying.

2. The relationship between research consultant and user will be mutually satisfying if:

   (a) the research consultant is generally high on consideration (i.e. he adopts, for example, listening, encouraging and reflecting behaviours) and yet is sufficiently flexible to adopt a task-centred, controlling style when appropriate (e.g. when expertise is demanded or the user needs structure)

   (b) there is clarity early in the relationship about each other's role, goals and motives and this information is freely discussed

   (c) moderate levels of achievement, affiliation and power motivation are present in both user and research consultant

   (d) the research consultant is less concerned with personal goals and more with task accomplishment

   (e) the differences in research experience/orientation and cultural background between research consultant and user are not great

   (f) the choice of researcher is mutually arrived at between user and consultant; and the research consultant has a wide knowledge of the researcher network in the area covered by the redefined proposal.

3. Utilization of the research will be facilitated:

   (a) where the researcher adopts an action-oriented approach and where the researcher is skilled in forming a working relationship (i.e. as in the case of the research consultant/user relationship, 2a to 2e above, apply), and

   (b) where the researcher succcessfully manages two potentially conflicting outcomes—solving the client problem and advancing general theory.

In order to address these questions we interviewed users, research consultants and researchers and attended meetings which occurred between them up to the research phase (Figure 2). During the research phase we took data from users and researchers at intervals.

Users and research consultants were both interviewed prior to their meeting together. Users were asked to identify the key aspects of their proposals, their goals, motives and success criteria and their expectations of the research consultant and the scheme. Research consultants were asked to speculate on the nature of their role, the characteristics of a 'good' research project, and their expectations of the user.

Meetings between users and research consultants were attended to clarify how roles were negotiated, how flexible was consultant style, how goals were set, and the extent to which perceived power was a factor in the discussions.

Subsequent to the meetings, both research consultant and user were interviewed to determine how any changes in the original proposal came about, how far the consultant helped, how far expectations of both research consultant and client changed (e.g. with regard to success criteria) and to what extent the user felt satisfied about researcher choice and the criteria used to identify potential researchers.

Finally, researchers were interviewed to discover their motives in becoming involved, their research orientation, and the feasibility of meeting both user and SSRC criteria in the proposal. Interviews of both researchers and users took place at intervals during the research phase to discover how the original proposal had been modified in the course of the research and by what processes. We were also at pains to discover what steps were being taken by users to use the research and how far the researcher had facilitated this process.

Of course, given the novelty of the scheme and its complicated procedures, researching it became, in part, an exercise in avoiding being drawn into content and procedural issues both as agents of SSRC and as researchers. Although our interviews were usually prefaced with a clear statement of our research role, this had frequently to be restated at various times during the course of a project.

The Open Door scheme during the pilot phase 1977–80

Twenty-four proposals were received from potential users by the SSRC during the scheme's pilot phase. These are classified in Table 2.

It is apparent from Table 2 that only about half of the proposals received by SSRC proceeded beyond the research consultant stage (Figure 2, Stage IV) and of these twelve proposals only five were awarded a grant. These ratios are, however, roughly typical of the SSRC's research grant scheme as a whole, so it cannot be inferred from them that Open Door proposals were either favoured or discriminated against. Certainly, the scheme enabled its pluralist objectives to be met, for the normal constituency of the council's Management and Industrial Relations Committee was widened to include research proposals which

TABLE 2
Classification of proposals by source and progress

Source	Stage of OD scheme to which a proposal proceeded (Figure 2)					
	II	IV	V	VII	VIII	Total
Managerial		7	1		1	9
Professional association	1	1*			1	3
Voluntary association			1	1	1	3
Trade union (national)	1			3		4
Trade union (shop floor)			1	2	2	5
Total	2	8	3	6	5	24

*In process, January 1981
II   = SSRC Office
IV   = Research consultant/user meeting
V   = Research consultant/user/researcher meeting
VII = Management and industrial relations committee
VIII = Research stage

were intended to benefit groups other than managers, such as voluntary organizations, professional bodies and trade unions. The last group has been particularly prominent in its use of the scheme for two of the five proposals which entered the research phase, and nine of the total of twenty-four original proposals were from this source. The large number of trade-union proposals is perhaps to be explained in several ways: the information network of the trade-union movement is effective, partly perhaps by being both informal and concentrated; trade unionists at the shop-floor level (five out of nine trade-union proposals) have limited resources to engage management consultants to tackle their practical problems and are, in any case, suspicious of them; finally, and tentatively, it may be that trade unionists stereotype academic researchers less negatively than do managers and regard them as more sympathetic to their goals. The proposals labelled 'managerial' (Table 2) need qualification. Only two of the proposals were from well known companies and one of these was initiated by the trade-union membership of a joint consultative committee. A manager in one company made three proposals successively and the remainder were from quite small organizations including a co-operative. Clearly, the reasons why managers did not make more use of the scheme include the converse of those reasons suggested earlier for the trade unions. The largest remaining group consisted of voluntary bodies and professional associations, both of which are generally short of finance for management consultancy and have had, in some cases, considerable positive contact with academic research.

Our research work into the Open Door scheme was primarily designed to see what type of interaction between the parties, the users, researchers, research consultants and the SSRC, most helped the initial proposal to proceed smoothly through the scheme's procedures and to result in useful output for users.

The effectiveness of the interaction between the parties to the Open Door scheme depends very much on what they each bring to the situation when they meet and how that meeting is managed. We, therefore, discuss the backgrounds, goals and expectations of users and research consultants prior to meeting and then the conduct of the meetings and their outcomes. Finally, the role of the researcher and the research stages of projects are discussed.

Users
Most users were unclear about the nature of the scheme. The managerial clients, in particular, expected a speedy process, the term research consultant perhaps signalling consultancy rather than academic associations and long time-scales. A number of clients, where they understood something of SSRC procedures and criteria, believed that the scheme would provide easier access to funding than normal research grant proposals. In the main, however, most users had only a vague understanding of the nature of the SSRC. Users were naturally expecting a practical resolution of their presenting problems and, for the most part, were not particularly interested in advancing general theory. In this context, they varied widely in their understanding of the research process; a few had used academic researchers before, and indeed some client groups consisted partly of academics. While these groups had a more sophisticated understanding of research than others, most of the research they had sponsored had been of the applied variety and they had had sole control of it. Others had had virtually no exposure to academic research.

Users also varied in the composition of the user group. On rare occasions one person represented user interests (e.g. in the case of a large trade union.) This, however, was exceptional for, in many cases, users consisted of a large group (e.g. in one extreme case a joint consultative committee composed both of managerial and trade-union representatives).

Users only vaguely understood the role of the research consultant. They believed the problems as they had defined them were already capable of research but were willing to consider amendments in order to satisfy research grant proposals criteria provided their main presenting problems continued to be addressed. Some users believed that their initial proposals were already adequate, while others (a minority) expected that the research consultant would help them narrow down and refine their initial ideas. In virtually every case, users had concerns about their future control of, and influence on, the research. Most overtly this was probably true of trade-unions groups which were suspicious of references to 'consultants' and 'management committees'. All users were, in varying ways, sensitive to the values and goals of potential researchers and, naturally, inferential judgements were drawn about the sort of researcher who might be introduced at the research consultant/user meetings.

In summary, then, the expectations and goals of users were not closely congruent with all the goals of the scheme and, despite their receipt of a well-presented brochure, they had only vague notions of its purpose and nature and of the role of the research consultant. The expectations of most users have been high at the beginning of the Open Door process but have later been brought sharply into touch with reality both in terms of lengthy and complicated procedures and eventual outcomes.

Research consultants

Twenty research consultants took part in the scheme, eighteen from the universities and two from polytechnics. Nine worked in the broad field of organizational behaviour and industrial relations, four were applied economists, three were operations researchers and one each worked in financial management and marketing. Knowledge of action research and research utilization processes were generally fairly sketchy and few had an academic interest in the theory of practice including consulting. None had had systematic experiential training in consulting skills.

Research consultants were appointed to projects on the basis of their research interests, geographical location and availability. While it was felt initially to be disadvantageous to the development of a project if the research consultant's research interests were too close to the proposed research area, this did not, with experience, prove to be a handicap. Rather it has been helpful to projects if the research consultant knew something of the proposed research and the researcher network in that area. Research consultants correctly anticipated that their first meeting with the user would prove difficult as users would not understand the nature of the scheme, the role of the research consultant, the need for research consultant help, and SSRC research grant procedures. Furthermore, it was anticipated that eventually both research consultant and user might find it difficult to sever their relationship and, in the case of the user, form a fresh one with the researcher.

Research consultants went to considerable pains to familiarize themselves with the background to proposals and client systems prior to the first meeting with users. Meetings generally began with an exchange of information. The research consultant explained the nature of the Open Door scheme and his part in it and the user elaborated on his proposal. Most meetings concluded with a discussion of potential researchers and ways of revising the proposal by narrowing it down to manageable proportions. At least one further meeting was usually necessary between user and research consultant to review the proposal in the light of modifications and to discuss potential researchers.

A number of issues predictably arose in all these meetings. Most user proposals were too wide-ranging and, in consequence, the clarity of research objectives and their feasibility were usually a matter for discussion as was subsequent publication of findings. Methodological issues were generally left to research consultants in that most users were not committed to particular methodologies. The main concern of research consultants, of course, was to integrate user needs for, say, unconceptualized data collection with the needs of the wider community for generalizable findings; the latter need being particularly crucial if, first a researcher was to be attracted to the work and second, if SSRC requirements were to be met in the eventual proposal to the research grant scheme. Proposals were modified in various ways though most commonly by research consultants re-drafting it and agreeing the draft with the user. Locating a potential researcher who would meet the often disparate requirements of proposal content, SSRC and user criteria, frequently proved difficult and, as has already been stated, was, of course, bound up with user control of the project. A number of projects were terminated either because appropriate researchers could not be located (this happened rarely), or because researchers subsequently were unable to meet the needs of all the parties.

A key matter for most research consultants was the appropriate point at which to withdraw from the project. Having gained the confidence of users, it was difficult for research consultants to make a smooth handover to the researcher. In virtually all cases, however, this was managed reasonably well, although both users and researchers continued to ask informal advice from research consultants after their formal withdrawal from the process. It remains to speculate on the extent to which generalizations are possible about the most effective ways of conducting user/research consultant meetings.

Research consultant/user meetings

It seemed to us that successful outcomes of the initial interactions between research consultants and users might, in part at least, depend on the degree of congruence of initial expectations and the way the research consultant managed the meeting. Of course, 'success' does not necessarily mean progress to a funded research project; in some cases, for example, users were pointed to alternative, more appropriate ways of funding and in others users themselves decided that the project would not be feasible. We evaluated each proposal in terms of the initial expectations of both parties, research consultant and user, according to their research orientation — the degree to which each was concerned both with the generation of theory and also with practical problem-solving, the extent to which the research consultant role was clear to both parties, an understanding of the time-scales of the Open Door scheme and research phase, and the locus of control of the research phase (See Table 3).

Clearly, where congruence on these dimensions was relatively high, proposals had a better chance of making progress than where there was relative incongruence of initial expectations. In the latter cases (Boxes II and IV, Table 3), much depended on other factors, particularly the style adopted by the research consultant. Indeed, it might be argued that a degree of dissonance between consultant and client might be more helpful to an integrated solution, though this has not been generally borne out.

TABLE 3

Open Door proposals classified by consultant style, initial expectations of the parties, source and progress through the scheme

Research consultant style	Initial expectations	
	Congruent	Incongruent
	I	II
Non-directive	$A^1 B^2 C^1 D^1$	$J^3 K^3 L^3 M^3$
	$E^2 F^5$	$N^3 O^2 P^3 Q^3$
		$R^4 S^3 T^4$
	III	IV
Directive	$G^2 H^1 I^1$	$U^3 V^2 W^2 X^3$

Classified by progress through the scheme
1: Proposals funded by SSRC
2: Proposals submitted to SSRC for funding and rejected
3: Proposals withdrawn before being presented for funding
4: Proposals withdrawn before research consultant stage
5: Proposals in process (January 1981).

Classification by source
Trade unions: A, B, C, E, G, K, O, T, V
Managerial: D, J, L, M, N, P, Q, S, U
Voluntary associations: I, W, X
Professional associations: F, H, R.

FIGURE 3
Multiple roles of the consultant

Objective observer/ reflecter	Process counsellor	Fact finder	Alternative identifer and linker	Joint problem-solver	Trainer educator	Informational expert	Advocate

CLIENT ⟍⟋ CONSULTANT

Level of consultant activity in problem-solving

Non-directive ———————————————————————————— Directive

Raises questions for reflection	Observes problem-solving process and raises issues mirroring feed-back	Gathers data and stimulates thinking interpretives	Identifies alternatives & resources for client and helps assess consequences	Offers alternatives and participates in decisions	Trains client	Regards, links, and provides policy or practice decisions	Proposes guidelines, persuades or directs in the problem-solving process

Source: Gordon and Ronald Lippitt, *The Consulting Process in Action*, University Associates Inc., 1978, p. 31.

The other variable we examined was the style adopted by the research consultant. Consulting style was considered on a continuum of directive/non-directive behaviour; for example, giving expert advice was considered to be more directive than helping users to identify alternatives or setting guidelines for problem solving (Figure 3). It might then be argued that given initially wide differences between the parties, a non–directive consultant style would better ensure that such differences were addressed and the problem solved. Of course, on occasions the research consultant would need to offer expertise although, in general, we came to the conclusion that research consultants need to adopt sufficiently flexible styles to meet the needs of the situation, while tending towards the non-directive. In practice, most consultants showed flexibility of style and were classified on the dichotomous scale, directive/non-directive on the basis of our overall impression of their predominant style (Table 3).

Proposals were, therefore, classified on a two-by-two matrix of initial expectations and predominant research consultant style. On this analysis, it might be predicted that the most likely proposals to proceed would be those in Box I (Table 3) and the least likely those in Box IV (Table 3). Proposals in Box III start with an advantage but suffer from an overly directive consultant. Box II is the condition in which most proposals might be expected and the evidence, as might be anticipated, is mixed. Some users were so unrealistic in their expectations and misunderstood the scheme so completely that it was clear almost from the outset that they could not be rescued. Of course, a number of proposals proceeded and others foundered irrespective of these criteria — e.g. failure to locate researchers, unrealistic, ill-conceived research grant proposals — but, nevertheless, there does seem to be some evidence that the two variables presented in Table 3 are significant. It is just worth mentioning, in addition, that both users and research consultants became more expert with experience. One user put up three different proposals before succeeding (proposal D, Box 1, Table 3). In his final successful proposal, he received the services of a research consultant who had previously unsuccessfully consulted on another project, but had learned from the experience.

The research phase of the Open Door scheme

Five proposals had proceeded to the research stage by the time our own research was concluded (see Tables 2 and 3).[5] Of these one has been completed, two are nearing completion, and two have very recently commenced. Despite this small sample, some common aspects of the researcher role are emerging.

The point has been made a number of times, with hindsight, that a degree of vagueness in objectives and methods in the initial research grant application needs to be accepted by SSRC in Open Door research grant proposals if the work is to proceed sensibly. User problems change rapidly with changes, for example, in the economic climate and appropriate methods then need to be found to meet emerging situations.

Initial lack of trust by users of researchers has led to the latter spending time on user problems, which have often been marginal to the main research objective, in order simply to service the user and so gain acceptance. Researchers have, therefore, with experience, come to the conclusion that longer time-scales than were originally proposed would have been more realistic.

The difficulty is, of course, connected with the much more fundamental, underlying problem of meeting the goals of the academic community and, simultaneously, user objectives. Research grant proposals have generally met user rather than academic needs and some have been rejected by SSRC partly for being 'consultancy'. We now turn to this issue in more detail.

Crucial to an understanding of the main issues in this type of research is field experience and familiarity with the action research literature. The major difficulty is 'contributing both to the practical concerns of people in a problematic collaboration within a mutually acceptable framework' Rapoport, 1970). An attempt to clarify this issue (and others) is shown in Table 1 by contrasting action research consultancy and 'pure' research (see also Heller's introductory chapter).

All researchers undertaking Open Door projects are faced with meeting both user needs and, through, for example, reports to SSRC, the needs of the wider research community. Where these needs are convergent — for example, in the rare cases where the user is as interested in advancing theory as solving idiosyncratic problems — the researcher is, of course, able to work most effectively. In at least one case there has been a close integration of user and researcher objectives from the start and user suspicions of 'academics' have not been great. The 'starting distance' between the user culture and the researcher's culture has apparently been small. This compatibility is helped by, on the one hand, the user being familiar with academic research and, on the other, the researchers having a primary academic interest in problem-solving on the one hand, and generalizing about the research process on the other.

In the cases of two projects, meeting user needs has been helped by the field researcher working closely with the user system and, in effect, primarily servicing it. The grant holder, on the other hand, is naturally concerned primarily with generalizing findings from the field-work in a final report to the SSRC. This role differentiation seems to have worked quite well in the case of these projects and may be a model for others in the future.

Ways have been developed to influence users to adopt findings from the research, particularly when they have been initially rather hostile to academic research. In one case short-stage papers have been written on various aspects of the work of interest to the user. These have later been discussed in workshops and accordingly have been added to, evaluated and utilized in the user's day-to-day activities.

Similarly, another researcher, concerned with a shop-floor trade-union group, has speculated about ways to involve the users in the work and so gain their acceptance of the data as a first step to utilization (see diagnostic stage of action research process in Table 1). Accordingly, he has, in his own words, provided a structure and advice to help the shop stewards collect their own data and then, with them, to classify and conceptualize them. This follows the action research strategies advocated by, for example, Sims (1981) and Ackoff (1975).

Most researchers have been flexible enough to renegotiate their role with the user during the course of the work and with more data it would be interesting to test Roff's suggested phase model of researcher role changing over time in the course of organizational research (Roff, 1981).

The future and a conclusion
Many of the objectives of the Open Door scheme were met during its pilot stage. Research opportunities were made available to researchers

which would probably not otherwise have come to light. Potential users were able to work with academic researchers and vice versa with the objective of mutually satisfying their goals. These points are equally, if not more, true of recent years. Perhaps most important of all, SSRC and its Management and Industrial Relations Committee had to focus on the criteria used to assess research grant applications in the light of pro-posals concerned with idiosyncratic problem-solving, using less tradi-tional methodologies, as well as with generating general theory. Many difficulties nevertheless arose in the course of the pilot phase of the Open Door scheme. In particular, long delays occurred in processing research grant applications through the scheme, especially where these did not conform to traditional academic research criteria.

As a consequence, some potential entrants to the scheme were diverted from it and only a small trickle of applications resulted. The future of the scheme was in serious doubt. It seemed likely either to be scrapped or to die of neglect under the burden of bureaucratic pro-cedure.

From 1982 onwards, however, a combination of circumstances, personalities and external pressures has dramatically revised and revived the Open Door to the point where in some quarters it was seen as a flagship for the Research Council as a whole. At the beginning of 1986 there were twenty-seven Open Door research projects under way at a total cost of £51,294. A half-time academic co-ordinator had been appointed and the budget for 1986-7 is some £94,627.

Seven factors may have contributed to this turnaround:

1. In 1982 the council revised its committee structure and the Management and Industrial Relations Committee was absorbed into a new and more powerful Industry and Employment Committee.

2. This committee, along with the five other new multi-disciplinary, problem-oriented standing committees, acquired its own annual budget and was able to allocate funds specifically to the Open Door scheme.

3. The 1982 Rothschild review, after which the council's title was changed to the present Economic and Social Research Council, recommended 'The SSRC to improve its links with industry'.

4. Several of the scheme's protagonists were by then in positions of influence. One of the key industrial members of the Banbury Committee was appointed to the Industry and Employment Committee and to the council. Its secretary was secretary to the committee[6] and the vice-chairman (and subsequently chairman) of the committee was himself committed to make the scheme work.

5. The Industry and Employment Committee then determined to improve the operation of the scheme not only as a mechanism for increased dissemination, but as a channel of communication with industry. The points about speed of decision-making were taken into

account. Funding on each project was limited to £2,000 to underline the exploratory nature of the research, and to allow more risks to be taken with the award decisions.

6. The council had a new chairman, appointed in 1983, who came from the business school community, and saw the scheme as a welcome mechanism for encouraging collaboration between academic institutions and local business.

7. The new chairman of council was also interested in the use of new media to present the council's activities and strongly supported proposals for television and radio advertising for the scheme, which has so far been carried out in East Anglia and South Wales and was continued in Scotland in the first half of 1986.

Nevertheless, even with this combination of resources and support, a scheme of this kind, which seeks to offer an alternative to the basic pattern of knowledge production and use, remains vulnerable to the indifference or even hostility of the academic community, to problems of standards, to industrial impatience with public sector bureaucracy, and to the many continuing pressures on the ESRC.

At a time of severe shortage of resources for research, this must remain a fragile experiment. It is due to be reviewed in 1987 and much will depend on the quality and interest of the reports written thus far, on the responses of the original 'clients' and on the continued willingness of present ESRC Industry and Employment Committee members to continue the radical line of their predecessors and the balance of power within the council.

In essence we return to some of the fundamental difficulties mentioned earlier which are encountered in bridging the academic and managerial cultures in our society. Clearly, any attempt which seeks to bring representatives of these cultures with their differing goals and expectations into contact, and demands reconciliation of these differences and the working through of ensuing ambiguities if both parties are ultimately to be satisfied, can only help increased utilization of academic research. The attempt perhaps puts more pressure on the academic researcher in the way he or she relates to the user in the course of the research and in the way these relationships affect utilization. Our research efforts into the early phases of the Open Door scheme indicated that the quality of the early relationships between research consultants, researchers and users were crucial in effecting outcomes.

Notes

1. The council's name was changed to the Economic and Social Research Council in January 1984.

2. For a critical review of the work of the Tavistock Institute of Human Relations, see Brown, 1967.

3. Heyworth Report, 1965; Rothschild Report, 1971; Dainton Report, 1971; Banbury et al., SSRC, 1974.

4. The field-work was undertaken by a group of staff (M. Foster, Dr J. Gill, J.D. Shipton, Dr J.S. Smith and Dr D.R. Tranfield) in the Management Studies Department of Sheffield City Polytechnic, who research and teach in organization development and behavioural science consultancy.

5. By the end of February 1986 a total of seventy-five proposals had proceeded to the research stage and of these thirty-one were completed and reported on.

6. I have been helped with updating the current position of the Open Door scheme by Chris Caswill, secretary of the ESRC's Industry and Employment Committee.

References

Ackoff, R. (1975) *Redesigning the Future.* New York: John Wiley.

Ansoff, I. (1977) 'The Pathology of Applied Research in Social Science'. (Unpublished paper to SSRC International Conference on the Utilization of Research.)

Argyris, C. (1970) *Intervention Theory and Method.* New York: John Wiley.

Argyris, C. and D.A. Schon (1974) *Theory in Practice — Increasing Professional Effectiveness.* San Francisco: Jossey Bass.

Banbury, J. (1974) *Report of the Working Group on the Relationship with the Consumer.* SSRC.

Beckhard, R. (1974) *The Dynamics of the Consulting Process in Large Systems Change.* MIT, Sloan School of Management.

Brown, R.K. (1967) 'Research and Consultancy in Industrial Enterprises — A Review of the Contribution of the Tavistock Institute of Human Relations to the Development of Industrial Sociology', *Sociology,* 1 (1): 33–60.

Cherns, A.B. (1968) 'The Use of Social Sciences', *Human Relations,* 21: 313–25.

Cherns, A.B (1970) 'Relations between Research Institutions and Users of Research', *International Social Science Journal,* 22 (2): 226–42.

Cherns, A.B. (1973) 'Can Behavioural Scientists Help Managers Improve their Organisations?', *Organizational Dynamics,* Winter: 65–9.

Dainton Report (1971) *The Future of the Research Council System,* Cmnd. 4814. London: HMSO.

Dale, A. (1972) *Coercive Persuasion and the Role of the Consultant',* Odmag, 1 (2).

Fineman, S. (1981) 'Funding Research: Practice and Politics', pp. 473–84 in P. Reason and J. Rowan (eds) *Human Enquiry: A Sourcebook of New Paradigm Research.* London: John Wiley.

Frohman, M. (1968) *Conceptualizing a Helping Relationship.* Ann Arbor Institute for Social Research, Center for Research Utilization of Scientific Knowledge, Mimeo.

Gill, J. (1978) *Client-Consultant Relationships in Management Review and Bibliography.* Bradford: MCB Books.

Glidewell, J.C. (1959) 'The Entry Problem in Consultation', *Social Issues,* 15 (2): 51–9.

Heller, F. (1976) 'Some Thoughts on the Utilization of Social Science Research'. (Unpublished paper presented to the SSRC's Consumer Relations Sub-Committee.)

Heyworth Report (1965) *Report of the Committee on Social Studies*, Cmnd. 2660. London: HMSO.

Hughes, J. (1977) 'Social Science Research'. (Unpublished paper presented to SSRC's Consumer Relations Sub-Committee.)

Klein, L. (1976) *A Social Scientist in Industry.* Farnborough: Gower Press.

Kolb, D.A. and R.E. Boyatsis (1970) 'On the Dynamics of a Helping Relationship', *Applied Behavioral Science*, 6 (3): 267–90.

Kolb, D.A. and A.L. Frohman, (1970) 'An Organization Development Approach to Consulting', *Sloan Management Review*, 12 (1).

Lippitt, R. (1959) 'Dimensions of a Consultant's Job', *Journal of Social Issues*, 15 (2): 5–11.

Rapoport, R.M. (1970) *Three Dilemmas in Action Research.* (Paper presented to SSRC Conference on Action Research, York, England, Mimeo.)

Remus, W (1977) 'Strategies for a Publish or Perish World', *Interfaces*, 8 (1): 64–8.

Roff, A. (1981) 'The Researcher Role.' (Unpublished working paper, Sheffield City Polytechnic.)

Rothschild Report (1971) *The Organization and Management of Government Research and Development.* London: HMSO.

Rothschild. 'An Enquiry into the Social Science Research Council'. Cmnd. 8554. HMSO, 1982.

Rowan, J. (1974) 'Research as Intervention', Chapter 5 in N. Armistead (ed.), *Reconstructing Social Psychology.* Harmondsworth: Penguin Books.

Sadler, P.J. and B.A. Barry (1970) *Organization Development.* London: Longman.

Schein, E. (1969) *Process Consultation: Its Role in Organization Development.* Homewood, Ill: Addison-Wesley.

Scott Armstrong, J. (1980) 'Unintelligible Management Research and Academic Prestige', *Interfaces*, 10 (2): 80–86.

Sethi, M. (1968) *Some Characteristics of an Effective Organization Development Consultant.* (Unpublished Master's thesis, Sloan School.)

Sims, D. (1981) 'From Ethogeny to Endogeny: How Participants Can Do Action Research on their Own Awareness', pp. 378–83 in P. Reason and J. Rowan (eds), *Human Enquiry: A Sourcebook of New Paradigm Research.* London: John Wiley.

Sinha, D.P. (ed.) (1979) *Consultants and Consulting Styles.* London: Vision Books.

Sofer, C. (1961) *The Organization from Within.* London: Tavistock Publications.

Steele, F. (1975) *Consulting for Organizational Change.* Amherst, Mass: University of Massachusetts Press.

Tranfield, D.R., J.S. Smith, J. Gill and J. Shipton (1975) 'Introducing OD. Some Problems and an Alternative Approach', *Journal of European Training*, 4 (3): 146–61.

Tranfield, D.R. (1978) *Some Characteristics of Organization Development Consultants.* (Unpublished PhD thesis, Sheffield City Polytechnic.)

van de Vall, M., C. Bolas and T.S. Kang (1976) 'Applied Social Research in Industrial Organizations — an Evaluation of Functions, Theory and Methods', *Applied Behavioral Science*, 12 (2): 156–77.

Young, M. (1975) SSRC *Newsletter*, 29 (November): 5.

9

Use and abuse of science

Frank Heller

My objective in the following pages is to draw attention — however briefly — to a variety of examples of 'use and abuse' which will complement the more detailed exposition in earlier chapters. It is not intended to produce a comprehensive coverage of this almost infinitely large subject. That would be absurd. Many more books will surely be written to document successes and failures and the more difficult area which lies in between.

Several vignettes lightly and quickly drawn in this chapter are based on extensive evidence which the resolute reader may wish to pursue through the appropriate references. Many will already be familiar with some of the case histories but may not have seen their close connection to our utilization theme. In any case, the task of persuading people to look at an old problem from a new angle can often be done very effectively through a story-telling approach. The chapter will discuss examples under the following headings: (1) abuse, (2) success or failure? (3) moderate successes.

Cases of abuse

The word 'abuse' in the title of this book was not chosen only to make people sit up and think. It is helpful to approach this topic by considering three fairly distinct alternatives. In the first place, research can be used; by which one means a positive attempt to apply or work with a finding or theory. Alternatively, there can be an absence of use. This is rarely deliberate; more usually there is a wide range of reasons, some of them well illustrated in previous chapters, why utilization is not achieved or even attempted. Finally, the term 'abuse' is appropriate in cases where research, theories or models are misused or wrongly used. This includes accidental or unconscious misuse as well as deliberate attempts to negate, distort, misapply or falsify research.

The utilization and evaluation literature has largely ignored this topic and consequently not too many examples are available, but it is important to look out for them. The reader has to approach this subject with some circumspection but I think that a few examples can be found in this book. First there is the account by Lengyel of the prevarication and bungling in Unesco which led him to resign as editor of the *International Social Science Journal*. Secondly, there is the way in which the National Coal Board (NCB) and some members of the accountancy profession attempted to discredit the work of a team of academic accountants who had questioned the conventional assessments of the NCB and the managerial decisions based on these assessments. Thirdly, the Jobs in the 80s research, which I will describe later in this chapter, used research funds for enhancing the public relations image of sponsors instead of for the original purpose of diffusing findings. Karapin's review chapter also gives two examples of misuse. The analysis by Rein and White (1977) shows that research can be used to suppress or delay action. The criticism by Casanova (1981) shows that research by ideologically homogeneous groups can distort the research design and lead to the omission of alternative hypotheses. I will come back to the problem of value distortions in the final chapter.

Abuses frequently surface in jokes and after-dinner speeches which may be apocryphal. One that I have heard concerns a managing director at a board meeting to discuss the results of a market research survey commissioned for £20,000 from an independent organization. The meeting could not agree on the results or recommendations, and the tone of the discussion had become agitated and aggressive. In the end, to make progress on other urgent items the managing director said: 'Gentlemen, I believe that for another £10,000 I can have the results of this survey expunged.'

Finally, there are of course a number of well-documented cases of deliberate falsification of research findings, usually by the researchers themselves. There is the very clearly documented case of fraud involving a very gifted biologist described in Arthur Koestler's book on the Midwife Toad (Koestler, 1971) and the well-known case of the famous psychologist Sir Cyril Burt which caused a major academic storm only a few decades ago. Burt was an acknowledged international authority on intelligence, and I remember well that as a student I had to write an essay on the theory of the declining national intelligence. The theory, based partly on Burt's findings, went like this: lower socioeconomic groups have lower intelligence than higher socio-economic groups but breed offspring in greater numbers. Consequently, over time the average national intelligence must decline. Thousands of students must have written essays or exam papers on this topic using statistical data from Burt's research. Then, suddenly, as a consequence of some painstaking work by Kamin at Princeton (Kamin, 1974), it became obvious that Burt had falsified or invented some critical statistical results and had even published papers with non-existent research associates. (For a full account, see Hearnshaw, 1979.)

Of course, such outright deception happens only very rarely but it is certainly not confined to the social sciences. A recent book (Broad and Wade, 1985) describes a large number of cases of intellectual theft and deliberate misrepresentation in most branches of science going back to Ptolemy, reputedly the greatest astronomer in antiquity, and including the Nobel prize-winner in physics, Robert Millikan.

Fraud will occur in every field of endeavour, particularly under conditions of intense competition, but the social and biological sciences are especially vulnerable because they deal with values and can therefore be influenced by pre-judgements. I mention the case of Burt because some readers of this book will remember reading his work and maybe even using it for one purpose or another. Burt was a fanatical believer in inequality and exerted a great deal of influence on public policy-making in the field of education and the treatment of delinquents. The work led to his knighthood, a rare honour for a psychologist. When the fraud was exposed, it turned out that it could have been discovered by any qualified researcher — including myself — over the preceding thirty years. Why did it take so long? One partial answer is that students as well as academics do not easily question the results of eminent people, particularly on the grounds of deliberate misrepresentation. Kamin's explanation is that Burt's theories confirmed what many people wanted to believe: 'Every professor knew that his child was brighter than the ditchdigger's child, so what was there to challenge?' (Broad and Wade, 1985: 210).

More significant than the omission to discover falsification of data was the reluctance of eminent professors of psychology to accept Burt's perpetration of fraud even after it had been exposed. Indignation and disbelief came from exponents of similar theories about the inheritance of intellectual inequality on both sides of the Atlantic. Herrnstein from Harvard said that the suggestion of Burt's fraud 'is so outrageous that I find it hard to stay in my chair.' Eysenck, sometimes said to be the best-known British psychologist, wrote to Burt's sister that the disclosures were 'just a determined effort on the part of some very left-wing environmentalists determined to play a political game with scientific facts' (Broad and Wade, 1985:207–8).

The influence of excessively strongly-held values and prejudice on research results extends to the medical and biological sciences. One extensively documented case concerns Samuel Morton, a well-known and respected American scientist in the nineteenth century who had collected 1,000 human skulls and, on the basis of apparently very exact measurements, formulated the theory that skull volume is a measure of intelligence. His ranking of races put whites on the top, blacks on the bottom and American Indians in between. Among the whites, Western Europeans were above Jews. Broad and Wade (1985:194) conclude that these findings became influential because they reflected, like Burt's theses a hundred years later, the prejudices of their time. Research results like this are not resisted; on the contrary, they are easily used for policy-making. In the case of Samuel Morton, his work was used to justify slavery.

Once again the fraud was not discovered for a long time, over a hundred and thirty years in fact. These and other examples of scientific prejudice and dogmatism were exposed by Stephen Gould (1981). The revelations chronicled by Broad and Wade show that the use of statistics and hard measurements are no safeguard against error or deception. Gould shows that scientists talk themselves into conclusions which reflect their beliefs and use the alleged obscurity of their procedures as a shield against criticism.

However, we must recognize that the exposures of abuse I have described were all made possible by the recalculation and/or reinter-pretation of statistical data and it is reasonable to suppose that non-quantitative research is subject to at least the same risk and is then more difficult to expose. However, safeguards exist. The most powerful one is replication, and its relative unpopularity in the social sciences is a major weakness of the discipline.[1] There are other safeguards, none of them, of course, infallible. One is team research. Most of the exposures of fraud or misrepresentation were committed by single researchers. Cross-discipline research may be even more effective and I have argued elsewhere (Heller, 1985) that multinational research groups often achieve — without too much deliberate effort — mixtures of discipline as well as plurality of values. The use of several investigators is parti-cularly important in case study or other non-quantitative research. Tape-recordings of interview or group discussion are also being used more extensively and should be kept for later inspection if necessary. A further safeguard, rarely used it seems, is to validate field research data by feeding them, and tentative interpretations based on them, back to the respondents who provided the data in the first place (Brown and Heller, 1981).

It is sad that all these safeguards are resisted by funding bodies, because of the extra expense involved.

Success or failure?

There are many cases where research is neither adequately used nor misused, but where high hopes for application or implementation just did not materialize. I shall briefly describe two examples: one has been written up and can be checked from the literature; the other will almost certainly never be formally written up.

The Shell policy project

In the 1960s, Shell UK was expanding its refinery business and encountered a number of problems like strikes, rising expectations and changing values. They set up an Employee Relations Planning Unit which started discussions with social scientists at the Tavistock Institute in London. Together they developed a plan based on drawing up and working through a policy document which clearly specified long- as well as short-term objectives. There were a number of unusual features. The company was working with new technology and encountered the usual demarcation disputes and resistance to manning reductions. Consequently, the planning document stressed the need for considering profitability long-term and the efficient use of all resources including manpower. More daringly they enunciated a 'principle of joint optimization of the social and the technical system'. This principle was based on the socio-technical model which had been derived from earlier studies in coalmines and has since become very widely known in the literature (Emery and Trist, 1960).

The implementation of what had become known as the company philosophy document was to be achieved by a large number of discussion meetings, starting with top management and then working all the way through the organization. The transition from philosophy to action was accomplished through pilot projects in Norway and Britain which developed a viable socio-technical analysis and this experience was later used in designing a new refinery.

A very detailed description of the project's development between 1965 and 1967 was fortuitously made available through a sabbatical year at Cambridge where Paul Hill, the Shell man responsible for setting up the project, wrote his book *Towards a New Philosophy of Management* (Hill, 1972). The story is by no means free of setbacks and complications but there is the evidence of a formal company evaluation in 1966 conducted by cost-conscious management. It seems that although the project had taken up 3 to 4 percent of management's time the benefits were thought to be quite substantial (Hill, 1972:172–82).

In 1967 the Suez Canal crisis had a profound effect on the oil industry and, maybe more importantly, the chief executive who had suppported the project throughout, took up another appointment. The two principal researchers from the Tavistock also moved out of the country and Paul Hill became an independent consultant following his sabbatical.

Twelve years later, a critical follow-up study took place which found a number of socio-technical changes, still in position, while others had evaporated (Blackler and Brown, 1980). Attitudes to the new management philosophy varied from appreciation to indifference but it was remembered and still positively commented on in a number of departments. The new refinery's organization was less innovative than originally planned but still recognizably different from other refineries. Altogether, it is probably fair to say that what could have been a landmark and unusual demonstration model of action research did not altogether fulfil its promise.

Blackler and Brown criticize the project on ideological grounds. They take the view that, contrary to the intentions of the Tavistock change agents, the work 'in practice seems to have successfully re-established management's control of its employees'. They go on to argue that this kind of action research is 'something of a cautionary tale for people ... interested in improving society by the application of certain scientific notions' (Blackler and Brown, 1980:6–7). It is an unusual criticism to make, but is worth mentioning in the context of utilization because it shows that there is a section of the social science community which is heavily imbued with what it calls 'critical science' values and consequently adopts criteria of success and failure quite distinct from those of the traditional clients of research, who in this case include the trade unions.

By most standards of evaluation, the Shell project could be described as moderately successful. This is certainly the position of Hill and even the critical evaluation of Blackler and Brown demonstrates that, despite the Suez crisis and changes of staff, there remained, twelve years later, substantial signs of the changes that had been introduced under the influence of action research. And these changes had been considered beneficial.

Jobs in the 80s

The second example will describe a research project which was conceived in very practical terms. It was planned and financed by business people and professionals, rather than by academics. The subject matter was also practical and had urgent policy relevance. The project was called 'Jobs in the 80s'.[2] It was designed to establish the critical problems relating to work in the next decade and to suggest viable policy options. The project was initiated by Daniel Yankelovich, a well-known American public opinion consultant, and in Europe it received the very active support of Pehr Gyllenhammer, Volvo's president. In the UK, Michael Shanks the chairman of the National Consumer's Council took charge of the British team. It was intended to include about ten countries but eventually settled for six.

To plan the cross-national work, several one-day meetings took place but there was very incomplete agreement on priorities. The American and Swedish teams were particularly keen on establishing a survey of job attitudes, changes in the work ethic and testing differences in work commitment. The British team would accept this as long as other projects would give emphasis to unemployment, regional planning and the 'black' economy. In the end, each country was to carry out a major survey on job attitudes and, in additon, do whatever else they deemed appropriate. The British programme included reports on youth un-employment, long-term unemployment, inner-city regeneration, early retirement, the expected skill requirements, the 'grey' economy and two projects on the impact of technology. None of these projects was carried out in the other countries.

The most innovative part of the original plan and the most important from the point of view of this book was the emphasis on imple-mentation. With the moral and financial support of the Public Agenda Foundation[3] and the Aspen Institute for Humanistic Studies[4] the inter-national effort was designed to spend at least as much time and money on dissemination and attempts to influence public decision-making as on the fact-finding part of the research. The idea was to engage with a number of defined interest groups from the very beginning and to feed-back research findings to them as they became available, take the assessment of the interest groups on board and in this way produce a prolonged dialogue and interaction between researchers and policy-makers. The interest groups included the professions, businessmen, trade unions, clergy, journalists and other media specialists and, of course, the local and national political system. It was an ambitious plan.

At the same time, in the late 1970s, a group of academics had begun a major eight-country comparative study of job attitudes and values, called the 'Meaning of Working' (MOW). The MOW group, of which I was a member, had heard of the Jobs in the 80s project which was assembling teams in the same countries (the US, UK, Germany, Japan and Israel)[5] and it was decided to make contact to see whether col-laboration could avoid overlap, duplication and save scarce financial resources. The effort succeeded only in the UK where Michael Shanks invited me to join the British team. In the other countries the survey of job attitudes was duplicated.[6]

Coming during the severe down-turn of the economic cycle, both groups had problems with finance. The MOW project was very tradi-tionally academic and in most countries succeeded in getting support from national research institutions which allowed it to complete very extensive field-work of two different kinds of samples with about 14,600 respondents.[7] (See MOW, 1981.)

Jobs in the 80s received some funds for international co-ordination[8] while each national team obtained its own resources. In Britain the money came from large businesses supplemented in the end with finance from a charitable trust.[9] A professional fund-raiser was engaged half-way through the project with very limited success. The UK project spent altogether about £280,000 (about $420,000 at July 1986 values)[10] but was always in financial difficulties. The British team consisted mainly of consultants and each member charged a daily fee based on the prevailing consultancy rates. These charges applied to planning meetings and conference attendance as well as field-work. Later, as money ran out the system was changed to a flat fee for each project assignment.

The work was structured round several committees and advisory bodies made up of well-known professionals, business executives and a few academics. The meetings were infrequent and failed to influence the progress of the work. Towards the end of the programme one of the large financial sponsors took over control, engaged an additional public relations consultant[11] and a young academic to rewrite and integrate some reports.[12]

In mid-1984, when the cross-national work had finished, Pehr Gyllenhammer and the Aspen Institute for Humanistic Studies invited the British to take part in a further study concentrating on policy options for work creation. The British sponsors refused and organized a final public meeting on 11 October 1984 to wind up the work. During this meeting, which attracted an audience of over 200 and some eminent speakers, very little attention was paid to the approximately fourteen research reports which the programme had accumulated. Most speakers talked about their own preoccupations with work, unemployment and training. References to the research reports were superficial and inaccurate.[13]

Lack of space prevents a more extensive analysis and comparison of the two projects. Having joined the Jobs in the 80s group because of its innovate emphasis on the action and policy-implementation component, my disappointment at its failure to achieve this is substantial.[14] I was probably too close to the project to give an explanation that would be accepted as unbiased, but certain facts are unlikely to be disputed.

In terms of visible product there is very little to show apart from the fourteen typed reports and none of it has or will enter the major policy debate on the future of work, nor is it published to be easily available to academics and researchers.[15] The international report was issued in a 145-page booklet by the Aspen Institute (Yankelovich et al., 1980). It is a curious publication, giving only a small fraction of the survey results without an explanation of the methodology, the actual questions asked or even the numbers in each sample. There is no breakdown by age, sex, job level or education.[16]

The most disappointing aspect of the three-year programme costing over a quarter of a million pounds is its failure to live up to the feedback dissemination objective. After the first nine months when preliminary meetings with a few policy-relevant interest groups had taken place, no time or money was spent on keeping in touch with these

groups on a regular basis or extending their number to what had originally been intended.[17] In spite of having two public relations consultants
available, the diffusion through the media was hardly greater than would
have been the case with any other much more conventional project of
this size and on such highly relevant public topics.[18] Although every one
of the UK reports was aimed at government policy, no attempt was
made to open a discussion with politicians or political parties.

One must not generalize from a single case, but unfortunately there
appears to be no written account of any other large, business-sponsored
cross-national research which had such high-level institutional support.
The hope that the practical, down-to-earth objectives monitored by
commercial clients rather than researchers would have achieved a
greater policy impact than the more usual academic project, has not
been fulfilled.

The Meaning of Working research will not achieve these policy objectives either, but that had never been its aim. The book (MOW, 1987) is
highly academic and will not be read by the people who planned or
sponsored the Jobs in the 80s programme. It took a little longer to get
its results which will be published in a number of academic journals. It
has already led to several doctoral theses, but no popular publication is
planned for the moment.

The contrast between the way these two projects were executed is
really quite extreme;[19] the end result from the point of view of utilization
may, however, be similarly unexciting.

Moderate successes
The Glacier project
Not many research or action projects last for over thirty years. The
Glacier Metals project in London started in 1948 and lingered on until
the principal researcher, Elliot Jaques, was eased out of the company in
1980.[20] The dynamic behind this work came from Wilfred Brown who
became managing director of the company in 1939, when he was thirty
years old. During the war there was a shortage of skilled manpower and
expectations about how employees should be treated had changed.
Brown initiated participative management practices and in 1941 set up
a works council. He wanted employees to have a voice in management.
In 1948 the British government formed a Human Factors Panel of
representatives from government, employers, unions and social science.
One of the outcomes of this initiative was the financing of a small team
of researchers under Jaques to carry out an investigation at Glacier
Metals, the results of which were published after two years (Jaques,
1951). Wilfred Brown valued the analysis-focused work and asked
Jaques to stay on. The two worked together as a team until Brown
retired in 1976 but Jaques stayed on under subsequent managements

and with the sanction of the works council. Both wrote books and pamphlets and there have also been several outside evaluations of the early and middle stages of the project.[21] The research has interested well-known American academics (see Argyris, 1964:208–11; and Katz and Kahn, 1966:411–15) but no systematic assessment of the thirty years has yet been carried out and this book is clearly not the place to do this.[22]

The combined Brown-Jaques team produced new managerial concepts and a language to go with it (Brown, 1960; Jaques, 1976). A company policy document evolved and was constantly updated; a training centre was established in 1961 and grew into an institute which took students from other companies and other countries. Three formal structures were established: a legislative, a representative and an appeals system and they have stayed more or less intact over three decades.

All this is written up in the literature, but for the purpose of our assessment I want to concentrate on two facets of the legislative and representative system which are unusual. One is the unanimous voting procedure and the other is Jaques's employment contract. After a brief initial period, Jaques requested and obtained a year-by-year contract from the works council as its social science officer. He was accountable only to the council and all projects had to be sanctioned by it. The works council was composed of elected members from all levels of the organization and met once a month, usually on Tuesday afternoons in company time. It was an open public meeting and I remember that for at least three years I took diploma students of management to each of these meetings and Wilfred Brown usually came along later in the course to hold a seminar on the Glacier project. Students and academics came from different countries, observed, took notes and later discussed among themselves what they had seen and heard. Most visitors, particularly managers, were incredulous about the unanimous voting requirement.

Glacier Metals was a highly unionized engineering business and had reached a written agreement with the unions to sanction the works council procedure which operated separately from the collective bargaining system. The unanimity principle meant that each representative had to accept every decision before it could become operational. Accepting a decision did not always signify agreement with it, but it implied the power to withhold agreement if necessary. The unusual assumption behind this procedure was that company policy had to operate in the context of different power groups, each of which could impose or withdraw its sanction either formally or informally. It was thought that since the survival of the organization depended on the continued support of each of its members, any change from the status quo should be made only by unanimous agreement.

Although the structures and procedures survived over periods of extreme economic stress, redundancies and a company merger, it should not be thought that conflict and crises did not occur. Several are documented in the literature but few people and certainly no outside observer can adequately assess the manipulation, power games, compromises and dissatisfactions that might have occurred out of sight, behind closed doors. In any hierarchical organization, and Glacier was no exception, senior staff are not aware of what really goes on at lower levels.

Although the purpose of this brief description is not to evaluate the project as a whole, some relevant observations can be made. Both Brown and Jaques believed in very careful definitions of concepts which created a specialized, somewhat stilted language which some groups failed to appreciate and sometimes ridiculed. Jaques's psychoanalytic training and personality led him to separate his formal role very carefully from informal relations and this created a distance between himself and staff which could be understood and respected but prevented warm, open relationships.

The pioneering work took place at the London factory and — as has happened so often in other experiments — failed to take roots in other Glacier locations to anything like the same extent.[23]

The intensity and fervour which accompanied the project in its heyday diminished over time and particularly since Brown left. This circumstance shows how difficult it is to evaluate success or failure reliably. An evaluation after the first three years would have been much more positive than during the last three years or at other phases where periodic difficulties were encountered. These were sometimes due to economic circumstances outside the control of the company.

A large-scale project like Glacier also highlights the problem of choosing an appropriate criterion variable. From the point of view of the chief executive, the project was evaluated very positively; it enabled him to direct the company with confidence since most major decisions had the formal sanction of all employees. He argued that this reduced friction to manageable proportions.[24] From an outside economic perspective, however, it can be argued that Glacier Metals was not very successful. It operated in the highly competitive and fluctuating motor car market and eventually had to be absorbed in a larger engineering conglomerate. However, even then many of the research-based concepts and structures survived.

On the other hand if the longevity of a project is used as a criterion of success, the picture changes. Glacier lasted three times as long as Hawthorne which itself set a record for survival (Landsberger, 1958).

The Glacier experience also shows once again why one usually has to be content to learn lessons from social science experience without succumbing to the temptation of copying or transferring ready-made solutions even if they are successful. The circumstances that gave rise to the research project at Glacier and sustained it might require a crisis like a war and a generous funding body at precisely the time when two ideologically and temperamentally highly compatible individuals can collaborate in a programme.

The Glacier project pioneered a number of important practical developments and theoretical concepts and it *inter alia* demonstrated the positive role which an independent social scientist adviser can play over a period of nearly three decades. Jaques was not an employee of the company in the way personnel managers are; nor was he a researcher paid by management or some outside body. He was an adviser to any and all members of the organization through a contract with the works council which had to be renewed yearly. Since the works council operated only by unanimous vote, any group in the company could veto his contract. Such an arrangement, which has not yet been imitated elsewhere, gives considerable strength to the argument in favour of action research.

In general, I believe that historians of organizational sociology will consider this project to have been unusually significant.

The Humanization of Work programme

Without doubt the most ambitious social science research programme in Europe was set in motion by the government of the Federal Republic of Germany in 1974. It has been continued in spite of different compositions of the political power structure and currently spends about DM 100 million a year (over £29 million or $45 million at July 1986 values).

When a new government came to power in 1970 it pursued a priority policy of improving working conditions and saw in the rapidly developing disciplines of physiology, general medicine, engineering sciences, psychology and sociology a means of achieving some of its objectives.[25] The more specific objectives can be described under four headings (Wilpert and Ruiz, 1984):

1. To develop better employee protection, improved safety norms and minimum standards for machines, building and work-places
2. To develop work technologies which harmonize with human needs
3. To search for appropriate models of work organization and job design
4. To diffuse and apply the emerging scientific knowledge and practical experience.

The main investment has undoubtedly been on research into the physical and physiological dimensions of work as set out in (1) above. It is less controversial than areas (2) and (3) and seems to have been well received. In the more socio-psychological field, conflicts between employees and unions are a partial explanation of the lower emphasis in the programme. Both sides agreed to accept 'proven work science knowledge'[26] (Wilfert, 1984:48). However, on a more general level, unions saw an extension of the co-determination system as the best approach while employers, who are opposed to such an extension, thought that a managerial interpretation of organizational and economic interests should prevail. This would eliminate or reduce democratic decision procedures which had received positive support from a variety of research projects.

From the point of view of our main topic it is worth noting that all three partners in the research enterprise seemed to agree that the major problem would be to transfer the newly-created knowledge into everyday working practice. Being somewhat legalistically minded they saw this as a challenge which would further the provision of Paragraphs 90 and 91 of the Works Constitution Act which deals with the utilization of 'substantiated labour science knowledge'. Other criteria which must be met before the government supplies in the region of 50 percent of the research cost are:

a. That national rather than purely company interests must dictate the design of the project and that the work would not be undertaken without the government subsidy

b. That projects must take off from the current state of knowledge and lead to broadening and new developments

c. That the area of work is recognized as entailing considerable scientific, economic or technical uncertainty and risk but that there should nevertheless exist a plausible prospect of success

d. That the results of the project must be transferable to a large number of working places rather than being applicable only in isolated cases

e. That neither the project nor its outcomes must cause redundancies or consequences that would entail significant disadvantages to those concerned with the work (unless even without the project such negative consequences would occur)

f. That the works council in each enterprise must give its agreement to the project.

In the ten years of this programme a very large number of projects have been undertaken and, in each major research area, a tripartite steering committee has had the responsibility of giving advice on the content and value of funding individual projects. Between 1974 and 1981 the following breakdown of the programme is given by Wilfert (1984:51):

481 projects costing DM 391.3 million for making work safer and easier

211 projects costing DM 170.6 million for creating greater opportunities for self-realization and skill improvement

202 projects costing DM 63.3 million for transforming and transferring
the knowledge gained from research

61 projects costing DM 26.0 million for broadly applied research and
miscellaneous aspects.

Given the expenditure of such large sums of money, it is natural that
several evaluations have taken place and quite severe criticisms are
made by trade unions, employers, government officials and academics.
It has led to the curious situation whereby, in spite of extensive
complaints, most reports recommend that the programme should
continue and the German government has agreed.

Most criticisms are very predictably in line with the time-honoured
opposition of basic interests between employers and representatives of
employees. Employers complain that unions treat projects as ammunition in collective bargaining and always try to insist that scientific
improvements should be accompanied by higher wages. Unions are said
to try to use their weight in works councils to obtain advanced confirmation on changes in work content that could result from a research
finding and then ask for the wage increases to be incorporated in the
experimental design. The employers say that the programme should aim
at improving working conditions and not at increasing wages even if job
enrichment and job enlargement improve the skill requirements of
labour. They regard this as illegitimate union pressure.

Trade-union criticism has come particularly strongly from IG Metall,
the metal-workers' union. They accuse some projects of leading to
increased work effort and/or speed up without wage compensation and
to rationalization which reduces employment. They also say that the
major beneficiaries of the Humanization programme have been the
scientific institutes and the academic community. Nobody seems to have
denied this last point.

From these criticisms it would seem to me that both sides are in
danger of misusing the research for partisan ends. Since the sphere of
disagreement is greatest on the socio-technical and psychological
projects in areas (2) and (3) above, the quarrels have led to an even
stronger trend to concentrate on safety, ergonomics and standards
agreements covered by area (1), and the present government seems to
support this.

There are some criticisms which transcend the vested interests of
management and employer. There is wide agreement that diffusion and
dissemination has not received sufficient emphasis or has been poorly
researched. In any case little has taken place. The quantity, quality and
style of the reports have also been almost universally condemned. Vast
quantities of paper bound in yellow folders have been churned out but

remain unread. Even academics agree. A study of the first twenty volumes of output by Wilpert and Ruiz (1984) says that 'their style and language addresses mostly scientifically trained readers'. They could have added that the different disciplines involved in these 955 projects make it almost impossible for the experts themselves to understand many reports written in the jargon of a particular speciality. From the perspective of the international scientific community, it is also a pity that, unlike Scandinavian research, the German sponsors do not seem to have allocated any funds for publications even of summaries in other languages.

Wilpert and Ruiz make a number of other quite specific criticisms. For instance, Volume 15 on artificial lighting lacks a comprehensive structure which makes 'it quite impossible for the volume to be used according to its objectives' (p. 188). Volume 3 'becomes a classical case study of a research process gone astray' (p. 180) and Volume 1, which was designed to be a critical self-description of the Humanization of Work programme, is described as catastrophically poor (p. 191). However, there is also praise. In view of the employers' desire for neutral research, it is instructive to learn from Volume 19 that 'the authors demonstrate convincingly that job evaluations are never devoid of vested interests and can never lead to a completely objective determination of job requirements' (p. 191). Volume 12 is praised, in spite of its 450 pages, for presenting a well-written case study of an organizational change project (p. 190).

Overall it is clear that what in Germany are called 'the social partners' have derived benefits from this prolonged process of research collaboration. Moreover, when the work becomes more easily available in readable form, the international social science community and research funding bodies will surely learn from the errors as well as from the successes. In retrospect it is easy to see that the experts were unprepared for such a large challenge at short notice. When politicians want to achieve results they sometimes throw money at problems to get quick solutions. It seems to have happened also in the United States. Difficulties of co-operation and dissemination are underestimated as is the time needed for planning a good cross-discipline research.

The Humanization programme may have paid a price for innovation; this often happens. It must, however, be praised for the clear realization in its original specification in (c) above that research is not worth sponsoring if it does not entail genuine uncertainty and risk. Many sponsors forget this and ask researchers to produce a specified project in a specified time with a minutely detailed budget as if it were a plan for a sausage factory.

Review

This last chapter in Part I briefly describes some examples of research which range from outright fraud, via misuse, to reasonably durable and successful applications. Two of the frauds, the Midwife Toad and the human skull classification come from physiology, and Ptolemy and Millikan from the even more respectable physical sciences. Most people have heard of the Piltdown fraud, but other critical misrepresentations or strongly suspected abuses cover all aspects of scientific inquiry (Broad and Wade, 1985). Two points can be derived from these delinquencies. One is that, in this respect, all scientific disciplines have to be equally on the alert to avoid deception. The other is the sobering realization that frauds are at least as easily applied and used as genuine findings.

When we look at examples of successful or unsuccessful utilization of genuine research, we have to make difficult judgements. In several of the cases we have mentioned, the evaluation will depend on the criteria we use. In both the Shell and Glacier projects, the action research approach led to substantial changes and lasted over considerable periods. Whether the changes were beneficial or not will depend on the point of view of the evaluator. This is also the case with the long-established German Humanization of Work programme, although in this case the criticism has come from inside as well as from outside sources.

The Jobs in the 80s project demonstrates the importance of criteria. Measured against the high expectations and original plans for engaging directly in prolonged feed-back discussions with policy-makers at the highest levels, the project failed completely and used up large sums of money ineffectively. But in the final meeting of the British sponsors, speeches by eminent industrialists appeared to be quite satisfied with what had been achieved and the two publications which purported to be a summary of the international data, were enthusiastic and dogmatic in most of their conclusions, although I believe that independent researchers would seriously condemn the quality of the material from which these conclusions were drawn.

The time perspective is also important. The Jobs in the 80s project was forgotten before it was finished, while I believe that the Glacier and, to some extent, the Shell project will probably occupy a permanent place in the literature; this could also be the case with some aspects of the Humanization of Work programme.

Notes

1. The unpopularity is due to at least three factors. One is academic respectability and promotion prospects which favour novelty. The second is that the abbreviated data presentation required by the most prestigious journals often precludes exact

replication; and thirdly, funding bodies go out of their way to inhibit replication by requesting reviewers to indicate whether similar research has already been carried out.

2. Later, the name of the project changed to 'Work and Society' when a charitable trust joined the original sponsors. For the sake of simplicity I shall stay with the original title.

3. The Public Agenda Foundation (president, Daniel Yankelovich) is a USA-based non-profit organization with the objective of informing the public on the functioning of democratic societies. It does not advocate any particular policy.

4. The Aspen Institute for Humanistic Studies is an international non-profit organization which, for more than thirty years, has brought together leading citizens from the public and private sectors in the United States and throughout the world to consider individual and societal values and issues.

5. In addition, both projects planned to work in countries where there was no overlap.

6. The Jobs in the 80s survey covered very similar questions though there were also differences of method, extent and emphasis. The duplication was nonsensical. In Japan, for instance, the Jobs in the 80s group had to be satisfied with a small sample while the MOW team obtained answers from 3,200 Japanese.

7. The countries are: Belgium, Germany, Israel, Japan, the Netherlands, the UK, USA and Yugoslavia. One set of samples came from ten 'target groups' like teachers, self-employed businessmen, tool and die-makers, the unemployed and the retired. The other came from national representative samples. For details see MOW (1987).

8. The German Marshall Fund, the Beatrice Foods Co., Harman International Industries and A.B. Volvo.

9. Among the business contributions, Shell, Rank Xerox and National Westminster Bank played a major role. The charitable fund was the Joseph Rowntree Memorial Trust.

10. This is about the amount of money which the MOW project spent in all eight countries.

11. This was in addition to two other public relations consultants who had previously helped with the programme. Only two of the three consultants were paid fees.

12. There was substantial discontinuity. The British survey was carried out by a professional firm of opinion research. Some criticisms were raised and an American member of the UK team offered to check results. However, a competing UK public opinion firm was engaged to carry out this work. Eventually a young university researcher was asked to re-analyse the data.

13. One of the main speakers who was deputy chairman of Jobs in the 80s mentioned two recent reports on manpower comparisons with Germany but omitted the report of Jobs in the 80s which had produced a similar analysis some time earlier.

14. It is relevant to mention the untimely death of Michael Shanks, in 1984, who had led the research effort, after which the directing influence moved even more firmly into the hands of one of the financial sponsors and the contribution of the research team was almost completely eliminated.

15. The different UK reports were typed and photocopied for a very small circulation. When the programme was wound up, the Institute of Manpower Studies at Sussex agreed to put on their own covers and include them in their publications list, but since they have their own reports in similar fields, it is doubtful whether they will give them much publicity.

16. It was clearly written in a hurry by four authors (see Yankelovich et al., 1983). The British contribution was not provided by the research team and was not checked by it before publication. The British research team is not mentioned in the publication. More recently, the same material, with very few improvements, was incorporated in a book (Yankelovich et al., 1985) which has received very little publicity.

17. Some contact — on a very sporadic basis — was continued with a Trade Union study centre and a couple of meetings with sponsors and members of the advisory committees took place.

18. When the press was invited on a couple of occasions to hear about the publications, the meetings specifically excluded the research team responsible for the reports. This may be an idiosyncrasy of the British scene and reinforces the comments made by some of the British chapter writers in this book about the low status of social science in the UK. However, it is sad that, in spite of this exclusion, the resulting press publicity was minimal.

19. For instance, planning meetings of the international MOW team took place at regular intervals in simple accommodation and never lasted less than one week. The Jobs in the 80s group met rarely and only for one day; accommodation was in luxury hotels and at least one team always travelled first class by air. In the case of the MOW research, the major article and the book were published under the reference 'MOW International Team'. The researchers are given full acknowledgement inside the volume. In contrast, the Jobs in the 80s publication lists as authors people who did not carry out the research and no acknowledgement is given to the researchers in any part of the report (Yankelovich et al., 1980).

20. A new director of personnel had been appointed. He came from an academic position and had no sympathy with Jaques's work.

21. See, for instance, Brown, 1960; Brown and Jaques, 1965; Jaques, 1976; Jaques, 1956. Two critical evaluations are by Kelly, 1968; and Gray, 1976.

22. Two members of the Tavistock staff, Alan Brown and Frank Heller initiated a monitoring-evaluation study in 1978 which continued until a new personnel director asked for it to be discontinued.

23. The lack of carry-over between departments and sites has often been described in the Norwegian and Swedish literature. See, for instance, Gustavsen's chapter in this book.

24. Analysis in terms of friction has a special significance for this company whose main product is frictionless bearings for the motor car industry. Wilfred Brown liked to explain that even a good quality bearing has, and to some extent requires, a degree of friction for successful operation (Brown, 1960; Brown and Jaques, 1965).

25. It also set about passing laws on works constitution, work-place regulations and work study norms (DIN).

26. In the introduction, I have already commented on the remarkably positive German predisposition toward the utilization of *Wissen* or scientific knowledge. The Humanization of Work programme clearly benefited from this.

References

Argyris, Chris (1964) *Integrating the Individual and the Organization.* New York: John Wiley.

Blackler, F.H.M. and C.A. Brown (1980) *Whatever Happened to Shell's New Philosophy of Management?* Guildford, Surrey: Saxon House.

Broad, William and Nicholas Wade (1985) *Betrayers of the Truth: Fraud and Deceit in Science.* Oxford: Oxford University Press.

Brown, Alan and F.A. Heller (1981) 'The Application of Group Feed-back Analysis to Questionnaire Data in a Longitudinal Study', *Human Relations*, 34(2):141–56.

Brown, Wilfred (1960) *Explorations in Management.* London: Heinemann.

Brown, Wilfred and Elliot Jaques (1965) *Glacier Project Papers: Some Essays on Organization and Management from the Glacier Research Project.* London: Heinemann.

Casanova, Pablo Gonzalez (1981) *The Fallacy of Social Science Research: A Critical Examination and New Qualitative Model.* Oxford: Pergamon Press.

Emery, F.E. and E.L. Trist (1960) 'Socio Technical Systems', in C.W. Churchman and M. Verhulst (eds), *Management Sciences, Models and Techniques*, Vol. 2. Oxford: Pergamon Press.

Gould, Stephen J. (1981) *The Mismeasure of Man.* New York: Norton.

Gray, Jerry (ed.) (1976) *The Glacier Project: Concept and Critiques.* London: Heinemann.

Hearnshaw, L.S. (1979) *Cyril Burt, Psychologist.* London: Hodder and Stoughton.

Heller, F. A. (1985) 'Some Theoretical and Practical Problems in Multi-National and Cross Cultural Research on Organizations', in Pat Joynt and Malcolm Warner (eds), *Managing in Different Cultures.* Oslo: Universitets Forlaget.

Hill, Paul (1972) *Towards a New Philosophy of Management.* London: Gower Press.

Jaques, Elliot (1951) *The Changing Culture of a Factory.* London: Tavistock.

Jaques, Elliot (1956) *Measurement of Responsibility.* London: Tavistock.

Jaques, Elliot (1976) *A General Theory of Bureaucracy.* London: Heinemann.

Kamin, Leon J. (1974) *The Science and Politics of I.Q.* Potomac, Md: Lawrence Erlbaum.

Katz, Daniel and Robert Kahn (1966) *The Social Psychology of Organizations.* New York: John Wiley.

Kelly, Joe (1968) *Is Scientific Management Possible?* London: Faber and Faber.

Koestler, Arthur (1971) *The Case of the Midwife Toad.* London: Hutchinson.

Landsberger, Henry (1958) *Hawthorne Revisited.* Ithaca, N.Y.: Cornell University Press.

MOW (Meaning of Working) (1981) 'The Meaning of Working', in Gunter Dlugor and Klaus Weiermair (eds), *Management under Different Value Systems.* Berlin: Walter de Gruyter.

MOW (Meaning of Working) (1987) *The Meaning of Working.* London: Academic Press.

Rein, Martin and Sheldon White (1977) 'Policy Research: Belief and Doubt', *Policy Analysis*, 3(2):239–71.

Wilfert, Peter (1984) 'The German Humanization of Work Programme: An Employer's Assessment', in *New Patterns of Work and Employment No. 7: Teutons and Travail.* Van Gorcum, Netherlands: European Centre for Work & Society.

Wilpert, Bernhard and Antonio Ruiz (1984) 'The German Humanization of Work Programme: Review of its First Twenty Publications', *Journal of Occupational Psychology*, 57:185–95.

Yankelovich, D., H. Zetterberg, B. Strümpel and M. Shanks (1980) *Putting the Work Ethic to Work.* New York: Public Agenda Foundation.

Yankelovich, D., H. Zetterberg, B. Strümpel and M. Shanks (1983) *Work and Human Values: An International Report on Jobs in the 1980s and 1990s.* Aspen Institute for Humanistic Studies.

Yankelovich, Daniel and collaborators (1985) *The World of Work: An International Report on Jobs, Productivity and Human Values.* New York: Octagon Press.

II
THEORY AND EXPERIENCE

10
Social research as participative dialogue

Bjørn Gustavsen

Throughout their history, the social sciences have been struggling not only with the problem of theory, but with the problem of practice as well. Looking at the natural sciences one can see the emergence of empirically well-founded and formally elegant theories, a parallel to which has been very difficult to create in the social sciences. Research on nature has, futhermore, had major practical success, as witnessed by the saturation of everyday life with technologies which represent applications of the theories. What impacts have the social sciences had? Clearly, they have had an impact. Equally clear, however, is that this impact is in no way comparable to that of research on nature. The conventional response to these two shortcomings in social research has been to try to create 'better theories' and found them on 'improved methods'. For a century answers have been sought along these lines. The goal seems, however, no closer now than two or three decades ago. In fact, the belief that the social sciences were on their way to a stage comparable to modern research on nature was probably easier to hold in the 1950s and early 1960s than today.

The search for a 'better theory' has not proceeded along one single line. On what constitutes a 'better theory' there have always been different views in social research. Some — often referred to as 'naturalists' or 'positivists' — have argued that it is necessary to move as close to the natural sciences as possible. Others — such as pheno-menologists and interpretative sociologists — have argued that the road to 'better theory' goes via the recognition that human and social pheno-mena are different from nature and consequently can *not* be understood through the same approaches and theories as are applied to nature. These discussions have long since reached stalemate. Recently, how-ever, there have been developments in social research which provide the foundations for pushing the debates about 'better theory' and adequate methods a step further. These developments have emerged when efforts have been made to use the social sciences to support reform and improvement programmes in working life. They are characterized by such concepts as participative research roles, local theory and the like. The basic new dimension which is added is a reassessment of the *boundary* between research and the people to which the research pertains. It is now a fairly common experience that it is very difficult — not to say impossible — to generate changes in working life if these changes are to be determined by a theory developed by research alone. For the necessary commitment from those concerned to emerge, it seems that the creation of theory has to be a *joint* process — an undertaking performed together by research and the people in those workplaces that are to be understood and developed. While naturalist and interpretative social science have both departed from the point of view that it is possible for research *by itself* to create valid theory, the new experience suggests that this may not be the case — at least not in the way traditionally believed. The debates about the role of social research must take into consideration that social research is not at all an autonomous activity but an activity which has to be performed in networks where other people also participate. It seems quite clear that this will have consequences for the discussions about what constitutes a 'better theory' in the social field. The purpose of this contribution is to indicate one of the developments which have led up to today's situation — action-oriented work research in Norway — and indicate some perspectives on the issue of theory and approaches in social research.

Democratization and general theory

Around 1960, a debate on 'industrial democracy' emerged in Norway. After about fifteen years of continuous rationalization of working life after the end of World War II, the time had become ripe for a discussion about the more basic characteristics of working life in the light of commonly accepted political ideals such as 'democracy'. As part of this discussion, a number of 'theories of democratization' were introduced. Among the theories, or models, which played some role in the Scandinavian debates as they unfolded in the 1960s we find, for instance, the Yugoslav self-management system, the Israeli kibbutzim, different versions of the 'human relations message', the organization development school, models drawn from political science (e.g. the balance of interest model) and the socio-technical school. On the whole, the theories were used in a structural way: to define what was wrong with Norwegian working life and to point at what changes would be necessary 'to set things right'. The main exceptions were the organization development school and the socio-technical school: in spite of a twist towards the structural, these schools also introduced ideas about how one should set about *making* the requisite changes. Here, the socio-technical school will be used as an example, not least because it achieved a not insubstantial practical importance.

In spite of its 'reformist' character, the socio-technical school — as it came to be applied in Norway — shares a number of basic elements with a Marxist position: first, the emphasis on the fundamental importance of the relationships of production. Secondly, the need to have a total theory, a theory encompassing all important aspects of society, and for that matter the whole Western world. Thirdly, the wish to create a theory that not only provided an interpretation but which also pointed out what action would be right. The theory — which was largely developed by Fred Emery — had, more specifically, the following main pillars: the first was socio-technical thinking in a narrow sense to restructure the relationship between the human and the technological element in production systems. The second was systems theory, which provided a framework for defining the enterprise as a place of work rather than exclusively as a system of social relations. As a place of work, the enterprise has, for instance, external transactions and dependencies which need to be reflected in the internal organization. The third level — the role of top management — was defined in line with the analysis of Selznick (1957) as the creation of solidarity around joint values. On the level of society, a theory of social ecology was introduced (Emery and Trist, 1972) where industrial democracy was defined and argued for as part of a strategy to deal with instability and turbulence due to environmental over-complexity.

In spite of the fact that this framework contained views about how to create changes, it can still be characterized as fairly structurally-oriented. This point is witnessed by the practical efforts to change working life being called 'field experiments' (Emery and Thorsrud, 1969; 1976), that is: they were meant to test, to demonstrate and to enrich the theory, but the major elements of the theory existed 'before' efforts were made to develop practice. The Norwegian effort was, more specifically, defined as a research-supported developmental programme with two main phases: first, a series of demonstration projects; second, a phase of diffusion. According to the logics of the theory, the introduction of new forms of work organization on the shop floor would initiate broader changes: it would 'roll back' the conventional enterprise organization to replace it with open systems rationality and joint values to guide the behaviour of the members of the enterprise, and more and more enterprises would eventually become involved in the process until a new rationality was in control of working life.

The first phase of the programme went quite well; four field experiments were conducted (for a report, see Emery and Thorsrud, 1976;

Thorsrud et al., 1976; see also Thorsrud, 1984). The diffusion phase, however, created problems, and here we will move directly to this phase.

The stagnation phase and
redefinition of the role of research

The stagnation phase was partly characterized by difficulties in creating a process of diffusion, but also by difficulties in protecting those changes that were achieved. A number of reasons have been suggested to explain why this development occurred.[1] Here, only one point will be mentioned.

The Industrial Democracy programme was developed as a consensual programme. It demanded agreement on a number of levels: the main organizations in working life, the national unions and corresponding employer organizations, and on the local level. It was, furthermore, not sufficient to attain this consensus once and for all. Instead, it had to be renewed and renegotiated on all levels a number of times. This was particularly the case when some sort of crisis emerged in one of the experimental sites, which happened now and then. On the local level the situation was often very complex in that the consensus had to include also lower and middle management who were either unorganized or belonging to unions not affiliated with the general Norwegian Federation of Trade Unions (LO). The researchers continuously faced this consensus maintaining pressure while it was, at the same time, highly difficult to produce platforms on which all interested parties could find a footing which was at least sure enough for them to be willing to keep up participation.

On the first level of analysis the problem can be called one of 'tactical overload'. However, there were deeper reasons which were not clearly seen at the time but which have emerged more distinctly in the light of later reflection. Among these, two are particularly important: first, that the general theory failed to provide a stable basis on which to build the necessary agreements and coalitions. Instead, the theoretical surface was experienced as slippery. Secondly, there was no reasonably efficient procedure for dealing with the problems. The traditional negotiations between the parties were insufficient while new mechanisms had not emerged to a sufficient degree. In this situation it was possible to go in three different directions.

First, to change theory. Numerous suggestions in this direction were put forward by the more or less friendly critics of the Industrial Democracy programme. Some suggested, for instance, that the efforts should be based on a theory of workers' control, while others suggested that the ideas should be converted into a management theory. When 'things do not work according to plan' it is common to revise the theoretical foundation for the plan. As mentioned initially, a number of theoretical frameworks were suggested in the debates about how to democratize working life. However, it was not easy to find examples of the successful application of other theories. Most of the views on democratization which were put forward in the debate in the early 1960s had not been put to the acid test of action at all, and those which had, did not seem to have fared better than the socio-technical framework. In fact, the situation was rather the opposite: in spite of the problems and setbacks, the socio-technical framework had been able to generate a number of successful demonstration cases and to initiate a broader movement in terms of debates and attention.

Secondly, the idea was put forward to modify the consensus demand. This suggestion is to some extent related to the first one, in that a more worker-oriented, or, alternatively, a more management-oriented, position would imply less emphasis on collaboration between the parties in favour of locating the motor of the change process under the wings of one side only. Of course, the general demands for collaboration according to, for instance, the Basic Agreement[2] would still prevail, but these demands were much more modest than the consensus demands of the Industrial Democracy programme. To redefine the programme into workers' controlled changes or management controlled changes would reduce the need for consensus and remove many of the pressing problems inherent in the tactical overload. To some extent this is what happened in Sweden, where a joint effort modelled after the Norwegian programme (Sandberg, 1982) ran into the same type of problem and was replaced by the management-initiated 'new factories' programme[3] and efforts at creating research-union collaboration.[4]

There was, however, also a third alternative, to place less emphasis on *any* pre-given theory. It was clear that the fact that the research group had a theory and relatively clear ideas about what created problems in working life and what should be done about them was a major contributing factor behind the difficulties in developing and maintaining agreement between a number of groups and parties in working life. The development actually went in favour of the last of these alternatives. Initially, this emerged as changes in practice rather than as a result of a more explicit reflection. The changes in practice occurred in relation to several different projects around the mid-1970s. One example is a job design workshop which was run from 1972 as a joint employer-union effort with support from the Work Research Institute. In this workshop six enterprises met several times, one group of enterprises being recruited each second year. The workshops were meant to initiate and support change programmes in the participating enterprises. Initially, they were largely used as arenas for the diffusion of the theory behind the Industrial Democracy programme and discussions of the experiences from the first field experiments. Relatively few viable projects emerged. Around 1975, however, a change started to occur in that the researchers placed less emphasis on pregiven theory and experience to open up for more influence from the participants, a more open view on theory, and greater emphasis on local variations and conditions specific to each enterprise. Table 1 gives a summary of the impact of the workshop in terms of the rate of successful projects to emerge out of each group of participants. It is seen that a 'turning of the tide' occurred in the period when the issue of what theory should control local development was made more open.

TABLE 1
Successful projects among participants in the job design workshop from 1972 to 1976

	1972–3	1973–4	1974–5	1975–6
Successful projects	1	2	5	5
No projects/unsuccessful projects	5	4	1	1

Projects have been scored as successful if the workers have actively participated in the redesign of their own jobs (participative design) *and* there has emerged new forms of work organization which gives more autonomy to the workers.
Source: Engelstad, 1980

The research role emerging out of this experience is often referred to as *participative*: research shares influence with the people in the workplace on a roughly equal footing. It is necessary to underline that this sharing of influence does not only pertain to the more practical questions of what measures to apply within each workplace but that it pertains to broader issues as well, for instance, why changes are to be performed at all. On the other hand, clearly, research has to maintain some elements as pre-set conditions. One idea maintained in the efforts of the Work Research Institute is that changes are to be developed on a model of participatory democracy and imply increased control for the workers over their own situation.

Since the mid-1970s the development towards new types of research roles has continued (e.g. Elden, 1979). In addition to the participative model it is possible to talk about a supportive model, where research gives support to developments which are mainly initiated and run by workers and management on the enterprise level themselves, and a model where research is responsible for what can be called the infrastructure of change. By infrastructure is meant support structures such as ongoing systems of conferences and the like which can function as a 'ground' out of which actual change processes emerge.

As mentioned above, these changes in the role of research initially occurred as a result of pressures from practice rather than as a result of a deeper reflection on the role of theory and research. More recently, however, these more basic issues have been taken up (Gustavsen, in preparation) leading to reflections along several lines, two of which will be pursued — albeit briefly — here: first, how the issue of democracy is to be understood, and, second, what role 'general theory' may have.

A re-conceptualization of the problem of (industrial) democracy

When people react against 'theories of democratization' to which they have not themselves contributed, one explanation may be that they — implicitly — identify democracy as the right to *create* the theory which is to prevail within their own workplace. General concepts seem mainly to function as building blocks and guidelines in the development of local understandings. It is rarely possible to implement theory as 'ready-made packages'. This also pertains to situations where new solutions look almost identical to the solutions created in other workplaces. There is, after all, often a limited range of logically possible solutions to any given problem, say, the allocation of tasks within a given production system. Still, there are at least two major reasons why the change process also in such cases has to be one of generation or creation rather than diffusion or application: Firstly, elements which may to an outside observer seem of secondary significance can often take on major proportions to those involved. Secondly, and mainly, people become much more committed to interpretations and solutions to which they have themselves contributed.

In this interpretation, industrial democracy is identical to *generative capacity*, to the ability to *create* solutions to problems of technology and organization, and not identical to any particular pattern of organization, be it autonomous groups, a particular representative system, or any other specific solution. Instead, democracy is seen as a generative principle — as a particular way of creating solutions. Democracy as a principle of generation versus specific patterns of organization is a conflict of interpretation which seems to have its roots in unclarities on this point in the writings of one of the founders of democratic theory: Rousseau. Today, however, the tendency is towards emphasising the generative aspect (Habermas, 1984). There are, of course, limitations to what forms of organization can be developed and used within a framework which is to bear the label 'democratic'. There are certain boundary conditions that cannot be transcended. For instance, solutions to problems of organization must not be sought which destroy the generative capacity as such. The clarification of these boundary conditions is an important task in urgent need of being undertaken. In principle, however, it is no different from the similar clarification with reference to democracy on the level of society, where there is already a rich literature, particularly within legal theory.

Research and theory
The development described above implies two things: first, the dissolution of a clear boundary between research and the people to whom the research pertains; secondly, a drift towards the local in terms of the content of theory. These two tendencies do not follow each other by necessity: it is possible for research and other people to collaborate in the development of general theory or for research alone to create local theory. In actual practice, however, there is a link between the drift towards the local and towards collaborative theory formation.

This development gives rise to two basic questions which in a pointed form, can be put like this: Is there any need for researchers at all — if it is so that 'people can do research' (Thorsrud, 1981) what is then the point of having 'professional researchers'? Secondly, what happens to general theory — is it to be abandoned altogether or will it survive in some form or other? These questions are far-reaching and no analysis in depth can be done here. Some indications of the answers can, however, be given.

The question of the continued survival of social research is easily dealt with. It is quite clear that the social sciences are highly useful and important partners in collaborative settings. There are a number of functions for research to fill: for instance, the feeding of concepts into the local processes, the transmission of experience between workplaces, the establishment of conditions out of which changes can grow, of support structures, etc. A number of analyses can be done only by research.

Not least, Scandinavian experience seems to indicate that a collaboratively-oriented work research can attain a very central position in relation to the development of working life (see, for instance, Emery and Thorsrud, 1976; Gustavsen and Hunnius, 1981; Gustavsen, in preparation). Arguing a collaborative role for research does not mean that research should perform no autonomous activities. The point is that the autonomous activities of research — for instance the development of potential theory — must not be confused with valid theory. A theory is valid only when it has received commitment from those concerned, because only then is the theory incorporated in the action of people.

What about the issue of general theory?

At this point a distinction must be made between two types of theory: on the one hand theory about the *content* of the solutions to problems of technology and organization in working life, and on the other theory about the *way* these solutions are to be created. The drift towards the local pertains primarily to the first of these issues. What becomes local is 'theory of organization'. In this way a long process reaches an end stage: a process which started with efforts at creating conceptual frameworks which could catch the salient features of all organizations — such as the various versions of 'bureaucracy' — proceeded to efforts at creating general alternatives to bureaucracy — e.g. 'organic organisation' (Burns and Stalker, 1961) — moved from there to contingency theory (e.g. Woodward, 1965; Pugh et al., 1968; 1969) to end with local theory (e.g. Elden, 1983). Along with this, 'theory of democratic organization' becomes local as well.

Turning to the mechanism which is to *generate* local theory, however, the picture changes. Here, theory will have to be general and it will be indicated — albeit briefly — why this is so.

In looking for concepts around which generative theory can be built, several possibilities present themselves. In particular, there are two concepts which have been suggested for such a purpose: *learning* and *dialogue.*

To locate 'learning' in a superordinate role has been suggested by, for instance, Bateson (1972). When a human being or a social system learns something of a more concrete nature, it also 'learns to learn': that is, a more general learning capability is developed which can be used for further learning in new situations. Through identifying the characteristics relevant to meta-learning one would also have a set of characteristics relevant to generative capacity. Among the architects of the socio-technical school, Emery (1982) as well as Thorsrud (1984) seem to go in this direction, a trend which generally has its firmest anchoring in North American social psychology (e.g. Argyris and Schon, 1978).

By 'dialogue' is meant an open discussion according to certain principles where everybody who is concerned by an issue can participate on an equal footing and where the outcome of the discussion influences decisions. Rational dialogue in a modern sense has its roots in liberal democracy where it was the main vehicle for the development of public opinion and public influence over the acts of the state (Habermas, 1962).

Dialogue and learning have elements in common: learning is an important part of dialogue, while dialogue can be a main prerequisite for learning. However, there are also differences. Dialogue refers not only to learning but to several other issues as well, such as the reaching of agreements in situations where this depends less on learning than on the way interests are pursued and balanced against each other. Solutions to problems of productivity and worker influence cannot advance without a considerable amount of learning. This notwithstanding, other elements are also strongly present such as the issue of interests and their settlement. In simple terms: the development of a new working life poses a number of problems which cannot be solved through learning alone. Consequently, the concept of the dialogue seems most appropriate as the main one. This is in line with tendencies within continental European thinking, as represented by, for instance, Habermas (1982) or Foucault (1982).

Now, however, we seem to be doing exactly the same as what traditional social science has been criticized for doing: introducing a concept which is then, by research, *elevated* to a general position. Why should it be possible to claim generality for such a concept as dialogue while most social science concepts are denied a general status?

To answer this question it is necessary to add another link to the argument, and to do this a brief look must be taken at another issue: from where does a social theory gain its truth or validity? The simple point of view is that a valid theory is a theory which *corresponds* to reality. It is easily seen, however, that this simple answer is fraught with problems. Reality reveals itself only through the investigation which lies behind the theory and there is nothing with which the theory can be compared for correspondence, unless the same investigation is done over again. To validate the results of this second investigation, a third must be done, etc. Consequently, there is a need to apply other criteria. A number of alternatives have been suggested. Most common has been to link the validity of a theory to the quality of the procedures which have guided the underlying investigation. By procedures has generally been meant 'scientific method'. The weakness of this position is that 'scientific method' is no unitary phenomenon where all approaches can be measured according to one single yardstick expressing 'the ideal'. After studies like those by Kuhn (1962) and Feyerabend (1970) of the history of theoretical physics and astronomy demonstrated that there are no 'ideal standards' within these disciplines, it seems futile to argue such standards within social research. This has led to the emergence of another type of procedural criterion — a social rather than a 'technical' one: the creation of a theory can be seen as a *social* process — also, the researcher who sits in his office and thinks is actually participating in a discourse with past, present and future partners — and the characteristics of this discourse can form a point of departure for evaluating the validity of the theory. In principle, a good discourse leads to a theory of high validity. The roots of this idea go back at least to Peirce (1955) who saw 'science' as a community of inquirers who operate according to certain rules which have to be proposed, argued and decided on in open and rational discourse. In more recent years, the basic idea has been further developed by Habermas (e.g. 1972; 1973) one expression being the concept of 'theoretical discourse' and Foucault (1982) whose 'discourse formation' is a network of people who share a certain language, an interest in certain topics, and conduct their discussions according to a set of rules on which there is a reasonable agreement.

What, then, is an open and rational discourse? In principle anybody can have his or her opinion on this. However, there is one reference point which suggests itself to anybody who is not favourable to pure subjectivism in the establishment of points of departure for research: *democratic thinking.* In democratic theory and practice, the dialogue is a key element, as indicated above. Rational discourse can, in other words, be equalled to democratic dialogue. Democracy, in turn, is part of a system for generation and legitimation of solutions on the level of society. Using the concept of the dialogue implies, in other words, that it is necessary to develop general criteria for what is a good generative mechanism. The way in which solutions are generated is actually what constitutes a society. Unless the same mechanism is applied throughout what is to be understood as 'one society', it would no longer be 'one society' but several.

It is a task for research to clarify the criteria for a rational democratic dialogue and find ways of making these criteria become operational in the creation of solutions to practical problems in working life, and for that matter also elsewhere. This is a major task. Research has clearly begun; there is, for instance, already quite a lot of experience, research and literature on ways of working in change programmes which can be interpreted in the light of the concept of dialogue and which can form the basis for further advances.[5]

Concluding remarks

Slowly but steadily the description and understanding of physical nature has become the task of specialized communities of inquirers who have been able to develop a more and more intensified relationship to their objects of study, until, today, they constitute large establishments continuously expanding the foundations for technologies, thereby deciding the fate of whole societies in peace and war. To a large extent the social sciences have been tailored on the same model. Consistently, however, their objects of study have refused to behave like physical nature. People 'talk back', they change the 'laws' which govern their behaviour and generally act in a way which creates difficulties from a research point of view. To grapple with the special problems emerging when the object of research is people, several alternatives to naturalist research approaches have been suggested, for instance that the task of social research is to interpret and understand, not to describe. Recently, however, there have emerged experiences indicating that the main problem does not lie in choosing between different schools of thought on how to create autonomous social theory but in reassessing the conditions under which social theory is at all *possible.* Social theory can neither describe nor control the behaviour of people unless people are committed to the theory and this commitment demands participation in its formation. Social research has a key role to play in collective processes of emancipation but cannot claim to perform this task 'on behalf' of the rest of society.

Notes

1. In all countries where systematic efforts at developing new forms of work organization have been made, diffusion problems seem to have emerged. There is now a broad literature on these problems. As concerns Norway, see Emery and Thorsrud (1976); Bolweg (1976); Gustavsen and Hunnius (1981a); and Sandberg (1982).

2. 'Basic Agreement' is a concept used in Denmark, Norway and Sweden with reference to a general agreement between the employers and the unions which functions as a constitution in the sense that it contains basic rules about negotiating procedures, the rights of worker representatives, etc. When these general agreements emerged — mainly in the 1930s — they represented the end of a period of much conflict and disquiet in working life and the beginning of the fairly stable and ordered labour relations system which characterizes these societies today. In recent years the importance of the basic agreements has to some extent declined because some of the regulations performed in the agreements have been taken over by legislation. This is particularly noticeable in Sweden. For further treatment of the basic agreements, see Gustavsen (1982); Gunzburg (1976); ILO (1984).

3. The development referred to as 'new factories' is a series of projects which occurred in a number of Swedish enterprises in the 1970s. They were initiated and run by management but received some professional support from the so-called Technical Office of the Swedish Employers Confederation. The internationally most well-known project within this framework is the Volvo Kalmar plant. For literature, see Agurén et al. (1976); Agurén and Edgren (1979); Lindholm (1979); Sandberg (1982).

4. In the Scandinavian countries there have been a number of attempts at creating projects on the basis of research-union collaboration. The majority have run into various types of difficulties and had a limited impact. The main exception is probably the Demos-project in Sweden and its successors (Sandberg, 1983).

5. Compared with, for instance, Peirce and Habermas, the community of inquirers is here defined so that it does not only include researchers but other people as well. This is actually one of the major points of this study. This author is, furthermore, not in agreement with Habermas in his view of the relationship between theory and practice. While Habermas uncouples theory and practice to a large extent, this author is of the opinion that they should be more strongly related.

This relationship must not, however, be achieved through reintroducing theory to control practice as in Marxism, but rather through increasing the influence of practice over theory. However, these issues cannot be pursued here; the interested reader must be referred to Gustavsen (in preparation).

References

Agurén, S. and J. Edgren (1979) *New Factories.* Stockholm: Swedish Employers Confederation.

Agurén, S., R. Hansson and K. G. Karlsson (1976) *The Volvo Kalmar Plant.* Stockholm: Rationalization Council SAF–LO.

Argyris, C. and D. A. Schon (1978) *Organizational Learning.* Reading, Mass.: Addison-Wesley.

Bateson, G. (1972) Social Planning and the Concept of Deutero-learning, in *Steps to an Ecology of Mind.* New York: Ballantine.

Bolweg, J. F. (1976) *Job Design and Industrial Democracy: The Case of Norway.* Leiden: Nijhoff.

Burns, T. and G. M. Walker (1961) *The Management of Innovation.* London: Tavistock.

Elden, M. (1979) Three Generations of Work Democracy Experiments in Norway: Beyond Classical Socio-technical Systems Analysis', in C. L. Cooper and E. Mumford (eds.), *The Quality of Working Life in Eastern and Western Europe.* London: Associated Business Press.

Elden, M. (1983) Democratization and Participative Research in Developing Local Theory, *Journal of Occupational Behaviour,* 4(1).

Emery, F. E. (1982) New Perspectives on the World of Work. Socio-technical Foundations for a New Social Order?', *Human Relations,* 35(12).

Emery, F. E. and E. Thorsrud (1969) *Form and Content in Industrial Democracy.* London: Tavistock.

Emery, F. E. and E. Thorsrud (1976) *Democracy at Work.* Leiden: Nijhoff.

Emery, F. E. and E. Trist (1972) *Towards a Social Ecology.* London: Plenum Press.

Engelstad, P. H. (1980) Developments in a National Strategy of Democratizing the Work Organization', in K. Trebesch (ed), *Organization Development in Europe, Vol I: Concepts.* Bern: Paul Haupt.

Feyerabend, P. K. (1970) 'Against Method: Outline of an Anarchistic Theory of Knowledge', *Minnesota Studies in the Philosophy of Science,* 4.

Foucault, M. (1982) *The Archeology of Knowledge.* New York: Pantheon.

Gunzburg, D. (1976) *Industrial Democracy in Sweden.* Melbourne: National Productivity Institute.

Gustavsen, B. (1982) 'Industrial Democracy', in E. Allardt et al. (eds.), *Nordic Democracy.* Copenhagen: Det danske selskab.

Gustavsen, B. (in preparation) 'Sociology as Action: On the Constitution of Alternative Realities' (draft). Oslo: Work Research Institute.

Gustavsen, B. and G. Hunnius (1981) *New Patterns of Work Reform. The Case of Norway.* Oslo: Oslo University Press.

Habermas, J. (1962) *Strukturwandel der Öffentlichkeit.* Neuwied: Luchterhand.

Habermas, J. (1972) *Knowledge and Human Interests.* London: Heinemann.

Habermas, J. (1973) *Theory and Practice.* Boston: Beacon Press.

Habermas, J. (1982) *Theorie des Kommunikativen Handelns.* Frankfurt: Suhrkamp.

Habermas, J. (1984) *Den rationalla övertygelsen. En antologi om legitimitet, kris och politik.* Stockholm: Akademilitteratur.

156   *The use and abuse of social science*

International Labour Office (1984) *The Trade Union Situation and Industrial Relations in Norway.* Geneva: ILO.
Kuhn, T. (1962) *The Structure of Scientific Revolution.* Chicago: University of Chicago Press.
Lindholm, R. (1979) *Towards a New World of Work.* Stockholm: Swedish Employers Confederation.
Peirce, C. S. (1955) *Philosophical Writings of Peirce*, ed. J. Buckler. New York: Dover Press.
Pugh, D., D. J. Hickson, D. R. Hinings and C. Turner (1968) 'Dimensions of Organization Structure', *Administrative Science Quarterly*, 13.
Pugh, D., D. J. Hickson, D. R. Hinings and C. Turner (1969) 'The Context of Organization Structure', *Administrative Science Quarterly*, 14.
Sandberg, T. (1982) *Work Organization and Autonomous Groups.* Lund: Liber.
Sandberg, Å. (1983) 'Trade Union Oriented Research for Democratization of Planning in Working Life - Problems and Potentials', *Journal of Occupational Behaviour*, 4.
Selznick, P. (1957) *Leadership in Administration: A Sociological Interpretation.* New York: Harper.
Thorsrud, E. (1981) *People Can Do Research.* Oslo: Work Research Institute.
Thorsrud, E. (1984) 'The Scandinavian Model: Strategies of Organizational Democratization in Norway', in B. Wilpert and A. Sorge (eds.), *International Perspectives on Organizational Democracy*, International Yearbook of Organizational Democracy, Vol. II. Chichester, Sussex: John Wiley.
Thorsrud, E., B. Aa. Sørensen and B. Gustavsen (1976) 'A Socio-technical Approach to Industrial Democracy in Norway', in R. Dubin (ed.), *Handbook of Work, Organization and Society.* Chicago: Rand McNally.
Woodward, J. (1965) *Industrial Organisation: Theory and Practice.* London: Oxford University Press.

11

Research and social policy: political, organizational and cultural constraints

Peter Brannen

This chapter examines the relationship between the social sciences and public policy at the level of the state. It is based upon the views of one social scientist derived from his experience over a decade in one government department; its method is, therefore, in part analytic introspection based on playing an observer as participant role.

There is an increasingly large literature on the use of social science within the policy-making process. Paradoxically, this literature has developed during a period when there has been growing unease about the policy impact of the social sciences. In part, however, this unease may have grown because of a limited set of assumptions about what constitutes utility and a degree of naivety about the barriers to utilization.

The paper suggests that an understanding of the use of social science must take into account the variety of elements which constitute the policy process and the different ways in which social science may contribute to these. More generally, it emphasizes that the use of social science is itself a social act which needs to be analysed within the political, cultural and organizational contexts in which it takes place. A full understanding of the factors which affect use needs to take account of both knowledge *potential* and the *propensity* of relevant categories of social actors to apply that knowledge.

The policy process
In abstract terms social science research might be seen as being useful to policy-makers at any point in a continuum of activities which include:
Policy area definition — the diagnosis of emergent issues which are likely to become policy relevant; social forecasting;
Policy area analysis — the description and analysis of areas in which it is already agreed that policy may or will need to be formulated;
Policy design — the provision of input into the actual formulation of policy in a particular area;

Policy implementation — assessment of constraints on the achievement of agreed policies and ways to overcome these;

Policy reinforcement — the provision of material in support of policy operations;

Policy evaluation — examining the operation and effect of particular policies.

At any point within the continuum outlined above, social science may contribute in a number of different ways through the provision of research, advice, concepts and techniques. This can be illustrated in Figure 1.

FIGURE 1

Social science inputs to the policy process

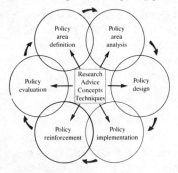

The debate about the relationship between social science and policy is usually couched in terms of *research*. Different types of research may, however, have different relationships to the policy process. *Basic research*, that is research aimed at theoretical and methodological development, is not usually seen as policy-related. However, the linkage of social science development with social development is so close that it is difficult to conceive of any category of social science knowledge as not in some way capable of application. Basic research, however, is best conceived as being one stage back from the policy process at any point in time; yesterday's basic research may, of course, become policy-relevant tomorrow. *Strategic research* is relevant to the beginning and end of the policy process; that is, to policy area definition and analysis and policy evaluation. *Tactical research* is research formulated to serve the needs of immediate policy execution; that is, to be relevant to the design, implementation, reinforcement or short-term monitoring aspects of the policy process. Finally, *informational research*, that is, the synthesis and analysis of existing information, is an activity which is relevant at all stages of the policy process.

These categories of research are not, of course, mutually exclusive. The same research project may have basic, tactical and informational aspects; so a project focused, for example, on the operation of youth labour markets may synthesize current information, provide data on the effects of special government schemes and contribute to theorizing on the nature of labour market segmentation. Nevertheless, it is clear that tactical and informational research are more susceptible to direct use and basic and strategic research more susceptible to indirect use within the policy process.

Policy *advice*, that is, specific prescriptions for change and action, is often seen as the main link between social science research and policy. A formally rational notion of the relationship between social science and policy is posited in the form: research knowledge leads to definition of the policy problem; this in turn leads to presciptions for action, the articulation and promulgation of a policy, and then research evaluation of that policy; the evaluation of the policy then leads to prescriptions either for redesign or policy abandonment. This type of model which is variously described as the instrumental (Peltz, 1978) or problem-solving model (Weiss, 1979) has been increasingly rejected in the literature (Husen, 1984). Nevertheless, the problem-solving use of research may be relevant to certain aspects of the policy process and to particular categories of research. There is, however, a growing appreciation that social-science-based advice can be diffuse rather than specific and can provide a background to decision-making rather than direct prescriptions for change. Implicit in this notion is the idea that advice can emerge not only from specific research projects but also from the corpus of published research, not only from substantive knowledge but also from conceptual and technical knowledge.

Social science *concepts* can and do aid and structure policy discussions. At a general level many of the concepts of the social sciences are part of the lingua franca of policy-makers. Within specific problem contexts particular constructs are drawn on to provide a vocabulary to help structure and clarify discussion and debate. The process by which social science influences policy-makers' ways of thinking and their language of discussion is subtle, but this contribution is nevertheless important.

In addition, the social sciences contain a large body of knowledge of *techniques* for gathering data (e.g. the controlled experiment, participant observation, the survey), on the limitations of these techniques, on the ways on which data collected through these techniques can be analysed and used. Social science methods can be and are used by non social scientists to collect data and information appropriate for their purposes. The survey method in particular is often used by policy-makers to collect administrative information.

Social science, therefore, may relate to the policy process at a number of different points and in a number of different ways. The influence brought to bear by social science on the policy process can be achieved through interaction between policy-makers and social scientists or through a variety of routes that include the published literature, the recycling of literature in the media, through pressure groups, through political parties, and through the parliamentary process including select committees. Whether the possible links between social science and the policy process are translated into actual links will depend on a wide variety of factors. The rest of this paper considers a few of the factors which affect both the potential for and the propensity to use social science in the policy process within a UK government context.

Political culture and knowledge potential

Political culture influences the amount of funding of social science research which in turn affects the amount of research undertaken; in this way it determines the knowledge *potential*. In most Western market societies the state provides a high proportion of the infrastructure for social science through its funding of institutions of higher education and through its direct and indirect financial support of research. Spending money on social science research is a necessary but not sufficient condition for utilization — no research means no use; of course, additionally, neither the total amount spent nor the direction of expenditure bears any *necessary* relationship to use. Nevertheless, the pattern of expenditure and the amount spent on research are indicative of the importance which societies attach to social science research. In that context it is useful to look at a number of trend figures on expenditure.

It is generally the case that in the post-war period prior to the late 1970s all developed countries increased the amount of expenditure on social science research, expanded the institutional base for social science research and operated on the common assumption that it was socially useful to do so. This assumption has been challenged in the new economic environment and in all countries questions are being asked about the utility of the previous expansion. Within a given economic context, however, the degree of financial support for the social sciences is likely to be related to the degree of support within the political culture. In the Scandinavian countries, for example, since the end of the 1970s the level of expenditure has been maintained and in some cases increased; in Britain, by contrast, it has been reduced. It is difficult to find accurate figures for trends in social science expenditure across the UK economy. The major part of that funding is provided by the state through the University Grants Committee or through the research councils or in research directly commissioned by government. In the following tables the external research expenditure patterns of the Department of Employment, and of the Economic and Social Research

Council (ESRC), are presented as proxies for the more general picture. (The figures are derived from the ESRC annual report and the annual Department of Employment Research report.)

Table 1 shows the annual expenditure of the Department of Employment on external research for the period of 1974 to 1983.

TABLE 1
DE research expenditure 1974–83 at constant 1983–4 prices

Year	Expenditure (£)	Year	Expenditure (£)
1975	909,000	1980	693,000
1976	1,002,000	1981	687,000
1977	998,000	1982	530,000
1978	1,200,000	1983	499,000
1979	1,300,000		

It is clear that after an increase in expenditure from the mid-1970s there was a decline between 1979 and 1983. Over the later period there was a tendency towards more short-term research, and an increased resistance to mounting medium- to long-term research. Furthermore, there was also an increased emphasis on research being clearly and directly related to well-defined policy needs. There was also, however, an increased emphasis on joint funding of certain kinds of projects between government departments and other agencies. In some ways these tendencies were both connected and contradictory. For example, the general tendency in funding industrial relations research was towards the short term and the directly relevant; at the same time the department took the lead in launching in collaboration with the Economic and Social Research Council and the Policy Studies Institute the most ambitious series of surveys of industrial relations at the workplace level ever undertaken in the UK (Daniel and Millward, 1983).

The trend in the pattern of expenditure for the ESRC is similar to that of DE.

TABLE 2
ESRC expenditure at constant 1983–4 prices

Year	Expenditure (£)	Year	Expenditure (£)
1975	23.7m	1980	25.8m
1976	24.8m	1981	23.5m
1977	26.8m	1982	21.9m
1978	26.8m	1983	22.4m
1979	25.1m		

The clear cutback in the amount of money available to the ESRC has been linked to a general inquiry into the functioning of that body set up by the government in 1982 and headed by an eminent scientist, Lord Rothschild.

The purpose of the inquiry was to consider whether the ESRC (then called the Social Science Research Council) should be abolished and some of its functions taken over by other bodies, both market and non-market. The inquiry concluded that the ESRC as an organization should be maintained and that the government should continue to fund social science research through it. In one part of the report Rothschild writes:

> The need for independence from Government Departments is particularly important because so much social science research is the stuff of political debate. All such research can prove subversive because it attempts to submit such policies to empirical trial with the risk that the judgment may be adverse. It would be too much to expect Ministers to show enthusiasm for research designed to show that their policies were misconceived. But it seems obvious that in many cases public interest would be served by such research being undertaken. (Rothschild, 1983)

The report was generally seen to be disappointing to the government but it agreed to accept its recommendations. Rothschild had pointed out that if the ESRC were abolished it would have to be reinvented and some new body would quickly spring up 'different no doubt in some ways from the existing one but in important respects identical to it'. One effect, however, of the inquiry was to reinforce a reorganization and reorientation of ESRC so that its internal committee structure became more oriented towards social and economic problems and a trend towards itself identifying areas on which it wished to generate research rather than simply being reactive to the needs of the scientific community.

The overall trend, therefore, within the UK has been a decline in the funding available for social science research, attempts to modify the institutional structure for funding, and as a consequence some re-orienting of the directions of research. In general there has been a decline in the amount of money available for disciplinary-based research, that is, research addressing problems arising from the theoretical development of the disciplines and growing pressure on the social science community to increase the relevance of its research output and to work across disciplinary boundaries. It is, however, the case that if governments and research councils aim to fund 'relevant' research this does not necessarily mean that the research will be used; nor if the social science community orients itself to influencing policy will it necessarily succeed in its aim. Policy-oriented research can and often does produce negative or irrelevant results from the perspective of the policy definition of the problem and non-policy-oriented research can be used in policy-oriented ways. However, the funding of research not only provides the knowledge base for use but is indicative of the propensity to use that knowledge.

Political culture and utilization propensity

Research is only one element in the decision-making process about policy matters; the salience which is given to research evidence as opposed to other types of input will itself be influenced by political culture; that is, political culture is also likely to influence the ways in which the role of the social sciences are defined within society and whether and in what ways they will be used. In order to examine this aspect of use, I want to look at one policy area — that of worker participation — and briefly contrast the position in Britain with Sweden.

Within the Department of Employment a programme of research into worker participation was set out in late 1973 and implemented as a series of projects over subsequent years (Brannen, 1981). The background of the programme was the continuing interest in Britain and in the European community in the issue, and the discussion of a variety of proposals which was taking place within the main political parties. The programme was designed to explore and monitor a range of institutional possibilities precisely because it was not clear at that time where political interest might coalesce. The inital project was a large survey of companies in which directors, plant managers and worker representatives were interviewed and data were obtained about practices and attitudes in relation to worker participation generally as well as specific mechanisms such as joint consultation, board-room representation, collective bargaining and information disclosure. Field-work for the project took place during the spring of 1976; planning and design had started a year earlier.

In February 1974 a general election had replaced the Conservative government with a Labour government which stated in its manifesto that it would 'repeal the Industrial Relations Act as a matter of urgency and then bring in an Employment Protection Act and an Industrial Democracy act as agreed in our discussions with the TUC to increase the control of industry by the people'. While action on the first two pieces of legislation was put in hand, the third, industrial democracy, appeared to have much less priority.

> Few Labour Ministers understood the subject and those that did were put off by the union power aspects or did not see much point in pushing the matter when a fair number of unions were opposed to the idea. In short it was too controversial and complex a subject for a government beset with many more pressing problems to take up voluntarily. (Elliot, 1978: 216)

However, a series of parliamentary accidents which allowed a private member's bill, launched by a Labour MP, to progress further through the parliamentary process than is normal, forced the government's hand. The TUC with the support of some Ministers urged the government to introduce its own bill immediately; other Ministers argued for a delaying committee of inquiry with very vague and open terms of reference, (Elliot, 1978: 217). In the event, the political compromise i.e. to inquire into the mechanisms for placing worker representatives on the board of companies. The committee was urged to report speedily; it began its work in December 1975 and finished its report in twelve months (Bullock, 1977). There was both a majority and minority report indicative of the tension surrounding the issue. The committee commissioned two reviews of European experience in the area (Batstone and Davies, 1976) but no original research. The report itself made very little reference to research evidence. In the same year in which the Bullock Report was published, a review in a scholarly journal of a research monograph on worker directors made the point that

> this study took 7 years from commencement to publication and Bullock (the Committee of Inquiry on Industrial Democracy) took well under 18 months; the Bullock report took no obvious account of this study despite the fact that one of the co-authors undertook a survey of the European experience of participation for the Bullock committee. It is a sad comment on the relationship between policy and research. (Cannon, 1977)

My own view is that this is an interesting though not sad comment. The predominant conclusion of the particular study reviewed (Brannen et al., 1975) was that if the purpose of putting workers on the boards of companies was to enable the workforce to influence decision-making in the board-room then in most cases the aim would be frustrated. The Bullock committee, however, had been expressly set up in order to suggest ways in which workers could be placed on the board of companies in order to democratize the control of companies. Although, in fact, most members of the Bullock committee had read the study in question they were unable to take account of it in the sense of acting upon its conclusions because of the political context in which their committee had to operate.

The research programme which the Department of Employment had mounted into the area of worker participation, although it covered some of the same area as Bullock, was also irrelevant to the inquiry. This was for a number of reasons. The Bullock inquiry arose quite quickly when the main parameters of the Department of Employment research programme were already set. The inquiry was originally going to report within twelve months and it would have been difficult to organize the collection and analysis of any large-scale dataset within that time period.

The time scales, therefore, were different. There were additional factors. First the Bullock inquiry was set up by the Secretary of State for Industry so that there was a natural bureaucratic distance between the DE research programme and the committee of inquiry. More importantly, however, it seemed likely, given the background to the inquiry, that the conclusions would be arrived at on political rather than research grounds; the costs of reorienting the research programme would not itself have been worthwhile.

I now want to turn very briefly to Sweden. Since the beginning of the 1970s there had also been a large programme of legislation in Sweden in the labour relations and labour market areas; this had covered, among other things, the role of trade-union representatives, health and safety, information disclosure, work organization, collective bargaining, representation on company boards and worker participation. These latter two areas provide the means of making an interesting comparison.

In 1973 provisional legislation was introduced on employee representation on the boards of management of companies. In parallel with this a monitoring programme was set up in order to examine the effect of legislation in relation to its aims, i.e. 'to give employees increased influence together with greater responsibility for making and executing decisions affecting the development of the undertaking'. The monitoring programme did not claim to be totally comprehensive. It did look, however, at the scope of the reform: that is, the number of companies involved, the take-up of the legislation, the characteristics of those who claimed exemption, the allocation of employee representatives to posts, the functions of the board within the overall organizational structure, working methods on the board, frequency of meetings, the role of worker representatives and issues such as confidentiality. The monitoring programme produced a report which incorporated a series of recommendations as to how the legislation might be changed to make it more effective. The provisional legislation was translated into the formal legislation which was passed in 1976 and this legislation seems to have incorporated most of the recommendations contained in the monitoring report.

In 1976 also the Workplace Codetermination Act was passed. It replaced three fundamental labour laws passed in the inter-war period, and legislated for the broad arrangements between management and workforce so that managerial authority was modified and the scope for negotiation and codetermination expanded. This Act was defined as working towards changing relationships in a problematic area and it was understood that its aims would not easily be achieved in the short term. At the beginning of 1977 the government set aside funds for the establishment of an organization for the study of working life questions *(Arbetslivscentrum)* whose major function was to examine through

research, and attempt to find solutions to, problems of the full implementation of the Act and related questions of industrial democracy. The
centre was funded to have about fifty full-time staff, the majority of
whom would be research workers, including three full-time research
professors.

While these short descriptions clearly oversimplify the relationship
between research and policy in both Britain and Sweden they do point
towards sharply differing orientations in their respective political
cultures. Of all Western market societies Sweden has the most influential working-class movement, the highest density of unionization
among manual workers, the longest continuous period of social democratic government (although the six-year period of Conservative government did not in any major way change its orientation towards research).
It is also a small country in population terms with a high degree of
industrial concentration and a centralized trade-union movement and
centralized employers' organization, both of which are able to exert
considerable control over their members. In the past there was bitter
conflict in the industrial relations area but for the last thirty-five years
there has been a high degree of co-operation and an emphasis on
mechanisms to engender consensus. In relation to labour legislation this
has meant that at the point when ideas about change are translated into
law, the goals of the legislation and the direction of change are generally
agreed, and support can be mustered around ensuring that the aims are
achieved. In this sense Swedish society is formally rational.

In Britain, by contrast, the degree of political consensus around
labour legislation between or even within political parties and between
and within unions and management is not great. While there are formal
relationships between the Labour Party and the trade-union movement,
a large proportion of trade unionists vote for other political parties;
there have also been frequent conflicts between the Labour Party (particularly when in government) and the trade-union movement over labour
relations legislation; there has also been no absolute coincidence of
views between management organizations and the Conservative Party
over labour relations legislation. Moreover, the central management and
trade-union organizations have relatively loose control over their
constituent member organizations. Finally, labour relations legislation
has largely been seen by government as a tool of economic policy within
an economic context of relative decline and instability.

Structural factors in Swedish society produce a political culture which
allows a more direct, planned and involved role for social science
research in the labour relations areas than does the British political
culture. Within Britain the fragmentation of interest and the adversarial
nature of relationships means that there is only weak support for, and
indeed a high degree of distrust of, social science research in the labour

relations area. Decisions, it is understood, are made politically; that is, in relation to beliefs modified by a pragmatic understanding of the balance of forces. There may be and indeed often is resistance to social research on the logically sound ground that any information on the subject could be an embarrassment. If little information or analysis is available then any views expressed cannot be challenged as untrue or irrational (Wilkins, 1964).

The policy organization and utilization propensity

Policy organizations will relate to social science partly as a reflection of political culture and partly as an outcome of their own internal systems. Much of the literature on the relationship between social science and policy is written by social scientists and reflects both a tension between the orientation of social scientists and policy administrators and a particular view of the policy world.

In particular, government policy-makers tend to be referred to as a powerful élite though in a largely undifferentiated and undefined way. What is often omitted in such analyses is a notion of the way organizations actually work. Pahl and Winkler (1974) in a paper on the economic élite commented that 'what is crucially missing in most power studies is any account of actual decision-making at the top (intrinsically difficult to obtain access to, of course, except usually long after the event).' They go on to suggest that this 'results in a very mechanistic description of power as if organizations really work the way they are drawn on the wall chart'. They argue that any serious consideration of decision-making must allow that decisions may be thrust up from below.

In this context I now turn to looking briefly at the characteristics and organizational arrangements of policy administrators within central government. The senior policy-maker is *typically* recruited directly from university, and socialized into having particular kinds of career aspirations and expectations. In addition, policy administrators are generalists by orientation and by training and usually have little or no acquaintanceship or understanding of social science research or its use as a tool of administration. The policy administrator is encapsulated in a bureaucratic structure in which his or her role is restricted and his or her responsibilities are constrained; the responsibilities are restricted to the functions defined in that role and he or she is not responsible for making connections between their own area of policy-making and other areas of policy-making. The time-span of policy-makers is bounded by the time horizons of the policy with which they are currently involved and the post they are currently filling.

Problem definition is therefore narrow and tends to be constrained within the context of 'feasible solutions', that is, ones that are both operational at government level and acceptable politically. Policy administrators will be sensitive to the fact that many decisions take themselves and there is little room for manoeuvre; that precise contexts for decisions are important and that research does not often link directly with such contexts; and finally that there are problems which in particular circumstances actually cannot in any way be solved. All of this tends to lead to a view of research which sees it as usually marginal and often a nuisance; where it is seen as useful the predominant demand is for short-term factual information.

This is, however, a stereotypical picture. Within a government organization there will exist a variety of groups which in different ways and at different times may have interests in research either in a positive or negative way. There are likely to be different orientations to research between departments and sections, and between senior managers and section managers. Even within senior management, while there may be common or accepted assumptions about objectives, there are likely to be different views about the ways of achieving these. The latter is also likely to be the case between senior administrators and their political masters. All of this will affect the potential for the use made of social science research.

One particular grouping, social scientists working in government, may have an important influence on the interactions between research and policy. This is more likely if members of this group hold senior posts in the bureaucratic machine: these confer status on the group; they also confer access to senior committees and to high-level information and they allow the possibility of the insertion of social science information at that level. Within the British civil service, while economists have such posts other kinds of social scientists do not. However, even without very senior posts social scientists may have other organizational advantages. They tend to stay in particular posts working in particular areas longer than policy administrators. They have therefore the advantage not only of expertise but also of the experience of issues over time; this is an organizational power resource. Staying in a post for a considerable length of time increases the range of personal organizational contacts; this is also a resource. These factors favour the use of social science but will operate only if the social science grouping is not isolated from the policy process. An influential in-house social science capability may, however, be threatening to administrative policy-makers in terms of career and status.

The use of social science research in government is more likely in conditions where a good working relationship is developed between social scientists and policy administrators. Such a relationship will involve constant exchange and negotiation between the two groups. This will include the exchange of short-term information services for longer-term research options and the discussion of policy problems and research problems at an early stage of formation. It will involve the education of policy administrators into social science categories but also negotiation with them around the protection of professional standards. Finally, it will involve the education of policy-makers in the acceptance of a tension between social science and policy-making and an understanding that such a tension is useful and potentially productive.

Conclusions

This paper has suggested that in trying to understand the relationship between social science and policy, constraints and possibilities at the cultural, political and organizational levels need to be considered. Within complex industrial societies the degree of support for social science research in a given political culture will influence both the funding of such research and the propensity of policy administrators to use it. The propensity to use research will also be influenced by factors within the policy organization. Van der Vall (1982) has argued that 'the creation of consensus — not the creation of controversy is the most important function of social research'. I would rather suggest that the use of social science research is most likely in consensual political cultures and also in those parts of the policy agenda where there is most agreement.

The approach in the paper emphasizes the contingent and political nature of the use of social science research within the policy process. This is, I feel, more typical of the reality of usage than the notion of use as a rational tool of social engineering. Within British political culture there has not traditionally been, nor is there currently, strong support for the social sciences. They are not seen as playing a major role in charting the directions of or the means of social change. This may be because there is a relatively weak sense of progress and social evolution within British political culture. It may be because of the adversarial nature of that culture. It may be connected to the structure and composition of British social science which in certain respects has tended to stand back from the policy process and to adopt a theoretical and critical stance (at least at its normative core) which has made policy administrators wary of it and which has led to loss of esteem for those social scientists who work within an applied mode.

While the propensity of policy organization to use the social sciences will in part be a reflection of political culture, it will also be in part an outcome of their own internal organizational systems. Within the context of British political culture the dominant tendency within the policy organization will be to use social science at those points of the policy process related to implementation and monitoring rather than to planning or long-term evaluation. The demand will also be for social science research to be informational or tactical rather than basic or strategic. It is easier at these points of the policy process for administrators to see a direct use for the outputs of social science and to justify within the organization the use of social science as a tool of effective administration. This is not, however, to argue that social science is not used in other parts of the policy process but that there is a lower propensity towards use and that use is more likely to be indirect rather than direct. The ways in which social science relates to the policy process varies both in relation to types of use, the stage of the policy process, the micro-politics of the policy organization, and the general stance of the political culture towards social science.

Note

Earlier versions of this chapter were given at seminars at the universities of Surrey and Bath and at a conference organized jointly by the European Centre for Social Welfare, Training and Research, and the Greek Ministry of Culture and Science. I am grateful to the participants at those events for their comments and also to Julia Brannen, Frank Heller and Ceredwen Roberts. Neither those mentioned above nor my employing organization are, however, responsible for the views expressed.

References

Batstone, Eric and P. L. Davies (1976) *Industrial Democracy: European Experience.* London: HMSO.

Brannen, Peter (1981) 'Developments in Employee Involvement', *Employee Gazette,* February.

Brannen, Peter, Eric Batstone, Derek Fatchett and Philip White (1975) *The Worker Directors.* London: Hutchinson.

Bullock, Lord (1977) *Report of the Committee of Inquiry on Industrial Democracy.* Cmnd. 6706. London: HMSO.

Cannon, I. C. (1977) Review, *British Journal of Sociology,* 28 (3): 410–11.

Daniel, W. W. and Neil Millward (1983) *Workplace Industrial Relations in Britain.* London: Heinemann.

Elliot, John (1978) *Conflict or Co-operation? The Growth of Industrial Democracy.* London: Kogan Page.

Husen, Torsten (1984) 'Issues and their Background', in T. Husen and M. Kogan (eds), *Educational Research and Policy.* Oxford: Pergamon Press.

Pahl, R. E. and J. T. Winkler (1974) 'The Economic Elite', in P. Stanworth and A. Giddens (eds), *Elites and Power in British Society.* Cambridge: Cambridge University Press.

Peltz, Donald C. (1978) 'Some Expanded Perspectives on the Use of Social Science in Public Policy', in J. M. Yinger and S. J. Cutler (eds.), *Major Social Issues: A Multi-disciplinary Perspective.* New York: Free Press.

Rothschild, Lord (1983) *An Inquiry into the Social Science Research Council.* Cmnd. 8554. London: HMSO.

van de Vall, Mark and Cheryl Bolas (1982) 'Using Social and Policy Research for Reducing Social Problems: An Empirical Analysis of Structure and Functions', *Journal of Applied Behavioural Science,* 18(1): 49–67.

Weiss, Carol H. (1979) 'The Many Meanings of Research Utilization', *Public Administration Review,* September–October.

Wilkins, Leslie T. (1964) *Social Deviance.* London: Tavistock.

12

Facets of 'relevance' in sociological research

John Eldridge

The call for research that is 'relevant' contains various resonances. It can be associated with notions of timeliness, usefulness and problem-solving. It may be thought of as research that is 'applied' rather than 'pure', of responding to 'needs' rather than 'developing knowledge for its own sake'. Such research may be seen as having policy relevance. These kinds of thing may be built into demands made upon scientists across the spectrum. From spheres as diverse as politics, commerce, industry, health and education, natural and social scientists are enjoined by many to be relevant. But what kind of imperative is this and what may be entailed? I want to look at the case of sociology and illustrate some of the ways in which work is defined as relevant and some of the difficulties which may flow from doing 'relevant' sociology. I shall refer primarily to research in Britain.

Consider first some aspects of research activity in industrial sociology. The work of the Liverpool University group and the Tavistock Institute group during the early post-war period provides an instructive comparison. Both groups exhibit an interest in the subject of technical change. A good example of the Liverpool work is W. Scott et al. (1956), a study located in a steel plant. This was a research investigation which took hold of an issue that had come to be defined as a problem — the adaptation of workers to technical change — and sought to provide information and indeed a conceptual framework that could be taken into account by policy-makers. The definition of what constitutes a problem comes not in the first instance from the researchers but from the contemporary debate on Britain's economic problems.

The rationale of the research is explicitly stated:

The selection of technical change seemed to combine both theoretical and practical requirements. The technical organization of production in a factory is a major and probably the main influence on its social structure and its study is therefore indispensable for the advancement of our basic knowledge of the social system of the plant; at the same time the maintenance and if possible the acceleration of the rate of technical progress in industry is generally considered to be one of Britain's main problems in the post-war years. Since resistances to change are to a large extent social in origin, it appeared that a study of technical change in relation to social structure might make a useful contribution to the development of industrial policy. (Scott et al., 1956:5)

The authors go on to state that they wanted to understand the factors which either facilitate or impede technical change. Relevance then operates in the selection of the topic and consciously responding through empirical research to a prevailing public definition of 'one of Britain's main problems in the post-war years'. One might add, of course, that interest in the topic of resistance to technical change was not exclusively British. Not only was it ante-dated in the work of American industrial sociologists such as Mayo, Roethlisberger, Dickson, Warner, Low, Guest and Walker, but was also taken up in a number of European countries, notably in a number of OECD publications.

Reflection upon the human aspects of technical change led research workers at the Tavistock Institute to the conceptualization of socio-technical systems. This was to encapsulate a concern for linking together in a good 'fit' the psychological needs of employees and the organization of tasks in the enterprise. A well-developed expression of this approach is found in Trist et al. (1963). As with the Liverpool group there is a strong interest in factors promoting or inhibiting productivity. In the Tavistock approach, however, consultancy is built in and the attempt is made to identify resistances to change with the aim of assisting in their removal or modification. The interest in organization design and in the monitoring of change in some instances over very extended periods of time (as, for example, in the much cited Glacier project, see Chapter 9) reflects a different research stance. It is client-oriented. The relevance of the research arises out of a conception of the needs of the client. There develops a collaborative relationship between researcher and client and indeed this serves as an early example of action research in British social science. Now this certainly did not mean that the researcher simply responded to the client's definition of his needs. One can see that the researchers interpreted their task in terms of re-education. The client must be led to understand things about the nature of organization and of the constituent groups within it. New concepts may provide new insights and come to be recognized by the client as being relevant to his organization. But who was the client? Typically, groups of senior managers or administrators and for this reason the Tavistock work has often been labelled as managerial sociology. Even if 'the problem' has to be conceptually redefined by the researchers it is still management's problem that is receiving attention and the relevance of the research activity is derived from that basic fact.

Let me at this stage refer to what I shall call the Joan Woodward phenomenon. Having already displayed an interest in the subject of technology and technical change as part of the Liverpool group she was later to pursue this independently in her south-east Essex study. The outline of her findings was published in the DSIR research pamphlet *Management and Technology* (1958). The impact of this study on management studies and industrial sociology proved to be very considerable and is worth pondering.

Woodward classified technology on a scale of increasing complexity: unit, small batch, large batch, mass and process production. Technology was treated as a critical variable in explaining organization structure and behaviour: '... technical methods were the most important factor in determining organizational structure and in setting the tone of human relationships inside the firms' (Woodward, 1958:4). From her survey of 203 manufacturing firms she concluded that different technologies imposed different kinds of demands on individuals and organizations and that these demands had to be met through an appropriate form of organization. Explicit in the Woodward approach, then, was the suggestion that firms with given technolgies might need to develop certain kinds or organizational arrangements if they were to be successful. This was of obvious practical interest to managers. Her work came to be treated as an effective demolition job on 'the one best way' of management myth. Hence the so-called principles of scientific management were challenged and no doubt caused disquiet among those who felt themselves to be the custodians of those principles.[1] The social science alternative was presented as one in which principles need to be modified to meet cases. Instead of starting with principles one started with the situation. But it was not just a matter of meeting every case on its merits in an ad hoc way. Rather, one could discern family resemblances between cases with similar technologies.

Here, then, was an answer to sceptical managers who wanted to know what use social science was to them. It could replace arid abstract principles of management by a concrete situational approach which was more realistic. Not only did this make it relevant to them, but in some respects they could even be reassured by it. They could come to recognize that some of the 'problems' they faced were not unique to them, they were endemic to firms with particular kinds of technology. This could diminish the scape-goating of managers. If certain problems are built into the structure and are intrinsically associated with that kind of technology, then it is no use blaming Tom, Dick or Harry, or even (blissful thought) yourself. It is a 'given' that one simply has to accept and come to terms with as part of the situation. A given type of technology will imply certain kinds of organization structure as being more appropriate than another. Within these structures there will be typical problems and points of friction that one may learn to expect and live with. To that extent managerial uncertainty is reduced.

The Woodward approach to organizational analysis leads me to comment on the relationship between *practical* relevance and *theoretical* relevance of research studies. After all, the claims of the approach were that in certain respects it superseded earlier management theories. It was, one may say, more practically relevant because it was a better theory. It served therefore as a better guide to action. But the theoretical claims themselves then come under further scrutiny by other researchers. What one finds in British industrial sociology after Woodward is that research investigations frequently built into their design her classification of types of technology. If its theoretical status could be effectively challenged then, of course, its practical relevance would be diminished. Woodward and her colleagues at the Imperial College Industrial Sociology Unit did come to accept the operational difficulties that were involved in measuring technical variables. One response to this was to introduce the concept of 'control system'. Attention is given to the way in which the control system explicates the link between task and organization structure. This leads to the exploration of questions such as: how are decisions made about the design and programming of production tasks and what is done to ensure that people actually do the work necessary to perform the tasks allocated to them? The control system is offered as an intervening variable between task and organization structure (and, predictably, one is offered a typology of control systems).

Again one can see the managerial implications. Just as the original typology of technical complexity was seen as increasing the manager's understanding of organizations (as opposed to formal management principles) so the intention of looking at control systems is to indicate which are the 'best fit' for the particular situations. The best fit will obviously be that which reduces uncertainty. While both the technology thesis and the control system thesis call earlier theories of scientific management into question, they both seem to me to retain a congenial relevance to managers and to some extent probably explain the general acceptability of a new approach. In so far as this kind of approach attempts to understand organizations in order that managers may more effectively control uncertainty, it may be regarded as highly relevant to management. Yet the analysis all takes place on the assumption that the existing distribution of power remains unchanged. Indeed, in my opinion, the political element in organizational life and the processes involved are very muted in the Woodward approach. Organizations are rather anaemic entities: impersonal mechanisms that require a little social engineering to get them in better shape. It is perhaps the questions that are not asked that in part enable one to distinguish between a sociology which is congenially relevant to an interested party and one which is critically relevant. If we neglect to ask what a particular form of technology is designed to do, in whose interests and with what consequences, it does save a good deal of unpleasantness. If we do not inquire into the structure of domination within which typologies of technology and control systems are embedded, then the critical relevance of the theory is diminished. The issue, which comes up again and again in sociological research, is how far one would put such questions in cold storage as one seeks to establish 'good' middle range theories. Is it a self-denying ordinance grounded on the principle of parsimony or is it a flaw in the fabric of the theory that omits the political dimension of organizational analysis? Does one have an obligation as a sociologist to try and relate organizational analysis to the society in which organizations are located?

The above discussion has suggested that a particular topic, in this case the significance of technology for organizational effectiveness, comes to be regarded as of some public importance. It has, one may say, a general relevance for society and is then responded to by researchers in various ways. These responses may seek to draw attention to neglected elements in our understanding: for example, the social origins of resistance to change. They may be directed at the generality of policy-makers, or at a particular interest group, say managers, or at a specific client. Such differences change the context and specificity with which we can speak of relevance. By different routes perhaps one comes to the destination: the relevant is the realistic. Once you have discovered what is realistic you may then go on to implicit or explicit prescriptions. What I think is important to emphasize here, however, is that what is realistic is never a matter of simply establishing 'the facts'. There is a complex interplay between the selection and definition of 'the problem', its conceptualization and theoretical elaboration and the deployment of facts and logical argument within the constructed framework. What is or is not realistic may therefore be highly contentious both politically and academically.

There are, then, typically contested answers to the question of what is relevant. I will try and explore some of the ramifications of this in the examples that follow.

The field of industrial relations provides one fascinating illustration, particularly the debate surrounding and subsequent to the Donovan Commission. Alan Fox's (1966) research paper for the commission had an academic and public impact somewhat parallel to that of Woodward's *Management and Technology*. The point I want to emphasize here is that the conceptual distinction between unitary and pluralist frames of reference carried with it a view of what was realistic and what was unrealistic in the conduct of industrial relations. This carried a prescriptive message with implications for management.

> Like conflict, restrictive practices and resistance to change have to be interpreted by the unitary frame of reference as being due to stupidity, wrong-headedness or out of date class rancour. *Only a pluralistic view can see them for what they are:* rational responses by sectional interests to protect employment, stabilize earnings, maintain job status, defend group bargaining power or preserve class boundaries. The unitary view must condemn them as morally indefensible: the pluralistic view can understand them and by understanding is in a position to change them [emphasis added]. (Fox, 1966:12)

In other words, facts have to be understood and connected within a conceptual framework and some frameworks are more appropriate, that is realistic, than others.

To illustrate the complicated nature of relevance in research, I want to draw attention to two seminal papers by John Goldthorpe. These are, 'Social Inequality and Social Integration in Modern Britain' and 'Industrial Relations in Great Britain: A Critique of Reformism' (Goldthorpe 1974; 1977). The thrust of the first paper is to suggest that it is not realistic to suppose that procedural reforms will make disorderly industrial relations orderly if, in the wider society, there are structured social inequalities which are widely regarded as having no moral legitimacy. This contention immediately changes the context within which the original problem is defined and consequently of what is relevant in terms of empirical research activity. Goldthorpe's paper does not actually make policy recommendations. Its relevance to policy is of the type: if you want x you will not get it by doing y but whatever else you must take into account z. In the second paper the attack is renewed. It is argued that it is not at all clear whose problem the reformist academics are purporting to solve or, where there are conflicts in the industrial relations arena, whose side they are on. One group's problem may after all be another group's opportunity. Hence, Goldthorpe suggests there is a danger of a 'problem-solving' approach having the character of rhetoric and masking the real problems.

> For even if they gain a wide measure of political approval, attempts at reform based on inadequate analysis will still face rebuff by the social reality on which they are intended to act. (Goldthorpe, 1974:191)

Goldthorpe comes to a radical conclusion, in the sense of trying to get to the root of the matter:

> . . . at the present time British industrial relations are simply not in any far-reaching way reformable — other than, perhaps, as part of some general restructuring of British society as a whole: that is, either in an authoritarian and corporatist direction, so that far more drastic sanctions than

are at present conceivable could be applied against workers; or in an egalitarian and socialist one, so that a more effective basis for workers' collaboration might be created. Within the existing form of society, however, a disordered state of industrial relations may best be understood not as pathological, but as a normal, condition. (Goldthorpe, 1974:215–16)

All this constitutes an uncomfortable rather than a congenial relevance for those politicians who would prefer a more manageable solution, rather than one which focuses upon the degree of legitimacy with which the present social order is invested.

The commitment to ethical neutrality in research plainly signifies that one regards the task of sociology as being something other than propaganda for causes with which one may sympathize. Yet ethical neutrality in research is not be equated with moral indifference. Indeed, such research may sensitize the investigator and the public to the range of political and moral choices that confront them. Something of what I have in mind is extremely well illustrated in the opening sentences of John Rex's *Race Relations in Sociological Theory*:

> The problem of race and racism challenges the conscience of the sociologist in the same way as the problem of nuclear weapons challenges that of the nuclear physicist. This is not to say that sociology can dictate to men and nations how they should behave to one another any more than that the nuclear physicist had some special competence to advise the American President whether or not he should drop the atom bomb on the Japanese. But it is to say that in so far as whole populations have been systematically discriminated against, exploited and even exterminated, the sociologist might legitimately be asked to lay the causes of these events bare. (Rex, 1970:1)

The research canon of ethical neutrality implies a stance of disinterestedness. The relevance of the research lies in the empirical adequacy of its findings and consequently the status of its theory. The call for a theoretically-grounded sociology is not therefore a luxury to be added if possible to some more relevant applied sociology: it is necessary if we are to have a more informed understanding of social constraints, political choices and the consequences of planned changes.

This may suggest to us that the straight contrast here is between the sociologist who stands on the sidelines in order to obtain an adequate view of what is going on and the sociologist who declares roundly whose side he or she is on and makes a commitment to that cause. However I am not sure that this really does justice to some sociologists who have participated in action research programmes. Take, for example the programme associated with the Plowden-inspired policy of educational priority areas. The general policy laid down was that positive discrimination for educational priority areas should be undertaken to achieve the ends of greater social equality of educational opportunity and attainment. But what was the relationship between the ends and the means? Action research programmes were set up under the directorship of A.H. Halsey to monitor and evaluate the effectiveness of planned changes in a number of designated Educational Priority Areas (Halsey, 1972). Halsey argues that

> ... it is necessary at every step to try to make explicit what are the implicit assumptions of political aims and the value-premises of sociological analysis. There is no final or ready-made procedure for either of these tasks. We have only imperfect aids beyond the injunction to constant vigilance. (Halsey, 1972:4)

No one should doubt the severe demands which this kind of critical scrutiny makes. In this case, for example, it involves examining alternative theories of poverty and of educational disadvantage. This was done both with reference to British experience and also to the development and rationale of compensatory education programmes in the USA. What I think is worth emphasizing is that again we see how original definitions of the problem and its proposed solution may shift in content and character. In summarizing the experience of American compensatory programmes Halsey writes:

> We can say that the movement began with what appeared to be a simple educational problem, the fact that certain social groups on average had a lower level of educational performance. Attempts to solve that problem were forced to go further and further outside the educational system, as the ramifications of the intitial problem were uncovered. In this process the most basic questions are raised about the nature of social organization, and about the reasons why lower social status should be associated with lower educational performance. These developments indicate that a purely educational response to the initial problem is unlikely to succeed ... Educational underachievement has become merely one manifestation of a series of social and economic disparities experienced by disadvantaged groups. The long-term solution must be a comprehensive policy which strikes at these political, social and economic inequalities. (Halsey, 1972:29–30)

The comment has direct application to the British scene and is a reminder that the relationship between social inequality and educational inequality is complex and calls for a fundamental analysis of social structure. At the same time, it is a clear reminder that unless the limitations of the effects of proposed changes are realistically appreciated, public expectations may be disappointed. My final illustration of sociological research is intended as a comment on what I shall call the sharp edge of relevance.

The long history and well-documented hostility to social science research of those who adminster the media is instructive. It can be traced back to the Lazarsfeld days in the USA as Burns (1977) has reminded us. Lazarsfeld wrote:

> If there is any one institutional disease to which the media of mass communications seems particularly subject, it is nervous reaction to criticism. As a student of mass media I have been continually struck and occasionally puzzled by this reaction, for it is the media themselves which so vigorously defend principles guaranteeing them the right to criticize. (Burns, 1977:xv)

Burns's own experience of the BBC's veto which for a very long time delayed the publication of his research is a classic illustration of the same disease.

The Glasgow University Media Group's (1976) study, of which I am a co-author, analysed through the use of videotape, the news output of BBC television and ITN over a five-month period. It was designed to examine how far the claims of television to be impartial and neutral in the presentation of news were justified. The evidence we provided to cast doubt on these claims was, it is fair to say, not well received by the news rooms or their administrators. The News and Current Affairs Committee at the BBC revealed its anger at this 'propaganda' in its minutes. The Director-General pointed out to his colleagues that one of the difficulties of mounting any counter-offensive was the necessity of having academic support for the counter-arguments in a field where it was difficult to find uncommitted academics.[2] But none of this addressed itself to the findings or the nature of the evidence. The Annan Committee on the Future of Broadcasting (1977) was later to endorse the view that the coverage of industrial affairs in television news was unsatisfactory in terms of the medium's own value system. As it happens, however, it was a public lecture by Lord Annan that encapsulated the flavour of hostility towards research. Giving one of the Granada Guildhall Lectures for 1977, he said:

> Our report was not a work of research, nor a book, nor a meditation on the works of the blessed Marshall McLuhan. We were not set up to provide jobs for the boys — that shadowy guerilla force which operates on the fringes of broadcasting, in higher education or in research units, or in international bodies — and which seems to regard the broadcasting organizations as bodies who should be subservient to their slightest whim in providing pabulum for research — all justified, of course, under the name of more scathing accountability. I willingly accede to the request of Mr Alan Protheroe, Deputy Editor of BBC TV News, that I should say that I have no sympathy with those who lobby to divert funds away from programme-making into research projects so that by the end of this century the broadcasters, depleted in numbers, may enter a sociological Canaan after subsisting for the intervening years in the desert on a diet of random opinions. (Curran et al. 1977:84)

The idea of a shadowy guerilla force of mass media researchers is, when considered in cold print, something which might excite the fevered imaginations of a few broadcasters but is intrinsically absurd. To describe researchers as justifying their activities by reference to 'more scathing accountability' serves the rhetorical function of dismissing research into the mass media and putting negative connotations on to the concept of accountability. No evidence was offered for the assertion. Precisely what lobby existed to divert funds away from programme making into research projects is not disclosed to us. The reality in Britain has always been that funding for mass media research has been extremely difficult and remains so with the outstanding exception of the kind of funding that goes into in-house audience research. Still, no doubt all this pleased Mr Protheroe.

If those in positions of power became so agitated by our research at Glasgow it occurred to us that perhaps we had something to say to a wider public. It is one thing to do research and quite another to communicate the findings. Because our work was a matter of some public interest we chose to speak to a wide range of groups: trade-union groups, schools, churches, as well as academic groups and media professionals. From those who work inside the media we have found an increasing sympathy with much of what we have done and we now maintain contact with a good number of working journalists and people concerned with programme production. For those outside the media, our work has had an educational function. At a simple level, routine media practices can be illustrated. For example, the jump in a speech can be shown where the editorial cut has taken place. This may be different from one bulletin to the next, yet to the uninitiated it looks like an uninterrupted flow of speech. Indeed, the professional aim may be defined in just those terms. Yet to replay the cut in different bulletins, especially if it makes a difference to the emphasis in the news text, makes people more aware of news as something that is manufactured. Similarly, it is not generally understood that interviews are not always as straightforward as they look. The interviewer, nodding earnestly and apparently looking at the interviewee, is often nodding to the camera long after the interviewee has departed. The film is spliced together to give the impression of a sequence that has not actually happened. In itself this is a small matter but it does remind the viewer that things are not always what they seem. Professional practices based upon naturalism do not simply reflect the world. They embody and express verbal and visual codes and invite us to think of what is going on in certain ways rather than in others.

While we have used the opportunity to explain our research to many audiences, it has been more difficult to do this on television itself. If we remember the millions of people that television news reaches each day, then the way that news is structured and organized is a matter of public interest. If research has something to say about this then it is at least reasonable to have the evidence shown and discussed on television. In April 1981 the Glasgow researchers made this request to the BBC and IBA. The letter was also signed by the general secretaries of twenty-two major trade unions, seventy-three Labour MPs and a number of academics with a particular interest in the mass media. The request was refused. However, a senior producer was reported as saying at a BBC news and current affairs meeting just after the letter had been received:

> The allegations made by the Glasgow group and others were permeating deeply into the consciousness of the general public, even down to influencing the way some of the BBC's own news trainees based their appreciation of its news coverage.

Subsequently, in July 1982, one member of the group was able to participate on the 'Man Alive' debate (BBC2) with the Labour MP Michael Meacher, when some aspects of the work were outlined and debated with an audience of journalists and broadcasters.

Since 1982, the primary interest of the Glasgow group has been in television coverage of defence and disarmament issues on television. Much of this has now been published in *War and Peace News* (Glasgow, University Media Group, 1985). The book explores the coverage of the Falklands conflict in 1982. It also looked at the coverage of arms control issues, the UN Special Session on Disarmament, the women's peace camp at Greenham Common, the Easter 1983 peace demonstrations organized by CND, and the Church of England's (1982) debate of its report, *The Church and the Bomb*.

Continuing interest in the group's work led to the opportunity of preparing an 'Open Space' programme on BBC2, which was shown in October 1985. This is an access programme and is supposed to mean that the group making the programme has editorial control. In this instance, however, editorial control was interfered with by the administrators in the BBC. The reason given was that the Glasgow group's use of the BBC's News and Current Affairs Committee minutes at the time of the Falklands conflict was selective and misleading. Although the substance of the argument and the relevant minutes were already in the published book, the BBC prevented us from showing this on television, thereby demonstrating the real limits of access programming. Moreover, when the group decided to show a card on screen objecting to this, the amount of time permitted was reduced from two and a half minutes to thirty seconds. So even the objection to censorship was itself censored without discussion. When it is remembered that these are the people who are responsible for interpreting impartiality in news coverage, clearly there was a sense in which the BBC was making our case for us.

Why were they so concerned? As Hugh Herbert, the *Guardian's* television critic put it the day after the programme:

> The special point about the Falklands crisis was that the Government was able to assume almost total control over what television reported to the public. And what in one sense is even more important is that the Government was also able to conceal the extent to which the manipulation of the news was taking place. Ironically, the attempts to influence last night's programme illustrate just what an established bureaucracy can achieve when it does control access to information. (*Guardian*, 8 October 1985)

There is a footnote to this episode which suggests that the public is sensitive to the relevance of these issues in a pluralist democracy. Over 500 people wrote to the Director-General protesting at this censorship. The audience research service BARB reported that 49 percent said the programme had changed their opinion of television news (44 percent said it had not and 7 per cent were not sure).

The experience of mass media research has taught me the soundness of Philip Abrams's distinction between clarification and advocacy in sociological research (Abrams, 1985:181–205). Embedded in a more extensive typology of uses, clarification and advocacy are both forms of sociology-as-enlightenment. Clarification is seen as

> taking the form of demystification, dispelling illusions and unmasking myths, of reformulating issues or problems by elucidating assumptions or revealing hitherto unperceived realities of social structure or meaning, or of changing the possibilities of social action by changing the language of social discourse. (Abrams, 1985:184).

While this may point to a connection between knowledge and action it is essentially passive, leaving the action to others. Surely someone out there is listening to the reasonable things sociologists are saying and this will lead to change. By contrast, Abrams points out, the advocacy model

> is thoroughly un-sanguine about the wisdom and goodwill of others. Sharing the basic enlightenment view that the relationship between knowledge and action is an argumentative, or political matter — that authoritative social knowledge is not to be had — it actively enters the arena of argument. In effect, this view of the use of sociology impels the sociologist to become a lobbyist for a preferred reading of sociological evidence. (Abrams, 1985:185)

In trying to follow through the implications of our own research for public debate we moved from the clarification to the advocacy stance. In doing so, our own sense of relevance in sociological work changed from the passive to the active mode. It is not a sheltered position yet, despite its risks and difficulties, it is the facet of relevance I would choose to emphasize. For, with Abrams, I conclude that we can bring sociology realistically into the realm of social action and into the arenas of power and policy.

Notes

1. Professor Eldridge is correct in assuming that Joan Woodward's findings 'caused disquiet'. The British Institute of Management was so upset about findings which suggested that the sacred universal principles of management were wrong that they asked her to come to their offices to explain and justify her conclusions. There were other protests and a correspondence in *The Times* newspaper. I wrote a letter defending her work on theoretical grounds and evidence from other research to sustain what is now called contingency models. The British Institute of Management and a lecturer in management studies at the Polytechnic of Central London attacked this letter. The row led to Woodward's book on this topic being delayed from 1958, when the pamphlet was published, to 1965 (Woodward, 1965). Joan Woodward told me later that she was shaken by the various attacks and went back to her original material to check her findings. They were substantiated. [Editor's note]

2. Uncommitted or not, there have been a range of criticisms of the Glasgow group's work to which I refer in the final chapter. [Editor's note]

References

Abrams, Philip (1985) 'The Uses of British Sociology, 1931–1981' in Martin Bulmer (ed.), *Essays on the History of British Sociological Research*. Cambridge: Cambridge University Press.

Annan Committee (1977) *Report of the Committee on the Future of Broadcasting*, Cmnd. 6753. London: HMSO.

Burns, Tom (1977) *The BBC. Public Institution and Private World*. London: Macmillan.

Church of England (1982) Report of a working party under the chairmanship of the Bishop of Salisbury, *The Church and the Bomb. Nuclear Weapons and Christian Conscience*. London: Hodder and Stoughton.

Curran, Sir Charles, Sir Brian Young and Lord Annan (1977) *Television Today and Tomorrow* (Granada Guildhall Lectures). London: Granada.

Fox, Alan (1966) *Industrial Sociology and Industrial Relations*, Research Paper 3, Royal Commission on Trade Unions and Employers' Associations. London: HMSO.

Glasgow University Media Group (1976) *Bad News*. London: Routledge and Kegan Paul.

Glasgow University Media Group (1985) *War and Peace News*. Milton Keynes: Open University Press.

Goldthorpe, John (1974) 'Social Inequality and Social Integration in Modern Britain', in Dorothy Wedderburn (ed.), *Poverty, Inequality and Class Struggle*. Cambridge: Cambridge University Press.

Goldthorpe, John (1977) 'Industrial Relations in Great Britain: A Critique of Reformism', in Tom Clarke and Laurie Clements (eds), *Trade Unions Under Capitalism*. Harmondsworth, Middx.: Penguin Books.

Halsey, A.H. (ed.) (1972) *Educational Priority, Vol. 1. EPA Problems and Policies*. London: HMSO.

Rex, John (1970) *Race Relations in Sociological Theory*. London: Weidenfeld and Nicolson.

Scott, W.H., J.A. Banks, A.H. Halsey and T. Lupton (1956) *Technical Change and Industrial Relations*. Liverpool: Liverpool University Press.

Trist, E.L., G.W. Higgin, H. Murray and A.B. Pollock (1963) *Organizational Choice: Capabilities of Groups at the Coal Face Under Changing Technologies*. London: Tavistock Publications.

Woodward, Joan (1958) *Management and Technology*. London: DSIR.

Woodward, Joan (1965) *Industrial Organization: Theory and Practice*. London: Oxford University Press.

13

Policy research under scrutiny

Albert Cherns

I start with the most sweeping generalization of all. Few things live up to the expectations held of them. And social research is no exception. In 1965, in both Europe and the USA, hopes and expectations were high. The sun of the social sciences had risen. If today it has not set, it has undergone an eclipse. Few would deny that some research has been shoddy and pretentious, that inflated claims have devalued the coin. But much has been sound but unused. If we are to learn from the experience of the last twenty years, we cannot avoid inquiring the causes of the failures. But the issue goes deeper. What do we mean, what should we mean, by 'use' and 'utilization'? Can we describe the process and refine our expectations accordingly? Can we generalize usefully at all about research?

A theory of utilization?
The natural science model
No one need be surprised that social scientists have sought to emphasize the *scientific* nature of their enterprise. The prestige of science has been high both as intellectual and as useful. In Britain in particular, money was found for science and for strengthening its base in the universities during the 1950s when other disciplines had to make do with far more modest encouragement. At that time psychology departments in universities showed great enthusiasm for its definition as a biological science. Those who obtained such recognition were rewarded with a more generous scale of financial support. It was the time when positivism was in the ascendant, with its doctrine of value-free social science. As Bulmer (1983, 355) puts it:

> A characteristic of early poverty studies was their fusion of analysis and prescription, of research and policy recommendations. In the United States . . . those who fused social science and ethics were eclipsed by those who favoured a more scientific approach to social questions. This new conception of social science first and foremost insisted upon the objective,

detached, and scientific character of the academic study of society, modelled (to some extent at least) upon the natural sciences.

In the USA:

> ... the claims made by positivists ... were extended during World War II and the Cold War. By the mid-sixties social scientists were regarded as political advisers capable of solving almost all the problems of the world. No problem was too big, and there was no shortage of promises for solutions to all problems. Sociology had become part of the administrative apparatus of the administrative welfare state. Positivism reached its peak period of expansion and economic success under state-supported contract research. (Vidich et al., 1981: 329)

Positivism more easily validates the claims for support of the social sciences than appeals on grounds other than utility. If the proper methodology is observed, the data are scientifically established and cannot be gainsaid, though we may disagree on what to do about it.

> A gap is hypothesized between knowledge producers and users, and, based on the 'understanding of the gap, means are offered to effectively link the two' ... this question arose largely out of the research on the spread of agricultural innovations ... The 'gap theory' was extremely popular, not least because it held out prospects of easily-managed technical solutions to the utilization problem. (Kallen et al., 1982: 8)

One way of looking at the utilization of research is as a problem of diffusion (Cherns, 1969; 1972). Certainly, before people can use any information, they have to know about it. It helps, too, if they understand it. Furthermore, they need to appreciate its relevance to their concerns. As Kallen et al. (1982: 9) say:

> In the fifties dissemination was thought of as a 'natural consequence of good research', in the sixties as a structured strategy with the object of making R & D results accessible to the lay user, but now it is described as part of an innovatory activity which must envisage increasing the user's problem-solving capacity ... the traditional linkage or diffusion model with its connotations of an active transmitter and a passive receiver has given place to a model in which the user occupies the central place as an active, inquiring, problem-solving entity.

Another concept that does not bear too much scrutiny is that of the 'policy-maker'. Those so identified by outside researchers tend to deny with some puzzlement that they are making policy or even decisions. Admitting to providing a contribution to those processes, they see themselves as part of a complex process, often with few opportunities to do more than find a way for a project through the machine, or to add a small increment to a long line of decisions. Such 'policy' as can be discerned is ex-post-facto. Looking back on a sequence or on a string of actions the historian detects a rationale which was not necessarily part of the actor's consciousness. When actor and historian are one the memoir conveys a meretricious appearance of high purpose. More prosaically Carol Weiss argues:

> ... models of utilization imply models of decision making, usually a linear rational one. But 'diffuse decision making' is a more incremental affair taking shape by jumbled and diffuse processes ... Only in retrospect ... do people become aware that a policy has been made. (Kallen et al., 1982: 311)

The utilization argument usually assumes that social research has a 'result'. But this suggests an altogether misleading sense of what a great deal of social research provides. Physical experiments and mathematical investigations produce 'results' which are authoritative until shown to have embodied experimental errors or fallacious reasoning, or to have been based on shaky premises. Nothing so straightforward is the lot of social research. Some psychological experiments qualify, but at the cost of a remoteness from ordinary life so that they are truly 'academic'. I am not saying that social research has no result; I am claiming that the word conveys inappropriate connotations. As we shall see, social inquiry has many outcomes, but they do not necessarily, even usually, take the form implied by the natural science model.

Government's needs

The more responsibilities government undertakes, the more information it wants. And the scope of government has widened and deepened as society has become looser and more complex. The welfare state is a different kind of society from the proto-industrial state and enshrines a different view of man. Its interactions with its citizens reach far beyond regulation and taxation. As William I's need for taxes generated the Domesday Book, so the modern state's concern with its citizens' welfare generated a multitude of surveys and a tower of statistics. As Britain finally embraced the comprehensive welfare state after World War II, so grew the appetite for statistics of every feature of social and economic life. And when government shouldered the responsibility for managing orderly economic growth, planning joined welfare. Much planning infrastructure was put in place during the war and, as controls were shed, was directed towards supporting less coercive and more persuasive and expansive functions. With each new technological challenge and each new symptom of malfunction, extra responsibilities and tasks are assumed, defying even heroic attempts to 'roll back' the functions of the state. And with each new task comes a new need for data.

It is interesting to note that unemployment, inflation, industrial

relations, drug abuse and race relations, to name a few of today's preoccupations, were not on the research priority list of the 1960s. The fact
is that we never run out of 'problems'. And each new problem generates
a wave of enthusiasm for research which eager contractors are only too
glad to undertake. Policy-oriented research appears to the cynic to be
less an indispensable investment than a luxury consumption.

> With hindsight, much of the policy-orientated research in recent years
> must be described as an appendage of the affluent society, a pleasing
> ornament to the welfare-state, rather than an essential ingredient of
> human happiness. (Kallen et al., 1982: 19)

Wollman (1984) has noted these developments in West Germany. He
describes how a Project Group on Reform of Government and
Administration (PGRA), formed in 1968, grew in the period of
'planning optimism if not euphoria' after the accession to power of the
socialist-liberal coalition in 1969. Social scientists were greatly influenced by US models. The pattern of events had parallels with that in
America: Germany's 'sputnik' crisis was the outcry over the 'catastrophe
in German education' which was held responsible for the decline in
competitiveness during the 1950s. That was followed by a university
expansion dwarfing that in Britain, from 130,000 to over a million students by the early 1980s. As the euphoria evaporated the members of
the Project Group returned to the universities where their focus of
interest shifted towards policy evaluation.

Governments' enthusiasm for policy evaluation was short-lived. Most
evaluation quickly assumes a critical if not adversary stance. At worst,
bad news is news, good news is not. At best, all policies have unwanted
and unforeseen consequences and are victims of bureaucratic goal
displacement. And since no policy is adopted unless dear to somebody's
heart, that somebody is more than reluctant to regard as unbiased
evidence of its failure.

The weakness is less in the techniques of the analyst, imperfect
though they are, than in the machinery for forming policy. Government
often sees problems or issues as belonging to particular departments,
and because of the complexities and uncertainties of interdepartmental
action, solutions are sought within the department's area of competence
and responsibility. This can make sensible research difficult. At the
other extreme, governments are also concerned with global problems.

One of the most significant contributions of economics to government
has surely been the development of models of the economy, not so
much because they claim to provide accurate forecasts (competing
models generate competing forecasts) as that they oblige those
responsible for economic policies to perceive the economy as a whole.

We have no corresponding model of society obliging those responsible for social policies to do the same. The work on social indicators which evoked a short-lived interest in government demonstrated the need but did not provide the means.

> In the work that has been done on indicators, the aims which are implied are usually extremely fuzzy . . . indicators only become fully useful if they are part of a model of some system. (Brand, 1983:243)

The most usable tool for policy which research could provide is a workable model of society, or, at least, models of coherent sub-systems. But that is a large and largely theoretical enterprise which would need a substantial infrastructure and a concerted programme whose duration cannot be estimated. Governments which want research that is immediately useful are unlikely to consider so long-term and chancy an investment.

Ideology and consensus

Policy research in Britain has expanded enormously. While much has satisfied its sponsors, serious strains have been evident, especially in sensitive areas. It is to those strains I now turn.

We came out of the last war with a belief in the possibility of social engineering on a large scale, a peaceful transformation of society. Planning of all kinds, physical, economic and social, would replace the fumbling of the past. There was no truce in the political battle but contention concerned the scale and pace of the means rather than the nature of the ends. Administrators could not mistake Conservative for Labour governments but could count on a degree of acceptance of common policies. The consensus of goals and the commitment to planning constituted an environment in which flourished what Peter Willmott (1980) has described as a euphoric sense that social research could change the world in a short period.

In that climate, 'action research' emerged as a mode of connecting research with action. The dilemma of action research is this. It assumes an objective shared by those concerned with action and those concerned with research. But it is in the nature of action research that new objectives emerge ambulando. The focus and thrust shift until they begin to appear alien to the original sponsor. As the researchers work with the 'subjects' of the research, their role has to be negotiated with them and, indeed, the subjects become the clients. The most prominent action researchers of the 1970s afford excellent examples of the consequences.

The national Community Development Programme (CDP) is one. A new concept of 'experimental social administration' was launched by the British Home Office in 1969. The Community Development Programme was an experiment in community development involving the field testing of new ideas in twelve local projects, each involving central and local government, the voluntary agencies and the universities. By 1974, when all were in operation, more than 100 action and research staff were involved. Mayo (1975) gives a concise account of its origins:

> CDP arose from an alliance of different interests — a group of civil servants concerned for administrative reforms, social workers galvanized by transatlantic examples from the American 'War on Poverty', to name only the most influential. Not surprisingly each group had its own conception of the problems and of the most appropriate solutions, and not surprisingly the end product was not remarkable for its unity of clarity of intention . . . [The assumption was that:] CDP could both extend the range of intervention to new fields and at the same time tackle some of the basic problems dogging existing forms of intervention. (Mayo, 1975:6)

A formidable apparatus of committees was constructed at central and local levels 'despite all the warnings from American experience about the problems of committee structures based on co-operation between widely different agencies and interest with quite different goals and policies, (Mayo, 1975:8). The programme suffered from all the usual contingencies of turnover of administrators, consultants and advisers, and the predictable struggles for control. The capture of the teams by those concerned to broaden their scope to absorb their objectives and viewpoints pressed them to the limits of the project's basic assumptions and 'badly strained the complex CDP machinery. This . . . was even more true at the centre which was quite unprepared for intervention on such broad and political questions' (Mayo, 1975:16). The problem may indeed have owed more to the manifold needs of the declining areas than to the 'influence of particular radical ideologies' (Mayo, 1975:15), but the latter must have contributed to the suspicions of those for whom social research was a dangerous weapon. Reading the accounts of the CDP one sees how researchers in such projects are able to survive only if they become useful members of local action groups. Smith (1975) describes how officials saw the projects as bringing additional resources to solve already perceived social problems, but not to act as a catalyst to promote critical awareness of existing services. Too often the role of the researchers becomes that of a ginger group, focusing temporarily the energies and enthusiasms of local activists. Too often the principal outcome of action research is a volume of case studies. Inevitably the case studies expose the deficiencies of co-ordination imposed by the departmentalism of bureaucratic structures; the proposed remedy often resembles a continuation, an institutionalization, of the temporary structures of the action research, which fails to recognize that the conflicts of interest which beset the research militate against the remedy.

In the case of CDP all the problems were indeed recognized but hope triumphed over experience.

> These warnings ... were treated as the inevitable academic small print and relegated to a mental footnote as CDP developed. The ... model ... left little room for the idea that the social scientist must remain as 'a critic of the social order' ... There was no obvious bridge betweeen the administrators' concern to retain a critical and independent stance ... An analysis which recognizes basic conflicts of interest ... led at least at a theoretical level to the rejection of the original model of field-tested observation ... not ... replaced by any clear alternative approach. (Smith, 1975:190)

And the honeymoon ended when it was realized that the programme had moved beyond its original brief and begun to develop alternative views of poverty and deprivation.

I have dwelt on action research because it appears to offer the best and the quickest route to application. As I commented some fifteen years ago (Cherns, 1969), action research is the most usable but least generalizable form of research; as a result of experience since then I would add that the more that action research influences action in its own context, the less it influences action elsewhere.

Policy research is less difficult if ideological perspectives are shared between the sponsoring department and the researcher. This confluence was singularly missing in another major social policy research under-taken at the behest of the then Secretary of State for Education and Science, Sir Keith Joseph. In 1972 Sir Keith asked the Social Science Research Council and the Department of Health and Social Security to commission a programme of research into the 'cycle of deprivation' of the disadvantaged in Britain. While Joseph perceived this 'cycle' as a property of the deprived families, most of the researchers viewed this as a dubious concept and located the problem in the structure of British society.

It was this difference in assumptions which contributed to the Minister's hostility to social science. Rudolf Klein (1982), who followed events closely, clearly believes that Sir Keith Joseph's instructions to Lord Rothschild (an eminent chemist and Fellow of the Royal Society) to conduct 'an independent review of the scale and nature of the Social Science Research Council's work' was influenced by his receipt of the final research report on Transmitted Deprivation. Klein comments on the deprivation research:

> The end-of-term report ... which involved over seventy academics working on thirty-four projects of various kinds ... is ... illuminating as a study of the relationship between social scientists and policy makers ... which the evidence would seem to suggest, is destined to end in a mutual sense of betrayal ...

> In responding to Sir Keith Joseph's initiative ... the social community rejected both his definition of the problem and its underlying theory ... The researchers set out to map deprivation in all its forms and dimensions. Against Sir Keith Joseph's theory of poverty rooted in family circumstances, they set a theory of poverty rooted in social circumstances: in the economic and social structures of society ...
>
> From his perspective, the programmes of research had been subverted, and used by the research community to pursue its own ideological preoccupations ...
>
> The trouble is that politicians and social scientists inevitably use different models of the world. (Klein, 1982)

I agree with Klein. I would add that in their effort to offer suggestions for action other than completely restructuring society, the authors could do little more than recommend strengthening practically every social and economic measure in force (Brown and Badge, 1982).

Before leaving this topic, I should add one point well made by Berthoud (1983) which indicates the extent to which the preoccupations of researchers can hinder the delivery of the answers they can give to the original questions:

> If the Transmitted Deprivation Working Party was clear on one point, it was that the centre of its programme should consist of the study of 'intergenerational continuities'. Astonishingly, this feature of 'deprivation' is not a central theme of the final report on the programme and there is no summary of the evidence on this point. Nevertheless, the evidence is regularly quoted in the chapter describing the extent and distribution of 'deprivations', and is so consistent that it is easy to summarize. For every single social characteristic for which any evidence on parent–child links could be found, there was some continuity. That is, the sons and daughters of 'deprived' parents were more likely to be 'deprived' in a similar way, than were the children of 'non-deprived' parents. This appears to be true of earnings and income (it is even true when a comparison is made between fathers and their daughters' *husbands'* earnings), of job levels, of housing standards, of educational achievement, of health (although the conclusion is less certain here), of criminal activity and of family life. But it is also clear that in all those fields, the parent–child link covers much less than half of the problem. The conclusion is that the correlation is important, but far from crucial. Nor is it clear, in any of these findings, why the link exists; and even less clear what could be or should be done about it. (Berthoud, 1983:151–69)

Sir Keith Joseph's experience with this work on transmitted deprivation must have reinforced his doubts as to the truly 'scientific' nature of the social sciences and his pressure on the Social Science Research Council to drop 'science' from its title.[2] I see little point in debating that issue; in a sharpened political climate the ideology of science is weaker than political ideologies in its hold both over the social science community and over its clients. One can conclude with Klein (1982) that:

the social sciences can expect niggardly support from *any* government unless politicians start valuing the academic community — against all precedent — in terms of its contribution to the quality of intellectual debate about policy, as distinct from looking to it for instant fixes for their immediate problems.

The consequences of
levelling off and cutting down

I have dwelt at some length on the causes of dissatisfaction and mutual disenchantment and misunderstanding that have occured in the zealous attempt to apply social science research directly to policy issues. In my view the right conclusion to draw is that policy-oriented research is perforce performed within a policy, a political, context. There is no escaping the fact that all research is a political act; the 'problem' is defined by an objective; research methods enshrine a world view. When the question is posed, 'Why do one million people in Ruritania commit offences?', it contains an assumption quite different from the one which asks, 'How is it that ninety-nine million people in Ruritania have never been charged with an offence?' Yet both refer to the same 'objective' data. A scientist is bound to rephrase an administrative question to reconcile it with his view of the world. So long as that is understood on both sides, a fruitful outcome is very possible. Government administrators and Ministers, like other clients, vary in their understanding and acceptance; social scientists vary in their percipience and understanding of the administrative world. Most of the work done for government both intra- and extra-murally is both scientific and politically acceptable, which does not mean that it produces reports which make the client happy. The examples of disenchantment on which I have drawn are important because they illustrate the perils of allowing expectations to rise too high.

To the scientist whose working experience has been gained in a period of rapid and continuous growth, its ending is a trauma. For those who can take a longer view, it provides no surprise. In Britain the 1950s were a period of slow growth of research; money was becoming available but was mostly absorbed in expanding the teaching base. In the 1960s and until 1975 the growth was rapid, drawing for research on the base laid in the 1950s. When the levelling out would have occurred had the 1973–4 oil crisis not supervened, is hard to say. What is fairly clear is that the capacity within government to interpret and use social research and to manage commissioned research had been, for the time, sated. That is not the same as suggesting that the need was satisfied; in any information-using system the capacity to generate information exceeds the capacity to process it. A plateau is reached. Eventually a qualitative or step change enables the system to process information at the next order of magnitude. That type of system change occurs unpredictably and at apparently random intervals — random because they are governed by a multiplicity of variables.

Levelling off is, of course, not only the consequence of channel overload. Much research is promoted by departments to lay the foundations for a branch of knowledge relevant to their operations. Thus, the Home Office promoted research in criminology and the Treasury promoted macro-economic modelling, both internally and outside. In time the discipline becomes established. It can either be strong enough to survive artificial respiration in the rarefied academic atmosphere or able to face the more bracing challenge of the market. Macro-economic modelling provides an excellent example of the latter. The Treasury has an obvious need to forecast and in however primitive a manner has been doing so and publishing its forecasts. The need for the best available, or not yet available, methods was obvious. As soon as economics had evolved adequate mathematical methods and computing advanced to the necessary level, the Treasury became interested in building a model of the British economy. And since any model requires a set of assumptions as its foundation, many models are possible. The Treasury evolved one; others were keen to do so using different sets of assumptions. Needing experts outside as interlocutors the Treasury supported work elsewhere, notably over many years in the National Institute of Economic and Social Research. Once modelling and its associated forecasting had advanced sufficiently it had a product to sell and a commercial market emerged. And for research and development as distinct from exploitation, the Social Science Research Council became a more appropriate sponsor than the Treasury; its macro-economic modelling consortium was the response.

In a climate of disillusion with social research and suspicion of social sciences it has been easier for government to swing its financial axe. The social science lobby has been less effective than, say, that for the Ordnance Survey. The axe has, however, not fallen evenly. Some departments of government have proved more doughty in fighting their corners than others. And they use different methods for compensating for what they are losing. Thus, as departments have less to spend on social research they become more inclined to press outside funding bodies to support the kind of work in which they are interested. In this way the independent funding bodies are brought into closer relationship with central departments with potentially greater influence on their research policies. It is too soon to discern how far that will develop or how welcome it would be to the social science community.

With the emphasis on contracting out has also appeared a preference for the commercial contractor, especially with the Department of Employment, although outside market research there are still very few. The more the research is closely related to policy requirements, the more pressing the time constraint, the more attractive becomes the commercial unit. From the scientific point of view their work may be no less respectable or rigorous, but they are not under the pressure to publish as are their university counterparts and are less likely to urge government to publish. Thus their work ultimately contributes less to the cumulation of knowledge.[3]

What is perhaps more disturbing is the effect on the quality of the research which departments are now prepared to sponsor. Less does not necessarily mean better; but in some departments there is a tendency to prefer short-term projects which are fact-finding for administrative purposes and make little contribution to research. Perhaps unsurprisingly this kind of research is most often encountered where the generation of research projects is handled entirely by administrators.

Politics and the misuse of values

The unavoidable, if unpalatable, conclusion is that, whether we like it or not, social science research cannot be sprung from its political context. We choose our ends to fit a model of society as we would wish it to be; to be effective we have to choose our means to fit a model of society as it is. But we are living at a time of sharp disagreement not only about the desirable shape of the future society but also about its present nature. Nor are the two unconnected. Those who most want an egalitarian society perceive ours as deeply stratified; those who regard freedom as incompatible with equality and prefer freedom, perceive our society as an open one.

When considering the relationship of research to policy we not surprisingly focus on government. But government is by no means the sole user of the research, nor is it the only body with social and economic policies. Other organizations are less constrained in their choice of research to sponsor. Government is criticized if it appears to favour research from one stable or of a particular stripe. It is spending public money. Other pipers can call their tunes. Few social policy pressure groups dispose of resources enough to sponsor research on a large scale but they can and do refract the findings of research conducted under other auspices including government itself. In that way they provide themselves with ammunition and force a public debate on the issues the research has revealed. As pressure groups become more adept at lobbying, so research obtains a more attentive hearing. A recent development is the founding by lobbies of their own think-tanks and research centres. Little attempt is made to disguise the ideological underpinnings of social and economic research. We do not expect too much Keynesianism from the Institute of Economic Affairs (a recently founded body strongly advocating the market economy), for example, nor much 'critical' sociology from the Social Affairs Unit (even more recently founded body, advocating the market system for social provision). While these examples come from Britain in the 1980s, similar trends have been observed in many other countries. This development is a clear consequence of the sharpening of the ideological split in our society.

Industrial and commercial organizations are the main customers for research outside national and local government. Here the researcher is under no illusion that his research will be the only or the main ingredient of policy. The closer he is to the organization, the more he recognizes the conflicts of interest within it and the dependence of the fate of his research on their power struggles. If he wants his recommendations to prevail he may have to enter the political process himself. And if he does he must guard against prevailing only to lose his base. Helping some to win means acquiring the losers as adversaries and losing the amount of 'objectivity' which has sanctioned his activities. This is not the place to discuss the politics of research in organizations at length, nor to lament the inability or unwillingness of unions to sponsor research. Goldner (1967) has described how an organizational researcher has to negotiate a role for himself; it is one that embraces more than research. If more researchers who aspire to influence government's social and economic policies could acquire this kind of experience, they might learn to be more effective.

And some within government have that opportunity as members of in-house research units. Unfortunately, the hierarchical structure and relationship of departments often confines those opportunities to the most senior levels.[4]

Conclusions

My conclusions are best seen within a model of the research process. For this purpose I am happy to refer the reader to the model described by Weiss in Chapter 15. I have given several illustrations of the wide variety of meanings that may be given to the notion of 'utilization'. What I have been at pains to argue is the need to recognize both its complexity and its shifting nature. The roles of the social sciences have been changing with changes in society towards greater politicization with the break up of, or, perhaps more fairly, the drift in consensus in recent years.

Much depends on whether one regards the abstractions of social research as revelations of more fundamental forces and relationships underlying surface phenomena, or as handy and temporary shorthand for grouping phenomena, to be modified as the phenomena change. Our understanding of 'science' has emphasized the former, our practice of empirical research has been closer to the latter. If we have claimed science and practised shorthand, we have confused ourselves as well as the users about what use means.

Notes

1. 'Scientism', as used by Hayek (1942) *The Road to Serfdom* (Routledge) to describe an unintelligent attempt to ape the natural sciences.
2. The investigation into the Social Science Research Council by Lord Rothschild came out in strong support of social science and the Council's work. Nevertheless, Sir Keith Joseph, the responsible Minister, ordered the word 'Science' to be dropped. It is now called the Economic and Social Research Council. [Editor's note]
3. See also Chapter 5 which reports a similar trend in West Germany. [Editor's note]
4. See chapter 11 for a similar view. [Editor's note]

References

Berthoud, Richard (1983) 'Transmitted Deprivation: The Kite That Failed', *Policy Studies*, 3 (3):151–69.
Brand, J. (1983) 'The Politics of Social Indicators', in M. Bulmer, 'Science, Theory and Values in Social Science Research on Poverty', *Comparative Social Research*, 6:353–69.
Brown, Muriel and Nicola Badge (1982) *Despite the Welfare State*. London: Heinemann.
Bulmer, M. (1983) 'Science, Theory and Values in Social Science Research on Poverty', *Comparative Social Research*, 6:353–69.
Cherns, A. B. (1969) 'Social Research and Its Diffusion', *Human Relations*, 22 (3):209–18.
Cherns, A. B. (1972) 'Models for the Use of Research', *Human Relations*, 25(1): 25–33.
Goldner, F. (1967) 'Role Emergence and the Ethics of Ambiguity', pp. 245–66 in G. Sjoberg (ed.), *Ethics, Politics and Social Research*. London: Routledge and Kegan Paul.
Kallen, D., G. Kosse, H. Wagenaar, J. Kliprogge, and M. Vorbeck (eds) (1982) *Social Science Research and Public Policy Making*. Windsor: NFER-Nelson.
Klein, Rudolf (1982) 'Pinpointing the Poor', *The Times Literary Supplement*, 7 December: 1401.
Mayo, Marjorie (1975) 'The History and Development of CDP', chapters 2 and 7 in R. Lees and G. Smith (eds), *Action Research in Community Development*. London: Routledge and Kegan Paul.
Smith, George (1975) 'Action Research: Experimental Social Administration?', pp. 189–90 in R. Lees and G. Smith (eds), *Action Research in Community Development*. London: Routledge and Kegan Paul.
Vidich, A., S. Lyman and J. Goldfarb (1981) 'Sociology and Society', *Social Research*, 48 (2):322–61.

Willmott, Peter (1980) *A View from an Independent Research Institute: Social Research and Public Policy.* London: Social Research Association.
Wollman, H. (1984) 'Policy Analysis: Some Observations on the West German Scene', *Policy Sciences,* 17: 24–47.

14

Policy research: an analysis of function and structure

Mark van de Vall

A theoretical framework

Academic social science has shown little interest in social policy research and utilization. The effect of this neglect has been twofold. On the one hand, absence of application has slowed down the advancement of the discipline of social science (Merton, 1963). On the other hand, lack of academic involvement has thwarted the development of a theory of social policy research (Trist, 1972; Larsen, 1980). A theoretical framework is necessary, however, for understanding and disseminating the potential and the limits of social policy research. One reason is that new information is more easily absorbed when presented in a system of theoretical conclusions (Caplan, 1975).

In the first part of this article, a 'realtypical' model is developed of two roles of social policy research in our modern social system (Baldamus, 1967): as an agent of planned change, and as an instrument of policy control. In the second part, the analysis moves to the micro-social level. An 'organizational context', variable is introduced based on the location of the researcher and the location of the investigated problem, inside or outside the client-organization. In this structural analysis we shall determine which type of organizational context provides an optimal condition for the two functions of social policy research described in the first part.

The role of social policy research
Planned social change

Few will dispute that our private and public institutions are confronted with an accelerating and diversifying process of change (Tofler, 1970). Coping with a growing number of uncertainties, today's organizations are increasingly converting retroactive policy action into planned, anticipatory programmes. In the next model, the role of social policy research is viewed from the wider perspective of applied social *science* as an agent of planned social and organizational change.

FIGURE 1

Applied social science as an agent of planned change

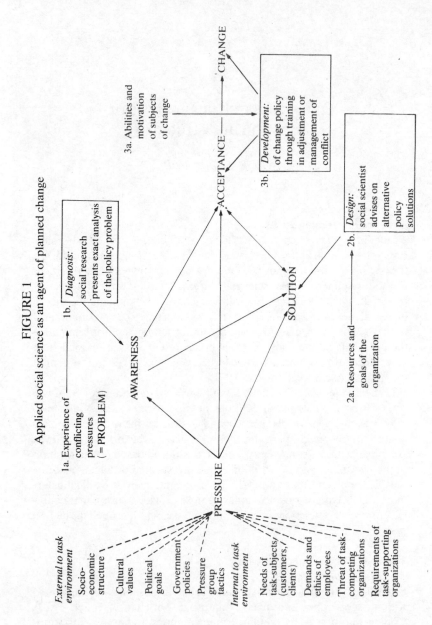

Diagnosis, design and development

Applied social science can play a role in three stages of planned organizational change (Figure 1). In diagnosis (1b), by increasing awareness of the problem by providing valid and reliable information about its origin, structure and scope (Parsler, 1978). In design (2b), by scanning the range of policy alternatives for ways to solve the problem (Mayer and Greenwood, 1980). In development (3b) by facilitating the implementation of a selected policy programme (Williams and Elmore, 1976).

In Figure 1 the steps 1b, 2b and 3b are part of *one and the same* process of adjustment to pressures within and outside the organization. This condition is important, as in academic social science each step has been appropriated by a separate discipline, with its own theory and concepts, methods and techniques, faculty and curriculum.

In diagnosis (1b) this is Sociology, with theories of social change and social problems, and methods of data-collecting and -analysis. In design (2b) it is Public and/or Business Administration, with theories of administrative behaviour, methods of policy analysis (Mitroff and Emshoff, 1979) and management by objectives. Development (3b) is appropriated by Organization Development and Policy Science, with methods of group feed-back analysis (Heller, 1973) and conflict management (Hornstein et al., 1970).

This division of an undivided process of planned change in three different disciplines has a negative effect upon the utilization of social science in policy-making. In fact, it is one reason why the impact of social science research is often found wanting.[1] It also explains the growing need for a 'clinical–engineering' model of applied social science (Ben-David, 1973; Rothman, 1980).

Social policy control

Policy programmes are concerned with the control and allocation of recources and, thus, the control of individuals and groups (Rule, 1978). In this situation, social policy research operates as a supporting control mechanism at three different stages of the policy process: input, throughput and output (Havelock, 1969).

Figure 2 shows how input-research is used as an instrument of pre-control or policy planning, how throughput-research improves current control or policy implementation, and how output-research acts as an agent of post-control or policy evaluation.

Figure 2 also illustrates that the scanning role of input-research requires little participation from the organization's inner circles, while throughput-research touches vital parts of an organization's goal-achievement, involving several hierarchical levels. Output- or evaluation-research may have two different results: improving the organi-

FIGURE 2
Social policy research as an agent of policy control

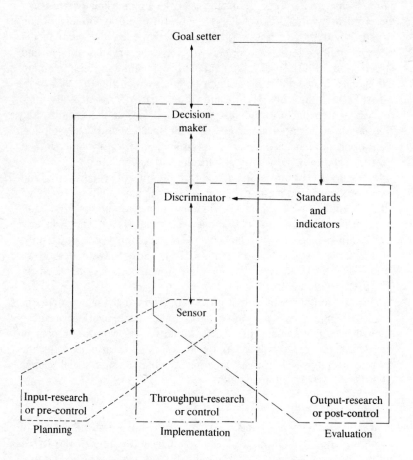

zation's procedures so they can meet current standards, or lowering standards so they can be met by current procedures. Choosing between these alternatives is often anxiety-provoking, acting as a barrier against the full utilization of evaluation research (Aguilar, 1967).[2]

Because each type of policy research plays a different role in the client-organization, using different methods and coping with different obstacles, we shall now analyse them separately.

Input-research: an agent of pre-control. Input-research belongs to the scanning techniques used by organizations to explore changes in or beyond their task-enviroment. An early and widespread method of environmental scanning is the social survey. Illustrations of input-research in urban and regional planning, labour and industrial relations, and social welfare and public health are presented in Table 1.

TABLE 1
Social input-research in three areas of decision-making

Regional and urban planning	Census research. Descriptive surveys of demographic trends. Surveys of supply and demand for low-cost housing, health facilities, recreation. Surveys of regional infrastructures, health conditions, traffic patterns, urban blight.
Labour and industrial relations	Surveys of plant location and manpower resources. Surveys of educational and health conditions in labour markets. Delphi surveys of possible changes in the organization's task environment.
Social welfare and public health	Diagnostic surveys of the needs or demands of particular clients (minorities, retarded, deviants, aged, migrants, addicts) for health clinics, rehabilitation programmes, training programmes, recreation facilities, social welfare services.

One reason why input-research often has a low impact is its peripheral location in decision-making, acting as a sensor at the earliest stages of the policy process. Also, social surveys are often conducted from a descriptive rather than a diagnostic perspective. In addition to describing, diagnostic surveys attune the analysis of the problem to the organization's resources, current operations and goals. It is only by adapting its research design to the organization's problem-solving potential that policy research can effectively contribute to a policy programme (Cyert and March, 1964; Hakel et al., 1982).

Throughput-research: an agent of current control. Throughput-research assesses the process of organizational goal achievement, whether consisting of manufacturing goods, educating disadvantaged youth, reducing small urban crime or providing welfare services.

TABLE 2
Social throughput-research in three areas of decision-making

Regional and urban planning	Research into designs, policies and procedures for country or city planning, new neighbourhoods, health systems areas, housing projects. Research into the operation, utilization or co-ordination of planning agencies.
Labour and industrial relations	Action research concerning production processes, industrial leadership and supervision patterns, promotion and mobility decisions, workers' motivation and morale. Studies of workers' participation in decision-making, union-management inter-action, adjustment to stresses due to technological change.
Social welfare and public health	Analyses of the operation of agencies and services. Studies of institutional goal attainment, the image or aims of welfare agencies, the co-ordination of private and public service organizations, of preventive and supervisory agencies, of social welfare and public health provisions, of mental health inpatient and outpatient services.

Although most widely used in industrial organizations, throughput-research is gradually moving into other sectors of policy-making.

Used by a growing number of private and public organizations, throughput-research has changed from a purely investigative method into a method of planned social intervention. This development is reflected in the increasing use of 'action methods' for reducing social and organizational problems (Donahue and Spates, 1972).

Action research. In action research, members of the target group — the ones who are expected to change their values and/or behaviour — take an active part in the various stages of the project of social policy research: diagnosing the problem, determining priorities, designing policy alternatives, implementing recommendations.

Several techniques have been developed to combine the requirement of participation with the epistemologial standards of social science research: community self-surveys (Wormser and Selltiz, 1952), self-recording of interpersonal communication (Hesseling, 1970), group feed-back analysis (Heller, 1970) and conflict intervention (Laue, 1981). In action research the policy researcher plays mainly an advisory role. By breaking it down in fourteen subsequent steps, Figure 3 presents a comprehensive analysis of the role of the researcher in action oriented social investigation.

The left-hand part of Figure 3 illustrates how co-ordinating the stages of diagnosis (Steps 2 and 3), design (steps 4 to 8) and development (steps 9 to 12) require the social scientist to master three sociotechnical skills: of social clinician, policy advisor and change agent.

FIGURE 3
The roles of the policy researcher in action-oriented social research

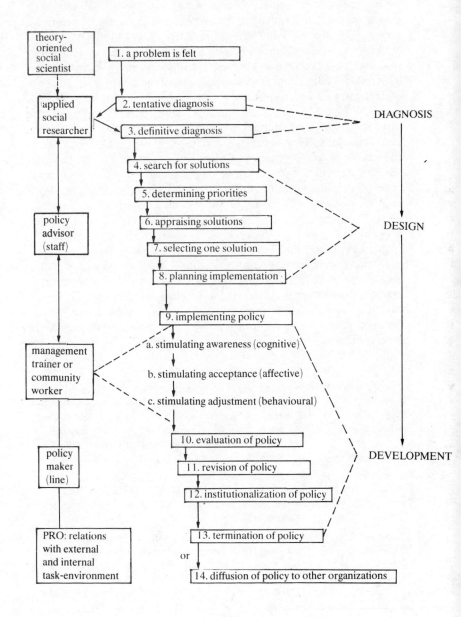

In this sequence, step 5 in Figure 3 represents one of the main non-scientific elements in social policy research: when the participants must evaluate alternative policy measures against the priorities of the organization, it is not scientific information but ideological and subjective values that will determine the latter. Without determining priorities, however, the process is unable to proceed from step 4 to step 6.

Finally, after the diagnosis is completed, the priorities set and a new policy chosen, the time has arrived for implementing the programme. This calls for adjustment from the members of the target group, which is often frustrated by cognitive, affective and behavioural barriers indicated in Figure 3 as 9a, 9b and 9c. Due to these barriers, new programmes are often accompanied by unintended effects and 'secondary' problems. This occurs especially when two groups within one role-set (employers-workers, providers-recipients, etc.) are compelled to develop their own role behaviour *and* adapt to the other's new role-conception. Consequently, it is usually after the programme has been implemented that we are in a position to understand its real contents. Thus, to obtain valid insight in the problem-reducing effect of a policy programme, it is not only necessary to diagnose the problem, but also to evaluate the programme's intended and unintended impact.

Output-research: an agent of post-control. With the spread of public health and welfare programmes in our modern social system, programme evaluation has become the most widely used method of output-research. In evaluation-research, the intended and sometimes unintended effects of a policy programme upon its target population are measured.

TABLE 3
Social output-research in three areas of decision-making

Regional and urban planning	Evaluation of municipal housing projects, inter-racial housing programmes, new neighbourhood designs, public transport systems, neighbourhood community centres, urban renovation projects.
Labour and industrial relations	Market research studies. Studies of the impact of industrial human relations policies, productivity bargaining, profit-sharing programmes, management training programmes, active manpower policies.
Social welfare and public health	Evaluation studies of welfare policies and programmes. Analyses of the effect of rehabilitation programmes and preventive measures. Studies of the use and effects of medical facilities, neighbourhood health clinics, dental care programmes, information and referral services for the aged.

In Table 3 we find examples of output-research in three areas of organizational policy-making.

Of the various methods of impact evaluation, methodologically most sophisticated is the 'experimental' approach, in which the assessment of a policy measure is restricted to a single feed-back loop. In this method, the researcher measures and compares before and after situations in both the target group and a control group (Rossi and Freeman, 1985). A disadvantage is its anxiety-provoking effect within the client-organization (Weiss, 1972).

Methodologically less developed, but probably closer to the daily realities of policymaking, is the 'process'-method of programme evaluation. In this approach, the respective effects of a sequence of policy-measures are monitored, sometimes without comparing with a control group. Researchers conducting process evaluation often use methods of data-triangulation, combining quantitative and qualitative techniques of data-collection and -analysis (Patton, 1978). They frequently communicate with the members of the client-system, using 'formative' methods of researcher-client interaction (Doerbecker, 1979). According to Dunn (1980) the more that social researchers encourage feed-back on the results of their research, the greater the knowledge utilization.

The different value orientations of academic social researchers and social policy researchers are probably best illustrated by their respective preferences for experimental vs. process methods of programme evaluation.

The structure of social policy research
A micro-model: organizational context[3]
Having analysed two functions of social policy research in our modern social system — planned change and policy control — we shall now raise questions about the structure of client-oriented social research. What is the most adequate organizational structure, for instance, for optimally executing those functions?

To answer this question, a conceptual model of four types of 'organizational context' will be developed. Organizational context is determined by two dimensions: (a) the location of the researcher, as a staff member of the client-organization (I) or as an external consultant (E), and (b) the location of the investigated problem, within the organization (I'), or in its task environment and beyond (E').[4] Together, they make for the following combinations, as below (see Figure 4).

In an analysis of 120 projects of social policy research in the Netherlands, each of the four variations of 'context' were found in the industrial and labour relations sector, in urban and regional planning, and social welfare and public health.

FIGURE 4
Organizational context

Location of the problem

		Internal'	External'
	Internal	I/I'	I/E'
Location of the researcher			
	External	E/I'	E/E'

Context and utilization

Exploring the relationship between organizational context and research utilization we constructed two different 'Overall Policy Impact' scores, one based upon ratings by the researcher, the other upon ratings by the policy-maker. Combining and averaging these two scores resulted in a more valid and comprehensive indicator, the (X/OPI–4) score used in this article.[5]

Comparing the impact of the research projects upon policy decisions in the four variations of 'organizational context', we found several trends in the three sectors of policy-making. They are shown in Table 4.

TABLE 4
Utilization of social policy research in four different types of organizational context, in three sectors of social policy-making (X/OPI—4 scores)

Organizational context of the research projects	Industrial and labour relations	Regional and urban planning	Social welfare and public health	The combined three samples ($n = 120$)
Internal researcher/ internal problem'	13.93	14.76	16.33	14.39
Internal researcher/ external problem'	13.25	13.33	10.30	12.15
External researcher/ internal problem'	11.83	13.03	10.12	12.17
External researcher/ external problem'	10.08	10.18	10.30	10.27

Our conclusions from Table (4) are:

1. There is a tendency for higher research utilization to be achieved when both the problem and the researcher are internal to the organization.

2. There is a tendency for higher research utilization to be achieved when problems are within the boundaries of the organization rather

than outside it. This finding bears out previous results by Chamberlain (1973: 202) who found that such a relationship also applies to the implementation stage of the research, in terms of action and change.

3. When policy research is conducted by in-house researchers rather than by outsiders, higher utilization is achieved. This finding would suggest that the numerous claims about the superiority of external consultants in client-orientated social research (Lippitt et al., 1958; Seashore and van Egmond, 1966; Gross et al., 1971; French and Bell, 1973; Segers, 1981; Snellen, 1981) appear not to be supported by our findings. Such a conclusion is also confirmed by one of the few other systematic studies on the subject: Bursk and Sethi (1975) compared the impact of internal and external agencies in a related area of advertising and found that in-house researchers have a consistently higher impact on management decisions than outside consultants. Bursk and Sethi mention that among the advantages of internal researchers is their greater success in communicating with middle-and higher-level executive policy-makers.

4. This hypothesis is supported by other results of our investigation, which showed that in all three policy areas, internal researchers communicate more frequently with policy-makers than external researchers (van de Vall and Bolas, 1981: Table 5).

5. The case for or against rigorous methods has often been debated. One way of formulating this issue is to decide whether researchers should spend more time on the niceties of methodology or on working closely with their clients, for instance through ad hoc meetings on policy formation.

Results from the 120 projects show that the amount of the researcher's time devoted to methodological problems does not correlate positively with utilization, while the portion of time devoted to ad hoc meetings on policy formation shows a positive correlation with utilization of the project's proposals (van de Vall and Bolas, 1981: Figure 2). This conclusion is easily misunderstood. It does not mean that methodological sophistication is not necessary in social research. But it does suggest that preoccupation with methodology is only one of several fundamental requirements, in addition to devoting time and attention to other issues, like policy design and development. In other words, attention to epistemological values is a necessary but not sufficient condition in social policy research.

6. The implementation phase of research has received relatively little attention. Yet the statistical results from our project, presented in Table 5, show that it is very important.

The data in Table 5 indicate that high utilization occurs more frequently in circumstances where the researchers were involved in policy formation tasks after the research report was submitted, than

TABLE 5

External and internal social policy researchers' involvement in procedures of policy formation after reporting to the client-organization, and the projects' impact upon organizational decisions (X/OPI-4)

| | Involvement in disseminating research results among interested parties | | | | | Involvement in advising policy recommendations after reporting | | | | | Involvement in co-deciding on policy measures after reporting | | | |
| | Ext. res. (E) | | Int. res. (I) | | | Ext. res. (E) | | Int. re'. (I) | | | Ext. res. (E) | | Int. res. (I) | |
Var.	Impact	%	Impact	%	Var.	Impact	%	Impact	%	Var.	Impact	%	Impact	%
Yes:	11.35	43	15.18	72	Yes:	13.37	40	14.74	65	Yes:	17.70	7	19.80	20
No:	9.72	52	13.18	28	No:	8.57	60	14.42	35	No:	9.91	93	13.37	80
		100		100			100		100			100		100
		(64)		(51)			(64)		(51)			(64)		(51)

when they were not so involved. Futhermore, since internal researchers participate more frequently in the tasks of policy formation, particularly in disseminating the research results and recommending specific policy decisions, their impact on utilization tends to be consistently greater than that of external researchers.

Conclusion
In this chapter two related questions have been answered, one about the major functions of social policy research in our modern social system, the other about its optimal structural context. The answer to the first question is that major functions of social policy research are facilitating planned change and supporting policy control.

The question about the optimal structure for executing these functions has only been partially answered, however. What is certain is that research of intra-organizational problems tends to be more highly utilized than policy research in the organization's task environment. However, in the course of our discussion, the question whether external or internal policy researchers achieve higher impact has gradually moved into the background. More important than which category of researchers excels as agents of policy formation is a more fundamental question: what variables account for the consistent finding that projects conducted by internal researchers are more intensively utilized?

The data indicate that the answer lies partially in a higher communication frequency between internal researchers and policy-makers, accompanied by greater consensus (van de Vall and Bolas, 1981). A second explanatory factor is the maintenance of a reasonable balance between the requirements of knowledge and those of implementation. Instead of concentrating exclusively upon methodological problems, effective social policy researchers, after reporting, should also assist the client system in translating the research results into feasible policy decisions. However, this professional requirement transcends the traditional academic role-conception of the value-free social scientist whose exclusive interest lies in enlightenment rather than in planned social change.

Notes

1. We found 398 research projects in the area of child-care and protection in the Netherlands for which no impact upon policies could be detected, either by the researcher or by the policy-maker. See also Adriani (1978).

2. For instance: 'The difficulty of convincing everyone that the purpose of an appraisal review is to *learn* and *not to blame* may well be the biggest stumbling block to successful adoption of this procedure' (Aguilar, 1967: 195).

3. Partially published in van de Vall and Bolas (1981).

4. The distinction between respectively internal and external problems (I and E) and internal and external researchers (I' and E') was for each project decided through the combined judgement of the researcher and the policy-maker and, in cases of discrepancy, a third observer.

5. For the construction of the (X/OPI–4) score, its validity and its reliability, we refer to van de Vall and Bolas (1981).

References

Adriani, P.J.A. (1978) *Jeugdwelzijn en Wetenschap.* Groningen: Wolters.

Aguilar, F.J. (1967) *Scanning the Business Environment.* New York: Macmillan.

Baldamus, W. (1967) 'The Category of Pragmatic Knowledge in Sociological Analysis', *Archiv f. Rechts- u. Sozialphilosophie,* I: 31–51.

Ben-David, J. (1973) 'How to Organize Research in the Social Sciences', *Daedalus,* Spring: 42.

Bursk, E.C. and B.S. Sethi (1975) *The In-house Advertising Agency.* (Unpublished report.)

Caplan, N.S., A. Morrison and R.J. Stambaugh (1975) *The Use of Social Science Knowledge in Policy Decisions at the National Level.* Ann Arbor: University of Michigan Press.

Chamberlain, N.W. (1973) *The Limits of Corporative Responsibility.* New York: Basic Books.

Cyert, R.M. and J.G. March (1964) 'The Behavioral Theory of the Firm: A Behavioral Science-Economic Amalgam', in W.W. Cooper, H.J. Leavitt and M.W. Shelly II (eds), *New Perspectives in Organizational Research.* New York: John Wiley.

Doerbecker, C (1979) 'Het iteratieve zoekproces en het cognitieve kader van de cliënt', *Tijdschrift voor Agologie,* 5: 355–68.

212 The use and abuse of social science

Donahue, M. and J.L. Spates (1972) *Action Research: Handbook for Social Change.* New York: Harper and Row.

Dunn, W. N. (1980) 'The Two-Communities Metaphor and Models of Knowledge Use', *Knowledge: Creation, Diffusion, Utilization,* 1 (4): 526.

French, W.L. and C.H. Bell (1973) *Organization Development.* Englewood Cliffs, NJ: Prentice-Hall.

Gross, N., J. Giacquinta and M. Bernstein (1971) *Implementing Organizational Innovations.* New York: Basic Books.

Hakel, M.D., M. Sorcher, M. Beer and J.L. Moses (1982) *Making It Happen: Designing Research with Implementation in Mind.* Beverly Hills, Ca.: Sage.

Havelock, R.G. (1969) *Planning for Innovation through Dissemination and Utilization of Knowledge.* Ann Arbor: ISR.

Heller, F.A. (1970) 'Group Feedback Analysis as a Change Agent', *Human Relations,* 23: 319–33.

Heller, F.A. (1973) 'Group Feedback Analysis', in D. Graves (ed.), *Management Research: A Cross-Cultural Perspective.* San Francisco: Jossey-Bass.

Hesseling, P. (1970) 'Communication and Organization Structure in a Large Multinational Company', pp. 40–70 in G. Heald (ed.) *Approaches to the Study of Organizational Behaviour.* London: Tavistock Publications.

Hornstein, H.A. et al. (1970) (eds) *Social Intervention: A Behavioral Science Approach.* New York: Free Press.

Larsen, J.K. (1980) 'Knowledge Utilization: What Is It?', *Knowledge: Creation, Diffusion, Utilization,* (1) 3: 421–42.

Laue, J.H. (1981) 'Conflict Intervention', pp. 67–90 in M.E. Olsen and M. Micklin (eds), *Handbook of Applied Sociology.* New York: Praeger.

Lippitt, N., A. Morrison and B. Westley (1958) *The Dynamics of Planned Change.* New York: Harcourt Brace.

Mayer, R. R. and E. Greenwood (1980) *The Design of Social Research.* Englewood Cliffs, NJ: Prentice-Hall.

Merton, R. K. (1963) 'Science and Economy in 17th Century England', *Social Theory and Social Structure.* New York: Free Press.

Mitroff, I. I. and J. R. Emshoff (1979) 'On Strategic Assumption Making: A Dialectical Approach to Policy and Planning, *Academy of Management Review,* 4(1): 1–12.

Parsler, R. (1978) 'Sociological Research and Its Implications for Social Policy', *International Journal of Comparative Sociology,* XIC (1–2): 114–29.

Patton, M. Q. (1978) *Utilization Focused Evaluation.* Beverly Hills, Ca.: Sage.

Rossi, P.H. and H.E. Freeman (1985) *Evaluation: A Systematic Approach.* Beverly Hills, Ca.: Sage.

Rothman, J. (1980) *Using Research in Organizations.* Beverly Hills, Ca.: Sage.

Rule, J.B. (1978) *Insight and Social Betterment.* New York: Oxford University Press.

Seashore, C. and E. van Egmond (1966) 'The Consultant-Trainer Role', in W. Bennis, K. Benne and R. Chin (eds), *The Planning of Change.* New York: Holt, Rinehart and Winston.

Segers, J.H.G. (1981) 'Sociaal Beleidsonderzoek', *Sociale Wetenschappen,* 24 (1): 69–89.

Snellen, I.T.M. (1981) 'Hebbelijkheden van Sociaal Beleidsonderzoek?', *Sociale Wetenschappen* 24 (3): 325–6.

Tofler, A. (1970) *Future Shock.* New York: Bantam Books.

Trist, E. (1972) 'Types of Output Mix of Research Organizations and Their Complementarity', pp. 101–37 in A.B. Cherns, R. Sinclair and W.I. Jenkins (eds), *Social Science and Government Policies and Problems*. London: Tavistock Publications.

van de Vall, M. and C. Bolas (1980) 'Applied Social Discipline Research or Social Policy Research: the Emergence of a Professional Paradigm in Sociological Research', *The American Sociologist*, 15: 128–37.

van de Vall, M. and C. Bolas (1981) 'External vs. Internal Social Policy Researchers', *Knowledge: Creation, Diffusion, Utilization*, 2 (4): 461–81.

Weiss, C.H. (1972) *Evaluation Research*. Englewood Cliffs, NJ: Prentice-Hall.

Williams, W. and R.F. Elmore (eds) (1976) *Social Program Implementation*, New York: Academic Press.

Wormser, M.J. and C. Selltiz (1952) 'Community Self-Surveys: Principles and Procedures', pp. 611–41 in M. Jahoda, M. Deutsch and S.W. Cook (eds), *Research Methods in Social Relations, Vol 2*. New York: Dryden Press.

15
Research and policy-making: a limited partnership

Carol Hirschon Weiss

It is a rare policy-maker who would cite the under-utilization of social science as a significant obstacle to dealing with national problems. Policy-makers know that public policies are not the product of rational problem-solving. They recognize the overwhelming pressure to take account of the political interests of important segments in society and to adapt to prevailing ideologies. While they also realize the importance of good information as a basis for wise actions, they usually believe that they are deluged with more information than they have time to absorb. Limited availability of social science information is not a concern which — except in the rare instance — weighs heavily.

Yet social scientists are frequently exercised about the neglect of research. They believe that social science can offer several vital contributions to the policy process. All public policies represent causal theories: if we do *a* (regulate, appropriate, set up a new agency, alter services), we will accomplish *x*, the desired result. Social science can provide data that describe the nature of problems and their prevalence, so that policy-makers can tell whether *x* is really needed. It can tell something about the factors that lead to the origin and perpetuation of the problems and thus answer the question: is *x* possible under current circumstances? It can examine the ways in which present policies are implemented and identify their successes and shortcomings.

Further, social science can examine and test the policy theory. Will *a* really lead to *x*? Will deregulation of airlines lead to lower costs to the traveller? Will merit pay for teachers improve the quality of teaching? Even if *a* does bring about *x*, will it also give rise to the undesired consequences of *y* and *z*? This type of information can be obtained through evaluation of the effects of past policies and analysis of the likely effects of current proposals.

A third kind of contribution that social science can make is the development of new policy theory. It provides new perspectives and new ideas. It offers ways of thinking afresh about societal conditions and re-combining policy elements into new schemes for action. While social

214

science is obviously not the only, or even the major, source of policy proposals (Kingdon, 1984), it has a respectable record in innovation and perhaps an even better record in making visible other people's ideas and legitimating them.

To use a computing metaphor, social science can not only provide inputs of data, it can also provide new computer programs to process and make sense of data.[1] That at least has been the recurrent promise that the social sciences have made.

With such a richness of offerings, one might suppose that policy-makers would welcome the gift with open arms, especially when faced with a series of almost intractable problems in field after field. Yet this volume, like many before it, is disconcerted by the relatively low levels of hospitality that policy-makers accord to social science. However pressed and harried they are, why should they not avail themselves more fully of its descriptive, causal and predictive knowledge?

Is social science overrrated as a source of practical help? Are decision-makers overly engrossed in bureaucratic and legislative politics? Are there chasms of misunderstanding and non-communication between practitioners in the two arenas? Or have social scientists misconstrued the nature of policy-making and the place of social science in its workings? There is probably some truth in all these contentions, but it is the latter position that I would like to develop here. First let us take a brief excursion through the recent past in the United States when government agencies made serious and intensive efforts to apply social science research to policy.

Great expectations
From the early 1960s until the early 1980s, both the US Congress and the federal domestic agencies that executed human resource policies made commitments to social science research. The most serious commitment was to research that evaluated the effects of new policies for their intended beneficiaries. During this period, most initiatives in education, social services, health, mental health, employment and housing, were accompanied by mandates for evaluation. Over all, the federal government spent hundreds of millions of dollars annually to learn how well human service policies were achieving the ends for which they were designed.

The upsurge in evaluation activity and expenditures had a rational cast. The presumed purpose of analysis was to improve the effectiveness of policy. Evaluation was expected to identify the programmes and policies that were working well so that they could be expanded, and locate the programmes and policies that were working poorly so that they could be terminated or modified. Evaluations that analysed the effects of component strategies of intervention — that indicated which components of policies were successful for which types of clientele under which conditions — would provide the basis for modifying policies and attuning them to the needs and life conditions of the participants. The enterprise, in short, was meant to use the methods and techniques of social science in the service of rational allocation of resources and the improvement of social policy.

American social scientists by the thousands were attracted to evaluation and associated policy studies. Not only did they find research funds available for the study of important and interesting social and economic phenomena, but the social consequences of the work also looked attractive: evaluation results were to be put to work to improve the lot of the needy. Despite reservations among a few social scientists about becoming technicians for the bureaucratic welfare state (Gouldner, 1970; Dye, 1972), policy studies looked like an ideal opportunity to combine research practice with social conscience. Researchers would be able to do good while they were doing well.

The uses of evaluation and policy research

Yet by the early 1970s, after about five or six years of relatively large-scale evaluation and policy studies, it was becoming obvious that study results were not having visible impacts on policy decisions. Programmes that evaluators had found relatively ineffective, like the Head Start pre-school programme, were continued and even expanded, programmes that evaluators had found effective, like direct federal loans to low-income college students, were cut back. And much of the detailed advice contained in the 'Recommendations' sections of policy studies reports simply went unheeded. Social scientists who had expected their work to shape future government policy became disillusioned. Not only were they not 'counsellors to the Prince', they were not even influential advisers to the bureau of vocational education. Given their general tendency to turn their experiences into 'findings', they began to contribute articles to the scholarly journals about the non-use and abuse of policy studies. During the 1970s there was a persistent recitation of the non-utilization tale — the resistance of self-serving government agencies to the lessons from research, the ignorance or inattention of legislators, the waste of social science wisdom, and the triumph of bureaucratic routine and special-interest politics.

Recent investigations, however, provide a different interpretation of events. It is true that cases of immediate and direct influence of research findings on specific policy decisions are not frequent. Examples can be found, but they remain relatively uncommon. But to acknowledge this is not the same as saying that research findings have little influence on policy. On the contrary, evidence suggests that evaluation and policy studies have had significant consequences, but not necessarily on discrete provisions nor in the linear sequence that social scientists expected (Weiss and Bucuvalas, 1980).

Rarely does research supply an 'answer' that policy actors employ to solve a policy problem. Rather, research provides a background of data, empirical generalizations and ideas that affect the way that policy-makers think about problems. It influences their conceptualization of the issues with which they deal; affects those facets of the issue they consider inevitable and unchangeable and those they perceive as amenable to policy action; widens the range of options that they con-sider; and challenges some taken-for-granted assumptions about appro-priate goals and appropriate activities. Often it helps them make sense of what they have been doing after the fact, so that they come to under-stand which courses of action have gone by default. Sometimes it makes them aware of the over-optimistic grandiosity of their objectives in light of the meagerness of programme resources. At times it helps them reconsider entire strategies of action for achieving wanted ends (e.g. investment in compensatory education as a means for altering the distribution of income). In sum, policy studies — and social science research more generally — have made significant contributions by altering the terms of policy discussion.

This kind of indirect conceptual contribution is not easy to see. It is not visible to the naked eye. Sometimes it is manifested only over lengthy periods of time and after numbers of studies have yielded convergent results. For example, scores of evaluations were done in rehabilitation programmes for prison inmates, most of which concluded that counselling, education and associated services had little effect in reducing subsequent recidivism. Correctional authorities paid little attention, and efforts at in-prison rehabilitation went on relatively unchanged for a long while. However, the research results percolated through relevant bureaux, agencies and legislative chambers, and in the past few years significant changes have been made. Not only correc-tional practice but also sentencing codes and judicial acts have been affected.

The state of California, for example, used to view correctional institutions as agencies of rehabilitation. Judges sentenced convicted offenders to indeterminate terms of imprisonment, leaving the date of a prisoner's release up to the decision of prison authorities on the basis of the prisoner's progress towards rehabilitation. In 1976, the California legislature officially gave up on rehabilitation. It changed the indeter-minate sentencing law, and provided instead for relatively fixed terms of sentence. The new law began with a statement of change of goals. The preamble, in a marked shift, stated that the purpose of imprisonment is punishment. Prison programmes aiming at rehabilitation continue, although more and more on a voluntary rather than compulsory basis

(Lipson and Peterson, 1980), but the state has absorbed the lessons of evaluation. It has scaled down its expectations of rehabilitation and shifted to a different rationale for incarceration. Research results played a large part in the change (Knott and Wildavsky, 1980).

In similar ways, social science results and social science concepts have had effects in many fields. It is not usually a single finding or the recommendation derived from a single study that is adopted in executive or legislative action (although this occasionally happens). More often, it is the ideas and general notions coming from research which have had an impact. Nor is it usually the particular 'decision-maker' for whom the study was done who uses the findings. Since few decisions in government are made by a single decision-maker or even a small group of decision-makers, and almost no decisions of sufficient scope to qualify for the category of policy, this is not the usual route to influence. Instead, what seems to happen is that generalizations and ideas from numbers of studies come into currency indirectly — through articles in academic journals and journals of opinion, stories in the media, the advice of consultants, lobbying by special interest groups, conversation of colleagues, attendance at conferences or training programmes, and other uncatalogued sources. Ideas from research are picked up in diverse ways and percolate through to office-holders in many offices who deal with the issues.

As the ideas from research filter through, officials test them against the standards of their own knowledge and judgement. They do not uncritically accept every set of conclusions they hear about, even if the conclusions bear the imprimatur of social science. They have many sources of information other than social science, ranging from their own first-hand experience to systematic and unsystematic reports from the field. The extent to which they accept a research idea, or give it at least provisional hearing, depends on the degree to which it resonates with their prior knowledge. If it 'makes sense', if it helps to organize and make sense of their earlier knowledge and impressions, they tend to incorporate it into their stock of knowledge (Weiss with Bucuvalas, 1980b).

This prevalent process of merging research results with other sources of information and ideas has two curious consequences. First, the merger often gives research results extra leverage as they shape officials' understanding of issues. Because research provides powerful labels for previously inchoate and unorganized experience, it helps to mould officials' thinking into categories derived from social science. Think of the policy effects of such category labels as 'externalities', 'aptitude test scores', 'deinstitutionalization', 'white flight' and 'inter-generational dependency'.

Second, because social science is merged with other knowledge, officials are largely unaware of when and how they use research. An investigator going out to study the uses of policy research quickly finds out that respondents have great difficulty disentangling the lessons they have learned from research from their whole configuration of knowledge. They do not catalogue research separately; they do not remember sources and citations. With the best will in the world, all they can usually say is that in the course of their work they hear about a great deal of research and they're sure it affects what they think and do. They can't give specific illustrations of their use of a specific study, because that is not how they work (Caplan et al., 1975; Weiss, 1980).

So if recent investigations of the consequences of research for policy leave us with greater respect for the influence of research, the influence appears to lie in affecting the shape and content of policy discourse rather than concrete choices. The nature of the effect has been called 'enlightenment' (Janowitz, 1970; Crawford and Biderman, 1969). Research modifies the definition of problems that policy-makers address, how they think about them, which options they discard and which they pursue, and how they conceptualize their purposes. For those who had hoped for greater direct influence on policy, it is a limited victory.

Elsewhere I have noted that even in the provisionally optimistic imagery of enlightenment, there lurk some dangers. For one thing, the research that policy actors hear about and come to accept is not necessarily the best, most comprehensive, or most up-to-date research. Sometimes they become aware of shoddy studies, outmoded ideas and unbiased findings. No quality control mechanisms screen the good and relevant from the partial and sensational. The phenomenon that has been discussed as enlightenment may turn out to be, in fact, 'endarkenment' (Weiss with Bucuvalas, 1980a).

Another limitation is that for all the potential power of shifts in policy-makers' awareness and attention, thinking differently is not the same as acting differently. While changed discourse is likely to result — eventually — in new modes of action, the process may be agonizingly slow and inexact. The policy action that finally emerges cannot be expected to correspond closely with the preferred state envisioned by the social scientist.

So much is prologue. The question to which I'd like to turn is why the use of evaluation and other social science research goes through such tortuous processes. Why isn't there more immediate and direct use of research results in the making of policy? Given the fact that government agencies responsible for particular policies sponsor studies with the avowed intent of improving those policies, how come they don't put the results to use directly?

Obviously the answers to this question are multiple and complex.

Some of them have to do with the inconclusiveness of the research. Many, probably most, studies are fragile guides to action, either because of limitations in the research, or the ambiguous nature of the findings, or — often most serious — the problematic relationship between the findings and any clear-cut policy recommendations. To move from data about what *is* to recommendations about what *should be* (and how to get there) usually requires an extensive leap. Researchers who have done a painfully careful evaluation study have been known to throw caution to the winds when they come to drawing implications for action and leap to unanalysed, untested, and perhaps unworkable recommendations. Other reasons for the lack of immediate adoption have to do with the nature of government agencies (e.g., their limited repertoire of available policy responses) and the imperative of policy decisions (e.g., the overriding need to reconcile diverse interests as well as to reach 'right' decisions). But one important reason has received little attention, and it is this reason that I want to talk about — the nature of political decision-making processes.

The nature of policy decision-making
Both the popular and the academic literature picture decision-making as an event; a group of authorized decision-makers assemble at particular times and places, they review a problem (or opportunity), they consider a number of alternative courses of action with more or less explicit calculation of the advantages and disadvantages of each option, they weigh the alternatives against their goals or preferences, and then they select an alternative that seems well suited for achieving their purposes. The result is a decision.[2]

There are five major constructs in this imagery of decision-making. The first is *boundedness*. Decision-making is, in effect, set off from the ongoing stream of organizational activity. It involves a discrete set of actors who occupy authoritative positions, people who are officially responsible for, and empowered to make, decisions for the organization. Decision-making is bounded in *time*, taking place over a relatively short period. It is usually bounded in *location*, with the relevant actors in contact with each other, or able to be in contact with each other, to negotiate the decision. The customary conceptualization of decision-making thus has much in common with the three unities of Greek drama.

A second construct is *purposiveness*. It is commonly assumed that decision-makers have relatively clear goals in view; they want to bring about a desired end-state or avoid an undesired state. Since Simon's (1947) seminal work, it has become accepted that decision-makers do not try to optimize decisions, but rather 'satisfice' (i.e. settle for something 'good enough'). Nevertheless, they are expected to have overt criteria for what is good enough and to seek a decision that promises progress toward attaining their purposes.

The third construct is *calculation*. Decision-makers are expected to generate (or have generated for them) a set of alternatives. In the past decades, scholars have recognized that no comprehensive set of alternatives is developed; limits on human abilities of cognitive processing preclude a complete canvass of options. But in the going imagery, decision-makers consider the costs and benefits of a variety of responses. Their calculation will often be informal and intuitive rather than systematic, as they proceed on the basis of experience, informed judgement, or gut feeling. Their goals need not represent only properly respectable public objectives, but will usually include such unexpressed aims as bureaucratic advantage, career interests and the furtherance of electoral chances. But however mixed the objectives and however informal the assessment procedures may be, it is assumed that decision-makers weigh the relative advantages of several alternatives against their goals and their formulation of desired end-states. The alternative that registers an acceptable balance of costs and benefits will be selected. Scholars have lowered their expectations for the rationality of the calculus employed, and they have tempered their assumptions of systematic and methodological assessment of trade-offs, but they retain belief that a process of calculation takes place.

Fourth, implicit in the concept of decision-making is a construct of *perceived significance*. A decision marks a step of some moment. People who make the decision perceive the act as consequential (i.e. having consequences). When the decision involves 'policy', whichever of the many meanings are invested in the term 'policy' (Heclo, 1972), the connotations of far-reaching importance are underscored, and a 'policy decision' is doubly endowed with intimations of significance. People who make a policy decision are viewed as self-consciously aware of registering a decisive commitment to an important course of action. Scholars have noted that some decisions involve a choice to do nothing, to leave the situation unchanged (e.g. Bachrach and Baratz, 1963). Yet even when this is the case, the choice is expected to represent a matter of consequence to those who make the decision.

Finally, there is an assumption of *sequential order*. The sequence is regarded as beginning with recognition of a problem. It proceeds to the development and consideration of alternative means for coping with the problem,[3] goes next to assessment of the relative advantages of the alternatives and ends with selection of a decision.

These five constructs — boundedness, purposiveness, calculation, perceived significance and sequential order — underlie most images of decision-making. And they capture essential elements of much of the decision-making that goes on at bureau, division and department levels, in executive agencies and legislatures, and in private and public organizations. Allison's (1971) account of the 'essence of decision' by President Kennedy and his small group of advisers considering the American response to the Cuban missile crisis is an archetypical decision of this kind. Similarly, a university deciding whether or not to construct a new building, the US Congress debating passage of tax-cutting legislation, an executive agency developing proposals for change in eligibility requirements for federal aid — all go through a process that may be well represented by these constructs.

Yet many policy decisions emerge through processes that bear little relationship to these descriptors. Much decision-making differs from the traditional model because one or more of the five characteristics is low or even absent. Policies, even policies of fateful magnitude, often take shape through jumbled and diffuse processes that differ in vital ways from the conventional imagery.

Government is a continuous bustle of activity, with people in many offices bumping up against problems, new conditions, discrepant rules, unprecedented requests for service and the promulgations of other offices. In coping with their daily work, people in many places take small steps, without conscious awareness that their actions are pushing policy down certain paths and foreclosing other responses. They do not necessarily perceive themselves as making — or even influencing — policy, but their many small steps (writing position papers, drafting regulations, answering inquiries, making plans, releasing news bulletins) may fuse, coalesce and harden. Over time, the congeries of small acts can set the direction, and the limits, of government policy. Only in retrospect do people become aware that policy was made.

While the people who engage in incremental adaptations are not necessarily conscious of participating in policy-making, officials at the top echelon may be equally convinced that they are not making decisions. From the top, it often looks as though they are presented with a *fait accompli*. Accommodations have been reached and a decision negotiated by people in the warren of offices below, and they have little option but accept. Only rarely, and with the expenditure of a considerable amount of their political capital, can they change or reject the advice they are offered. To them, the job often looks like rubber-stamping decisions already made.

Even in legislatures, the quintessential locus of decision-making, individual legislators have limited options. In the United States, committees receive drafts of complex legislative bills from the executive agencies. Committee staffs may identify controversial points in the light of legislators' general preferences and work out accommodations with agency staffs. From time to time, particularly interested and influential legislators get particular provisions added, amended or deleted. But when the lengthy bills come up for vote, no individual legislator can be familiar with more than a handful of provisions. By and large, he or she must either vote against the entire bill or accept it. To the participants, their own influence on policy often looks marginal.

Given the fragmentation of authority across multiple bureaux, departments and legislative committees, and the disjointed stages by which actions coalesce into decisions, the traditional model of decision-making is a highly stylized rendition of reality. Identification of any clear-cut group of decision-makers can be difficult. (Sometimes a middle-level bureaucrat had taken the key action, although unaware that the action was going to be — or was — decisive.) The goals of policy are often equally diffuse, except in terms of taking care of some undesirable situation. Which options are considered, and which sets of advantages and disadvantages are assessed, may be impossible to tell in the interactive, multi-participative, diffuse processes of formulating policy. The complexity of government policy-making often defies neat compartmentalization.

Alternative routes to policy

Yet policies do get made. If government often proceeds to decisions without bounded, purposeful, sequential acts of perceived significance, how do decisions emerge? Some of the undirected strategies appear to be these.

1. Reliance on custom and implicit rules. Officials do what the agency has traditionally done. Even if a situation is unprecedented, officials may interpret it to fall within customary procedures. In doing so, they in effect make new policy by subsuming the novel contingency within a familiar rubric.

2. Improvisation. Another tactic is to improvise. Confronted with an unanticipated situation, officials may exercise their ingenuity, stretching a point here, combining a few tried and true procedures there, adding a dash of novelty, much like a chef concocting a new recipe. Through impromptu accommodation, an agency may begin to fashion new policy.

3. Mutual adjustment. As Lindblom (1965) has indicated, office-holders who lack any sense of common purpose ('partisans' in his term) may reach desisions by simply adapting to decisions made around them. If one office has invoked convention or made improvisations, other offices can adjust their actions to accommodate to the situation.

4. Accretion. Once officials have extemporized under the press of events, or adapted to actions taken in other offices, they may repeat the procedures when similar — or even not so similar — situations recur. The first responses provide a precedent and, if they seem to work, they will be followed again. Over time, when numbers of cases have been handled in like fashion, or when several different contingencies have been adopted to deal with an array of exceptional circumstances, they may coalesce and rigidify. Like skeletons of millions of tiny sea creatures building up into giant coral reefs, the result can become fixed.

5. *Negotiation.* When authority is fragmented and agencies have over-lapping and discrepant mandates, overt conflicts may arise. Many are settled by direct negotiation among the interested units. Threats and promises, discussion and debate on the issues, trade-offs of advantage and obligation — these are the currency of bargaining. The aim is less to reach a rational decision in the usual sense than to work out an arrangement that will at least minimally satisfy the key interests of each of the parties. Through processes long familiar in the Congress (log-rolling, horse trading), a bargain is arranged.

6. *Move and counter-move.* If bargaining breaks down, an agency may take a unilateral move to advance its position. Other affected agencies counter with moves of their own. This kind of antagonistic adjustment is particularly likely when present policies leave some new policy territory unclaimed (cf. agencies' scramble to move into the field of 'children's policy' during the Carter administration). The series of competitive moves may continue until mutual adjustment reaches stalemate, or until resolution is shifted up to higher levels. Move and counter-move is an accustomed mode of decision in international relations.

7. *A window for solutions.* Not infrequently, the solution precedes the identification of the problem. In fact, it can be argued that unless a plausible solution is envisioned, the issue will not be identified as a problem. It will be considered a 'condition' that has to be endured, like death, the weather and (for many centuries) poverty. Officials become wedded to pet remedies and they seek opportunities to implement these remedies. One group may want to install a computer system, and they engage in a search for places and occasions that would justify its intro-duction. Another group may be wedded to the idea of deregulation as an all-purpose panacea and scour the federal system for areas amenable to regulatory roll-back. These are cases where the solution is in hand, and partisans actively seek a 'window' that will provide an opening for their ready-made nostrum.

8. *Indirection.* Another route by which policy emerges is as a by-product of other decisions. In this case, policy outcomes are unintended, but because of decisions made to achieve other desired ends, they nevertheless come about. Federal guarantees of home mortgages, under-taken after World War II to help families purchase their own homes, led to an exodus from city centres and the massive growth of suburbs. Federal aid to education, designed to improve the quality of education particularly for disadvantaged and low-achieving students, has led to some shift of authority over educational practice from local to state and

federal education agencies. No decisions were consciously made to create such shifts, but they emerged by indirection.

This list of non-decisional processes that produce policy outcomes is probably not exhaustive. Nevertheless, it indicates a variety of ways in which major outputs can issue from government without considered review or rational assessment. In time, ad hoc agency actions may have to be formalized by legislation. But often the early response is decisive and legislative action merely ratifies the decisions that have already emerged. At some periods and in some areas it is only a slight exaggeration to say that ratification of the status quo, and allocation of funds to support it, is a main function of legislation.

The place of research

If government policy can 'happen' without a set piece of formal decision-making, how does policy research get a hearing? When decisions take shape over long periods of time, through the incremental actions of multiple actors, and often without participants' awareness that they are shaping decisions, the opportunity for formal consideration of research information looks distinctly limited. In such situations, research data on constituents' needs, the benefits and costs of policies, and the effectiveness and shortcomings of programmes seem to have little chance for impact.

Yet one of the interesting facets of the situation, verified repeatedly in empirical investigation and borne out by the record, is that United States officials value social science research. They say that it is important and useful, and they sponsor large numbers of studies. If opportunities to use research results as a guide to policy are limited by the diffuse processes of government decision-making, there must be other purposes that research serves. It seems important to identify them.

One possible reason for officials' allegiance to research, we can conjecture, is that research serves as a device of control. In a federal system, federal agencies set policy and allocate resources but local agencies deliver direct services. With day-to-day control of education, health services and welfare in local hands, there can be a wide gap between federal intent and local performance. Only when the federal agency has good information about what local services are doing — their structure, the processes of service delivery, and the outcomes for clients — can it begin to exercise the authority that rule-making and resource allocation allow. Evaluation and policy studies can become the mechanism by which federal agencies keep informed.

Federal education officials, intent on ensuring compliance with federal purpose, can find out whether local school districts are actually spending funds provided under Title 1 of the Elementary and Secondary Education Act to enrich educational opportunities for low-income and low-achieving students. Federal health officials can find out the extent to which neighbourhood health centres improve the health status of low-income clienteles. If local agencies are found to be performing poorly, the federal agency can institute stricter controls over recipient agencies, tightening up rules and even terminating particular local grants. Research results may become the basis for control, and the mere decision to undertake research can serve as an implicit threat that stricter control is impending. The United States Congress sometimes seems to write evaluation provisions into legislation for just this kind of purpose — to serve notice on agencies that it will have the capability to review the effectiveness of their operations — even if it never does.

Another possible purpose that policy research can serve is to provide support and vindication for current policies. Federal officials often expect research to justify at least some of their claims — that large numbers of people are in need of their services, that programmes do some good, and that constituents like the attention and want services to continue. Even an evaluation showing little direct benefit to clients will often yield some positive evidence of this kind. The agency can use findings selectively to buttress its case for legislative reauthorization and additional funding.

A third possibility is that decision-makers support research because the use of objective information is one of the hallmarks of rationality. They go through the motions of commissioning studies and searching for evidence in order to lay claim to the mantle of intelligent choice. In effect, they seek to demonstrate the quality of their decisions, in situations where criteria for 'quality' are highly ambiguous, by appropriate performance of the rituals of information processing. As Feldman and March note:

> Command of information and information sources enhances perceived competence and inspires confidence ... A good decision-maker is one who makes decisions in the way a good decision-maker does, and decision-makers and organizations establish their legitimacy by their use of information. (Feldman and March, 1981:177–8)

There may be high symbolic value in requesting research and justifying decisions on evidential grounds. Even when the actual linkage between research input and policy output is weak, political actors can signal their commitment to the ideology of rational choice by taking an appropriate posture regarding research. In this way, they seek to bolster their reputation for intelligent and unbiased decision-making.

If these reasons for continued sponsorship of policy research seem unduly sceptical, a fourth basis can be advanced. It is possible that federal officials support research because they recognize that every agency, even the most progressive, tends to grow musty and stale. It settles into a rut, taking old assumptions for granted, substituting routine for thought, tinkering at best with policy minutiae rather than venturing in new directions. To overcome hardening of organizational arteries, they may welcome the fresh insights and critical perspectives that good research brings. By subjecting conventional practice to evaluation, they may seek to help the agency renew its sense of mission and adapt to changing conditions.

One may hope that some part of the reason for high levels of research support comes from motives of this latter sort. But even if the thrust for evaluation and policy studies springs from less high-minded sources, even if it is the result of adversarial forces (department heads checking up on the performance of bureaux, the Congress checking up on departments, agencies seeking legitimation for their programmes), even if it represents only rhetorical commitment to the norms of accountability and rational procedure, even then it has consequences. The regularized practice of evaluation and analysis has become embedded in government structures. Offices of research and evaluation exist at the bureau, division and department level in many federal agencies. Their professional staffs do what evaluation and analysis staffs know how to do — continue and expand the flow of research information to the agency. Even the United States General Accounting Office, which used to serve the Congress only as financial auditor, now has its Institute of Program Evaluation. As procedures develop to transmit the results of policy studies routinely to officials throughout government, an important mechanism for learning becomes institutionalized.

The importance of the inclusion of evaluation and analysis units in departmental structures should not be underestimated. They are institutionalized mechanisms for collecting, sponsoring, synthesizing and disseminating research and evaluation information. The informational function that they represent is embedded not only in the agency's table of organization but also in procedures, the flow of paper, and the division and co-ordination of work. Members of evaluation and analysis units sit on agency committees that discuss present programmes and future policy; they prepare position papers and option statements, marshalling the evidence for and against specific proposals; their reports and analyses circulate to key officials and are discussed in meetings; and their comments — and in some cases, their approval and sign-off — are built into the processes of agency work.

In many ways, the incorporation of evaluation and analysis units into agency structures represents an organizational commitment to the use of information. The knowledge that they provide goes beyond the level of *individual* learning. It is not only individuals here and there in the agency who become enlightened by the results of evaluation studies. The evaluation process is embedded in the procedures and routines, in the *dailiness*, of agency work. It represents a mechanism for organizational learning.

The view from outside

Outside researchers who engage in policy-oriented studies under government sponsorship are often disillusioned by their experience. They rarely see the slow and indirect uses of their research that I have been describing, or the learnings that accrue to government agencies as research findings wend their way through bureaucratic channels. They are much more aware of the *absence* of dramatic response in the short term. This is probably particularly true for researchers in universities who undertake evaluation and policy studies with the expectation of making an immediate contribution to policy-making. They see that the research is done and then nothing much seems to change.

The message of this paper is: don't leap to the conclusion that research is ignored. The expectation of direct and immediate policy effects from research is frequently unrealistic. Since policy decisions often accrete through multiple disjointed steps (and for other reasons as well), looking for blockbuster impact from research results represents a misreading of the nature of policy-making. If you stay around long enough — and close enough to the decision apparatus — you are better able to gauge the real consequences. It may still turn out that research leaves few ripples behind, but it is premature to make that judgement without a long-term and close-up view of the issue arena.

Are there some things that researchers can do to facilitate the use of their research? After all, shouldn't the policy process, however diffuse, accommodate the more accurate description of conditions and incisive analysis of events that research at its best provides? Those of us who hanker for rationality look for strategems that will enhance the power of research as a basis for policy decisions.

In the local case, there are undoubtedly acts that can lead participants in decision-making to pay greater attention to research. The literature is replete with admonitions: locate the potential users of research in advance, understand which policy variables they have the authority to change, concentrate the study on the feasible (manipulable) variables, involve the potential users in the research process, establish a relationship of trust, demonstrate awareness of the constraints that limit their options, report promptly, provide practical recommendations, write results clearly and simply, and communicate results in person. All of these prescriptions are directed at influencing one decision-maker, or a small group of decision-makers, to use research in making a direct, concrete, immediate choice.

While one or another of these precepts, or all of them combined, may indeed pay off in increased consideration of research conclusions, they provide no guarantee that even in a small hierarchical organization research will carry the day. Officials are not blank pages on to which research transfers truth. Officials have their own body of information, their career interests at stake, their patterned assumptions and ideological positions growing out of the sum of their life experiences. While they can usually be induced — through the nurturance of good relationships and the logic of scientifically reputable analysis — to attend to the evidence that research produces, they will not automatically cast aside all other influences and embrace the researchers' conclusions.

Nor do researchers always want to abide by the restrictions embedded in the traditional prescriptions for influence. To accept officials' formulation of the problem or to limit the study to alternatives that are politically and organizationally feasible often represents undue constraint on the scope and focus of investigation. Studies too tightly tied to current operating 'realities' rapidly become obsolete. If they lose their one shot at immediate application, they have little left to say.

Finally, it is as well to acknowledge the limits of social science research. Policy studies address a small sub-set of the issues involved in any decision of moment. They inevitably omit a variety of factors that responsible officials have to take into account, such as the reaction of constituency groups, budgetary implications and contests over programme turf. Policy studies, too, are shaped by implicit value assumptions. They do not represent mirror images of some reality 'out there'. As Merton (1968) has noted, data are not 'given' but created. Which variables are considered, how they are conceptualized and measured, and the completeness of the explanatory model, all influence the nature of the results.

Moreover, different investigators studying the same phenomena often come up with divergent, even conflicting, conclusions, and even well-accepted research generalizations can be undermined over time as the sweep of contemporary events overtakes and discredits them. The claims of social science studies to the status of eternal truth are tenuous indeed. Participants in decision-making view the study results critically not only because they are self-seeking or poorly informed or prey to pressure groups (although they may sometimes be all of these things), but also because careful scrutiny is a responsible act.

Decision accretion and knowledge creep
If all of these factors can limit the influence of policy studies in a small localized agency, the distractions are far greater at more rarified levels of policy-making. A significant feature of the policy process, as we have noted, is the diffuse manner in which decisions often accrete. When policy seems to 'happen' without synoptic review and rational choice,

few occasions exist for careful review of relevant policy research. Officials respond to situations by hunch and experience, drawing on whatever mix of knowledge — and of course much else besides knowledge — that they have on hand.

But there are ways other than formal review of study reports by which research gets a hearing. Officials absorb a great deal of research knowledge through informal routes. They read widely, go to meetings, listen to people, discuss with colleagues — all without necessarily having a particular decision in mind. Research information and ideas filter into their awareness, whether or not they label it research as they absorb it. This diffuse process of enlightenment contributes to their stock of knowledge. When they engage in a stream of activities that aggregate into policy, they draw upon the knowledge that they have gathered from a variety of sources, including research, and apply it to their work.

The diffuse process of research use that we are calling 'enlightenment' is highly compatible with the diffuse processes of policy-making. It informs the work of many policy actors in many locations as they perform their bits and pieces of policy work. Unlike the usual notion of a single research sponsor who acquires a directed set of findings for a particular decisional purpose, it does not suggest a monopoly on research knowledge by the bureaucrat who funds the study. Many different people, with different interests and ideologies, inside and outside government, can be enlightened by research, and they can exercise their knowledge at many points, co-operatively or adversarially, as policy takes shape.

Of course, the enlightenment image represents no ideal model. When research comes to people's attention haphazardly, the process is unorganized, slow, wasteful and sloppy. Some policy actors may fail to hear about relevant research; others may fail to take the research they hear about seriously. Some people may become enchanted with catchy, faddish, irrelevant, obsolete, partial or invalid findings, or latch on to only the sub-set of findings that supports their predispositions and policy interests. The whole process reeks of over-simplification. People tend to forget the complexities and qualifications and remember the slogans ('the poverty programme failed', or 'a guaranteed income leads to little reduction in work effort'). Diffuse enlightenment is no substitute for careful, directed analysis of the policy implications of research. Ways still have to be found — and used — to improve targeted applications of targeted research as well.

Nevertheless, the fit between the diffuse processes of policy-making and officials' diffuse absorption of research is noteworthy. It seems to represent one of the most important contributions that social science makes to public policy. The ideas derived from research provide organizing perspectives that help people make sense of experience.

These ideas offer frameworks within which problems are interpreted and policy actions considered. Retrospectively, they help people understand what government has been doing and what the consequences have been. Prospectively, they help raise the possibility of alternative courses of action. Perhaps most valuable of all, research can be a medium of criticism. Subjecting old assumptions to empirical tests and introducing alternative perspectives are vital contributions. Even when officials themselves have suspected policy shortcomings or negative side effects, research crystallizes the suspicions and makes them visible to others; the review of research results provides an occasion for mapping new responses. Of course, specific findings may be questioned, and the implications that researchers single out for attention may not be accepted. Research cannot be expected to prevail over all contending influences. Yet even in cases where officials dispute the particulars, they often find themselves using the concepts and frameworks of the research to reconsider accustomed practice.

To the extent that such contributions to the public arena are important, they suggest different lessons to policy researchers from those associated with direct research application. Concern about pleasing — or at least satisfying — the immediate client is secondary when dozens of other actors will affect the shape of policy. Being practical and timely and keeping the study within feasible boundaries may be unimportant, or even counter-productive. If the research is not completed in time for this year's budget cycle, it is probably no great loss. The same issues, if they are important, will come up again and again. Keeping the study within the accepted constraints of one set of actors will often imply irrelevance to the concerns of other sets of policy actors. In the enlightenment tradition, the research is well advised to broaden the scope of the question and take time to do quality research.

Other scholars have noted that research contributes to the policy process in ways far different from the traditional 'rational' image, and they have urged that its realistic potential for influence should be exploited. Lindblom wrote years ago about the use of policy analysis in government:

> Policy is analysed not in an unrealistic attempt to reach conclusive determinations of correct policy, but simply to persuade. (Lindblom, 1968:117)

More recently, Cronbach and associates wrote about programme evaluations:

> Instead of promoting single definitive studies that promise unquestionable guidance on a narrow issue of policy, evaluations should be contributing to the slow, continuous, cumulative understanding of a problem or an intervention ... What is needed is information that will facilitate negoti-

ation of a compromise rather than information that can be cranked into a decision rule. (Cronbach et al., 1980: 47, 116)

In fact, this lesson may be the most important implication from the recent studies of the uses of social science research in decision-making. Researchers need to be aware that the work they do, no matter how applied in intent and how practical in orientation, is not likely to have major influence on the policy decision at which it is purportedly directed — at least not if policy actors' interests and ideologies are engaged. Adherence to all the traditional strictures — acceptance of decision-makers' constraints, focus on manipulative variables, timeliness, jargon-free communication, and the like — seems to increase the actual application of research results only marginally. Of course, improvement at the margin can sometimes be significant. But when competing with other powerful factors, such as officials' concern with political or bureaucratic advantage, one limited study (and all studies are limited in some way) is likely to have limited impact.

On the other hand, the stream of social science research has consequences. The generalizations, the *ideas*, that emerge from social science research help to shape the assumptions on which policy is based. Ill-conceived and slipshod research will yield conclusions of questionable value; quick and dirty ad hoc studies, which cut methodological corners in order to meet an arbitrary deadline or satisfy an impatient client, are more likely to muddy than to clarify the issues. To serve the longer-term policy needs of officials, research should be grounded in relevant theory and existing knowledge; it should look at issues comprehensively in all their multivariate complexity; it should be done with the greatest methodological skill that advances in research and analytic techniques have made possible.

Basic research

Prescriptions such as these sound suspiciously like a return to business-as-usual for social scientists. To ground research in theory, to conceptualize problems broadly, to use sophisticated methods of study — these are the hallmarks of basic, rather than applied, research. Does our analysis of 'knowledge creep' lead to advice that social scientists go back to doing the kind of research that most of them prefer to do anyway? Can basic research be expected to have as great an impact on public decision-making as research undertaken specifically to answer decision-makers' questions?

From a study of the use of fifty mental health studies by US federal, state and local decision-makers, I have unpublished data that bear on this question. All the studies in our inquiry were funded by the National Institute of Mental Health, so they had to promise some modicum of applicability to policy or practice in order to receive federal funding. However, thirteen of the fifty studies were requested by the Institute in order to address specific questions framed by government officials. The government issued a request for proposals outlining the type of study desired, officials selected the winning bidder, and the study was funded by contract. The other thirty-seven studies were initiated by researchers on issues of their own formulation; peer review committees composed of non-governmental scientists approved the proposals; the studies were funded by grants.

We collected measures of the usefulness of the fifty studies from 155 mental health officials in high-ranking federal and state positions and in top positions in local care-giving institutions. At least six decision-makers rated each study. Thus, we can compare the mean usefulness ratings given to practically-oriented research funded under contract with the ratings accorded to studies with a more basic orientation initiated by researchers and funded by grants.

The data show that differences are small. The contract studies received somewhat higher ratings on usefulness than studies funded by grants, but the differences did not reach statistical significance. This dimension was nowhere so important as the quality of the research. Studies that were rated high on methodological quality were judged significantly more useful by decision-makers (Weiss with Bucuvalas, 1980).

Basic research can be as useful to decision-makers as studies specifically designed to provide direction. Yet the fact that contract studies had a small edge in this sample of studies should sound an alert. Research has to address issues that policy-makers care about. It has to be relevant to the institutional structures and the cultural themes that order the making of policy. It has to take account of the contour of social discourse. When the substance of the research deals with relevant issues, policy-makers can often gain significant insight from basic research.

Reprise
This is not a call for retreat to the ivory tower. It is not a surrender to the preoccupations of the academic disciplines. Nor is it a plea for studies that go on year after endless year without reaching conclusions. Researchers must recognize that decision-makers cannot wait for certainty and authoritativeness (which social science may, in fact, never be able to provide), but have to proceed on the basis of the best knowledge available at the time. Nor do I want to suggest that researchers abandon all commissioned studies or all efforts to serve specific decisional needs. Some government-defined policy studies have been and no doubt will continue to be highly influential.

234   *The use and abuse of social science*

The key point is that social scientists have a responsibility to convince government agencies to allow them the opportunity to do the best social science of which they are capable. The critical ingredients are independence of thought, conceptual sophistication, understanding of policy issues and methodological rigour. And when research has produced something worth saying, researchers have a responsibility to make serious efforts through many channels to get its message heard by the multiple participants in policy-making.

Notes

This chapter is based on the article 'Policy Research in the Context of Diffuse Decision Making', *Journal of Higher Education*, 1982 (53):619–40.

1. I thank Harry Levit for suggesting this metaphor.
2. There was a time when the characterization of decision-making was considerably crisper than this. In what is commonly referred to as the rational model, several additional assumptions were made (e.g. explicit goals consensually weighted, generation of all possible alternatives, explicit calculation of all costs and benefits for each option and selection of the optimal option). Scholars from the several disciplines engaged with decision-making have been chipping away at the formulation for over a generation in the light of actual organizational behaviour. The statement above is what generally remains.
3. Despite the ubiquity of the phrase 'problem solving', most people understand that current-day government problems are rarely 'solved' once and for all, or even for long periods of time. Any solution is temporary, as likely to generate new problems as to remove the condition that it is intended to solve. And many problems, such as poverty or insufficient oil resources, are so deep-rooted and intractable that government action can at best make modest inroads. Therefore, I have selected the word 'coping' rather than 'solving' to characterize the kinds of alternatives that officials consider.

References

Allison, G.T. (1971) *Essence of Decision: Explaining the Cuban Missile Crisis.* Boston: Little, Brown.
Bachrach, P. and M.S. Baratz (1963) 'Decisions and Nondecisions: An Analytic Framework', *American Political Science Review*, 57:632–42.
Caplan, N., A. Morrison and R.J. Stambaugh (1975) *The Use of Social Science Knowledge in Policy Decisions at the National Level.* Ann Arbor: Institute for Social Research.
Crawford, E.T. and A.D. Biderman (eds) (1969) *Social Scientists and International Affairs.* New York: John Wiley.
Cronbach, L.J. and Associates (1980) *Toward Reform of Program Evaluation: Aims, Methods, and Institutional Arrangements.* San Francisco: Jossey-Bass.
Dye, T.R. (1972) 'Policy Analysis and Political Science: Some Problems at the Interface', *Policy Studies Journal*, 1:103–107.
Feldman, M.S. and J.G. March (1981) 'Information in Organizations as Signal and Symbol', *Administrative Science Quarterly*, 26:171–86.
Gouldner, A.W. (1970) *The Coming Crisis in Western Sociology.* New York: Basic Books.

Heclo, H.H. (1972) 'Review Article: Policy Analysis', *British Journal of Political Science*, 2:83–108.

Janowitz, M. (1970) 'Sociological Models and Social Policy', pp. 243–59 in M. Janowitz, *Political Conflict: Essays in Political Sociology.* Chicago: Quadrangle.

Kingdon, John W. (1984) *Agendas, Alternatives, and Public Policies.* Boston: Little, Brown.

Knott, J. and A. Wildavsky (1980) 'If Dissemination is the Solution, What is the Problem?' *Knowledge: Creation, Diffusion, Utilization*, 1 (June):537–78.

Lindblom, C.E. (1965) *The Intelligence of Democracy.* New York: Free Press.

Lindblom, C.E. (1968) *The Policy Making Process.* Englewood Cliffs, NJ: Prentice-Hall.

Lipson, A. and M. Peterson (1980) *California Justice Under Determinate Sentencing: A Review and Agenda for Research.* Santa Monica: Rand Corporation.

Merton, R.K. (1968) *Social Theory and Social Structure.* New York: Free Press.

Simon, H.A. (1947) *Administrative Behavior.* New York: Free Press.

Weiss, C.H. (1980) 'Knowledge Creep and Decision Accretion', *Knowledge: Creation, Diffusion, Utilization*, 1:381–404.

Weiss, C.H. and M.J. Bucuvalas (1980) 'Truth Tests and Utility Tests: Decision Makers' Frames of Reference for Social Science Research', *American Sociological Review*, 45 (April):302–13.

Weiss, C.H. with M.J. Bucuvalas (1980) *Social Science Research and Decision-Making.* New York: Columbia University Press.

16
What's the use of social science?
A review of the literature

Roger S. Karapin

Every day, hundreds of thousands of social scientists go to work. Meanwhile, most of the rest of the world believes that social science is frivolous and useless. More to the point, even those in government and business who sometimes hope to use research frequently complain that social science is irrelevant, incomprehensible or of low quality. Researchers are usually unable to cite specific instances of their work being used.

Social scientists are frustrated that their work is not used as they think it should be, and dismayed that they do not share the social esteem of natural scientists. Sometimes this situation may endanger research funds. With their economies in trouble, nations like the US and Britain have begun to decide that social science is an expendable luxury. As a result, the 'under-utilization' of research has received a surge of new attention, although the field has already had citations increase fifty-fold in the twenty years preceding 1976 (Human Interaction Research Institute, 1976: vii).

This chapter reviews some of the recent literature on the uses of social science research. It is selective, attempting to include and emphasize the most important, penetrating and widely relevant contributions to the field. Some of them approach the subject in general, while others address, or at least draw on the experience of, action research, evaluation research and organizational behaviour.

To start with, this field is still groping to define its central terms. If no one knows exactly what 'utilization'[1] looks like, how can anyone be sure that there is too little of it? There are probably many different kinds of 'utilization' and of 'social science research'.

Research can be usefully categorized according to how theoretical or empirical it is, how general its findings are, to what extent researchers intervene to promote the use of their findings, or what kinds of institutions are sponsors and audiences, e.g. academic, business and government.

However, most writers act as if these differences did not bear on utilization questions. They often write of 'research' in the aggregate, although most of their examples may come from a particular area such as policy analysis. Even the field's central term 'utilization', is usually not explicitly defined. The few times when it is, notably in making the distinction between 'instrumental' and 'conceptual' utilization, the definitions are problematic and incompletely operationalized. These definitional failures, which will be discussed in parts 1 and 6, are serious obstacles to studying the field and solving utilization problems.

An equally serious problem is the amount and type of evidence cited by the authors in support of their arguments. Most of them rely on anecdotes or their personal experience with research utilization. The few existing empirical studies are very limited in scope. Very few researchers in this field have used advanced research methods for studying organizational decision-making, the content of social science research or cases of potential research utilization. Without good evidence to support them, most of these writers' stated conclusions are more like hypotheses which have yet to be tested, and which it is unclear how to test.

As hypotheses about why utilization does not happen, the writers' main themes fall into several categories, including: positivism in social science, the separation of theory and observation, the nature of collaborative relationships, and political influences on research. These themes overlap and many authors use more than one in the same or different works. They provide a rough guide to the diversity of speculation which largely constitutes the field today.

The first of this chapter's six main parts presents some attempts to define and measure utilization. Part 2 deals with positivism as a block to utilization and Part 3 with the split between theoretical and empirical research. A need for collaboration is posited by both action researchers and evaluation reseachers, who occupy parts 4 and 5 respectively. The writers in part 6 focus on how politics and policy-making shape the biases and uses of social science.

1. Definitions and measures of utilization

A previous review[2] of the literature on research utilization (Larsen, 1981) complains that many different definitions of the term abound, it is often not clear what an author means and this results in confusion. Another review, by Laura C. Leviton and Edward F. Hughes (1981)[3] tries to offer some help. They propose that any instance of utilization must meet two 'bottom-line' criteria. First, the policy implications of the research must be made clear; second, the research must make a difference to the thoughts or actions of those who make policy. This distinguishes utilization from what they call 'impact', in which research influences a modification in a programme or policy, and from 'utility', which refers to the relevance of the research to an area of policy. They identify three types of utilization which meet the bottom-line criteria and can be observed. 'Instrumental' use is of a particular piece of research to make a specific decision, in a way that can be documented. 'Conceptual' use occurs when research affects the thinking of policy-makers, for example their attitudes, arguments or level of certainty about a question. 'Persuasive' use involves using research to try to convince others of a political position (Leviton and Hughes, 1981).

According to Leviton and Hughes, most empirical work uses case studies or interviews with selected policy-makers, but the nature of utilization makes it difficult to detect by these means. Problems include time lapses between research and use, the highly informal character of much utilization, and the lack of a base rate for comparisons. The authors neither suggest how to deal with these problems, nor provide any indicators or measures for their own definitions.

There is also considerable ambiguity about their concept of persuasive use. For this really to be a case of utilization, the research must be discussed seriously (Leviton and Hughes, 1981), but it is hard to see how to distinguish a case where it is from one where social science is used cynically, to 'legitimate' a political position. The definition of 'instrumental' utilization also suffers from ambiguity, since policy-makers may document their 'use' of research in order to justify or legitimate decisions on which the research has no effect.

'Conceptual' utilization presents the greatest dangers, however. The definition does not distinguish between policy-makers' thinking which affects their organizational tasks and that which does not. In the absence of any way of measuring it, the definition is very vague and tends to exclude the important possibility that research is not utilized at all. The significance of one kind of conceptual utilization, i.e. the adoption of social science terms by policy-makers, is criticized by several authors in part 6.

These deficiencies notwithstanding, the instrumental/conceptual distinction seems to be the state of the art of defining utilization, and a recent international conference held in the Netherlands (Kallen et al., 1982) used it heavily. Henk C. Wagenaar's (1982) paper introduced the International Workshop on Educational Research and Public Policy-making and drew on the pre-submitted contributions. He describes how a boom in Dutch education research led to disappointment that it was not being used. The government then insisted that the research be designed closer to its specifications, but this did not increase utilization. The government's view is that policy-makers define problems and social science provides the missing information or knowledge needed to solve them. Wagenaar attacks this 'engineering' or linear problem-solving model as inadequate for understanding either social science or the making of policy. Social science facts are really based in theory, there is little consensus about theories, and all scientific knowledge is inherently uncertain. Government decision-making is never fully rational, decisions are shared among policy-makers and made incrementally, and both programmes and traditions help shape policy. Wagenaar believes that social science's real contribution to policy lies in the provision not of facts but of theory. He advocates a conceptual model of utilization. Wagenaar also favours research on how policy affects social science; most, so far, have been looking for the opposite effect (Wagenaar, 1982).

Nathan Caplan's (1982) paper at this workshop tried to steer participants towards the idea of conceptual utilization. He points out that recent research in this field has made social scientists more conscious of utilization without increasing it much. It is popular to describe a 'gap' between researchers and users and to suggest 'linkages'. But the approach is not very helpful. Defining the audience for research is one problem. Another is presented by the example of Finland, where no gap can be found and neither can much utilization. Gap-filling must in any case be ad hoc, not based on univeral rules. Caplan suggests that it would be more profitable to look at the nature of utilization.

In Caplan's (1980)[4] study of 204 US government administrators, he divides their 575 reported instances of utilization into instrumental and conceptual categories. There is good linkage in instrumental cases, where problems are narrow in scope, but Caplan sees two drawbacks: policy-makers may miss the wider implications of the research and the instrumental model is misleading for looking at larger-scale decisions and at other types of utilization (Caplan, 1982). When decisions affect the entire nation, research becomes merely one of many information sources which affect thinking. In such conceptual utilization, general (or 'soft') social science knowledge is more important than 'hard' specialized research. 'Social science knowledge is used like the news' (Caplan, 1982: 184). Soft knowledge acts to change the over-all orientation of policy, so it is difficult to trace specific effects. Further, knowledge has a life cycle and time lags are likely if organizational politics require ideas to be 're-invented' or 'bureaucratized'. The kind of input-output model used to study instrumental utilization is poor for understanding conceptual utilization (Caplan, 1982).

Other empirical studies included in Carol H. Weiss (1977) follow designs and reach conclusions broadly similar to Caplan's. For example, Robert F. Rich's (1977) limited study of the US government reports some conceptual utilization of certain pieces of opinion research.

2. Positivism in social science

Running through much of the literature is dissatisfaction with not only

the utilization of social science but also the (social science) understanding of the situation. Theories which focus on the shortcomings of
social science offer to explain both problems. Some see 'positivism' as a
barrier to both utilization and an understanding of it.

Martin Rein's book *Social Science and Public Policy* (1976) attacks
the positivist idea of value-free social science and develops a 'value-
critical' approach. Positivism advocates the empirical observation of
facts to formulate general laws according to a scientific method, says
Rein. Such a science claims to be free of values, but since values
underlie any observation, positivists actually choose values arbitrarily.
Marxist critics choose their values consciously, but adopt an uncritical,
'value-committed' stance. Rein advocates instead value criticism, which
takes values themselves as objects of study and focuses on their consequences for research and on the conflicts among them in ways that the
other approaches cannot.

In his version of value-critical social science, Rein aims at understanding through story-telling and metaphors. A good story describes
true events and interprets them in a valid way; a good metaphor rests on
a relevant analogy. Social science has three roles: to create narratives
and proverbs which reflect both empirical observations and moral
concerns; to translate these stories into programmes of intervention;
and to criticize stories and values as well as theories and facts. Rein
thinks this more appropriate than positivist science, because social
phenomena are not stable or universally observed and both the purposes of research and an orientation to action are crucial.

Rein's is clearly a value-laden social science. He identifies three 'value
screens' which affect policy analysis. Researchers may concentrate on
the malfunctioning of institutions (either particular bureaucracies or
broader social structures), the failure of people to cope with their world,
or the existing power structure. Though they may shift their attention
among these screens each one biases them towards certain kinds of
social change. Being self-conscious about their values and adhering to
standards of story-criticism may help researchers to counter their biases
(Rein, 1976: 80–5).

Rein sees three main barriers to utilization. First, conflicts are
inherent in political decision-making and second, social phenomena are
very complex to study. The third problem is that policy takes place in
frameworks of values and theories, and these 'paradigms' protect
themselves against counter-evidence by reinterpreting it so that it fits.
Further, there is no coherent, shared policy framework to match with
the dominant paradigm in social science (Rein, 1976: 96–138).

According to Rein, a sceptic would say that research cannot help to
choose between competing policy paradigms, and that policy dictates
social science. The optimistic view is that a common framework allows

some utilization and that in the long term, social science helps to introduce new frames. Rein distinguishes three types of research which aim at three different kinds of use. Government contracts for 'consensual' research, which judges whether policy achieves what it tries to achieve. 'Contentious' research asks whether the ideals of the policy paradigm are being applied. New imagery is important for convincing others about ideals, and journalists and fiction writers are better at this than social scientists (Rein, 1976: 96–138).

Finally, 'paradigm-challenging' research criticizes policy at the broadest level and may take a long time to be effective. For example, the British Poor Law reforms of 1834 tried to drive the able-bodied to work. Research criticizing its effects continued through the nineteenth century and eventually led to a theory of entitlement and the reforms resulting in the welfare state in 1948 (Rein, 1976: 96–138). Rein distinguishes between dialogue, which occurs within a particular frame, and discourse, which is communication across different frames. The mass media play an important if ill-understood role in such political discourse, communicating the different frames and interests of experts (Kallen, 1982: 342).

Rein sees three options for social scientists. They may ignore politics and continue with their research, oblivious to whether or not it is used. They may give up some autonomy and do applied work for the government or some opposing interest. Or they may try to establish their prestige as an independent source of political influence (Rein, 1976: 125). Rein supports his argument with illustrations from areas of policy analysis, including two chapters on the extended examples of equity and health policy.

Gerald I. Susman and Roger D. Evered (1978) offer action research as an alternative to positivist social science. Action research also addresses the utilization problem by trying both to further the goals of social science and to solve concrete problems in collaborative relationships (Rapoport, 1970: 499).

Susman and Evered (1978) find positivist science grossly inappropriate for studying society. Value-neutrality is clearly impossible with human subjects, and treating people as objects ignores their capacities to diagnose and act on their problems. Positivist science is least appropriate where the subjects are self-reflecting, the definition of the situation affects the relationship between subjects, and subjects have helped to define the problem.

Action research consists of five stages occurring in repeated cycles: diagnosing a problem, planning action, taking action, evaluating the results of action, and specifying the learning that has taken place. This cyclical process is regulated by the client at the same time that it develops the client. The advantages over positivist science include its future-orientation, its collaborative rather than elitist character, the development of self-regulating systems which require less intervention, and the close connections between theory and action.

But according to positivist criteria, it is not scientific since it works in only one organization at a time and relies on local knowledge rather than on strict application of general laws to specific cases. However, the authors explain how philosophies other than positivism support the action research claim to scientific legitimacy, e.g. praxis, hermeneutics, existentialism, pragmatism, process philosophies and phenomenology (Susman and Evered, 1978: 594–6).

According to the authors, action research provides understanding without general laws. It is more concerned with making things happen than with accurate prediction. It reasons through speculative conjectures, rather than inductively and deductively. It is engaged in action instead of detached in contemplation. Action research creates new knowledge in the form of action principles, 'enables' organizations with new skills, and creates conditions for the development of others.

Marc T. De Mey (1982) supports the connection between knowing and acting with findings from cognitive science, a field which has recently developed along with artificial intelligence research. A naive view of scientific knowledge has led to expectations that social science could provide instant solutions to problems. The actual results have been disappointing. A more realistic, 'cognitive view' stresses preconditions and social factors in knowledge production, i.e. the context of knowledge. The world view of the knower determines how knowledge is interpreted. De Mey presents the psychologist Jean Piaget's model of how a child develops through action and conceptualization. The knowledge generated is self-knowledge as well as knowledge of objects. Knowledge is subjective; knowledge and action are intimately related.

Like Rein, Frederick E. Emery (1976) sees the social scientist's options as three-fold. He prefers a collaborative role to the alternatives of either being disinterested in the purposes of social science or putting social science in the service of manipulation, as often happens in management consultancy. Collaboration, on the other hand, requires the resolution of value conflicts. For example, an advertising campaign accused all drunk drivers of being criminals and potential killers. Since under the law they were not criminals and since many were not potential killers, social scientists at the Tavistock Institute refused to collaborate on the campaign unless the content were changed. It was (Emery, 1976).

Both academic social scientists like Rein and action researchers like Susman and Evered think that positivism obstructs research utilization. So do applied researchers like the industrial psychologist Virginia R. Boehm (1980). Boehm complains that because industrial psychology is unable to live up to the textbook model of scientific method, academic psychologists ignore applied research and applied researchers ignore academic work. She diagrams an alternative model of scientific method which intends to solve performance problems rather than find knowledge and takes account of the complexity of researching in an organization. If this model were acceptable, Boehm believes that applied researchers and 'pure' social scientists could both benefit from interaction. For example, applied research findings are likely to be very reliable, because they are well-tested in practice, while theoretical advances in statistical methods may be useful in organizations (Boehm, 1980).

Though 'positivism' is clearly the villain for the writers in part 2, it is less certain that social science researchers actually use positivist methodologies in their work. These writers seem to take their notion of positivism from the philosophy of science, which is not an empirical discipline. They offer little evidence for the claim or assumption that social scientists follow textbook models of positivist scientific methods.

3. The separation of theory and observation
Another utilization problem seen as internal to social science concerns the sharp split between basic (or 'pure') and applied research. Eric L. Trist (1976b) argues that while the natural sciences first generate pure research findings and then apply them, social sciences require application in order to make theoretical progress. This is because the social scientist must 'reach his fundamental data (people, institutions, etc.) in their natural state', and to gain that access must prove 'his competence in supplying some kind of service' (Trist, 1976b: 46). In this way, practice is to improve theory, which permits improved practice, etc.

Trist's position is typical of the influential, unified approach to action research which has been developed at the Tavistock Institute of Human Relations. In this chapter, the Tavistock contributions are reviewed in different places because the approach seems to raise two separate issues. Part 3 deals with the complaint that theoretical social science often has little contact with the concrete data of social reality while empirical work tends to ignore theory. Trist's second argument for action research is that access to valid data requires collaboration. This is also the long-standing position of Argyris (1968; 1970). The issue of the researcher's involvement in practice, research implementation, collaboration, etc., occupies parts 4 and 5.

After systematically analysing the content of ten recent years of American economics literature,[5] Eugene J. Meehan's *Economics and Policymaking* reports that over 90 percent of it is utterly devoid of value for policy-makers, and that the rest of it is nearly useless. Economists study the analytic constructs of the 'economic system' and the 'market' rather than any practical problems. Their theorizing relates only to other economic theories and is connected to real world data very tenuously or not at all. Economics imitates theoretical physics but lacks a grounding in observation equivalent to experimental physics (Meehan, 1982: 117–74).

Meehan says that although economists are quick to advise policy-makers, their conclusions are usually only postulates, unsupported by any data. If data are used, they were often collected by a public authority for a purpose unrelated to those of the researcher who synthesizes them into new indices. Actual descriptions of economic phenomena are extremely rare. On to their synthetic variables economists slap everyday labels, which make them seem more real. The 'definitions' cannot be challenged by reference to observable things. Yet almost all economic concepts are defined in this way (Meehan, 1982: 117–74).

Economists produce many models, but 80 percent of those Meehan studied had no applications and few of the remainder were geared towards guiding human intervention or being tested by observation. The assumptions of the models are empirically either dubious or plainly false, e.g. the 'rational economic actor'. Ninety to ninety-five percent of major articles in econometrics deal with purely technical problems. The remainder present models of correlation rather than causation, and therefore are useless for designing intervention (Meehan, 1982: 144–69).

Meehan argues that the uselessness of economics for policy-making is inherent in the purposes of current economic inquiry. He develops a pragmatic, instrumental theory of knowledge which construes knowledge as tools for pursuing basic human purposes, which are to predict and control the environment and choose among alternative actions.[6] Knowledge must be judged by pragmatic criteria, i.e. 'the accuracy and reliability with which specified purposes can be achieved under stated conditions using particular instruments' (Meehan, 1982: 36).

Meehan aims to improve economics at the level of its epistemology and methodology. He urges that only a theory of knowledge can allow a discipline to develop instruments that could help policy-makers make reasoned choices (Meehan, 1982).

According to Meehan, policy requires certain instruments. It involves applying a priority system to the options available in a particular situation, by using rules of action. The content of available options is an empirical question depending on both the situation and human capacity, while the priority system must be constructed with normative variables — which define and measure the values important to human life. Both these instruments plus the rules for action must be articulated so they can be improved in practice. Economics does not provide these instruments for policy-makers (Meehan, 1982: 41–82).

Meehan provides detailed, technical descriptions of the tools or instruments which social science must produce if it is to be of use to policy-makers. They include adequately operationalized concepts and classifications, descriptions, forecasts and testable causal theories. Forecasts permit mere prediction while theories provide a basis for intervening in a situation. The failure of economics, despite great mathematical sophistication, to develop and test instruments like these accounts for its uselessness for policy-makers. Unfortunately, Meehan provides no evidence that policy-makers actually do not use the results of academic economic research. His argument amounts to saying that policy-makers cannot use them successfully.

Meehan's emphasis is on the corrigibility of these instruments because they are very difficult to construct yet can improve greatly over time (Meehan, 1982: 83–116). He stresses that his theory of knowledge must itself be tested and improved, and offers three tests.[7] What is remarkable about Meehan's book is that it is based on a broad empirical study of a social science discipline and attempts to explain the causes of its ineffectiveness. Meehan also provides well-defined remedial procedures, and does all this by using a fairly simple and accessible theoretical structure which can be tested independently. Apparently no one else has done anything comparable in the field of research utilization.

Martin Bulmer's *The Uses of Social Research* (1982) describes the split between theoretical and empirical research in the history and institutions of British social science. The first English social research was fact-finding about poverty conditions in nineteenth-century cities. Researchers like Booth, Rowntree, and the Webbs sought these facts to support their advocacy of new governmental policy. They clearly favoured social reform and were sometimes effective. The Webbs helped found the influential London School of Economics in 1895, and their tradition of 'empiricism' has remained strong. Empiricism assumes a very sharp division of labour and ideas between theoretical and empirical research and an engineering model of social science's contribution to policy. It often operates within the value framework of social democracy or 'social administration'. Research conducted or sponsored by the British government is firmly in this empiricist tradition: descriptive, factual, statistical and not very theoretical.

Bulmer criticizes empiricism and the engineering model. Social science must always oscillate between theories and facts. An 'enlightenment' model of utilization recognizes that policy-making is not rational, that social science does not yield general, reliable theories, and that social science is really part of the problem-solving and -defining process, not an input feeding into it. He uses the extended example of 'deprivation analysis' to show how theoretical choices (e.g. in defining a concept and choosing a research area) have enormous consequences for empirical results (Bulmer, 1982: 50–67).

According to Bulmer, the engineering model of social science has benefited from the lack of a strong, independent, coherent social science in Britain. Research organizations and professional orientations are highly fragmented, graduate student training is poor, social science is not a well-recognized profession, and teaching remains higher in status than research.

He finds that ad hoc royal commissions in Britain and presidential commissions in the US display further difficulties in getting social science theory past the theoretical/empirical divide. These commissios consist of well-known people who work independently and then advise the government. The government excludes social scientists with extreme views and ignores the commissions' findings if it wants to. Lawyers often dominate these commissions, and their methods are not very scientific. They marshal facts in order to advocate a position, and like to hold theatrical oral hearings. The commissions strive for consensus and are easily 'captured' either politically or intellectually. They may function more to legitimate existing policies, manipulate research, and allow groups to sound off than as open-minded, scientific inquiries (Bulmer, 1982: 94–127).

Bulmer provides something rare and valuable in this field: an empirical description, in this case of the historical, institutional development of social science in Britain. While this is a vital first step in exploring the theory/observation split, there is not enough evidence here to evaluate Bulmer's claims. Although he seems to argue that empiricism is the problem and his examples or stories about deprivation analysis and health care are consistent with his view that empirical social scientists are ignorant of the theoretical decisions their work requires, Bulmer does not give direct evidence of 'empiricist' researchers.

Suzanne Berger (1980)[8] claims that new theory may be the most important social science contribution to policy. Changes in theory underlie the changing importance of facts. When dual labour markets theory emerged in economics, it gave new importance to data on migrant labourers. It also suggested new policy based on improving inferior jobs, rather than inferior workers (as classical labour market theory has implied).[9] She sees this as the kind of paradigm-challenging work described by Rein (above), which has the highest potential pay-off for government but is also the most difficult to fund.

Frank A. Heller (1976) addresses a slightly different aspect of the pure/applied problem: a gap between general and specific research findings. Heller offers a partial solution in his technique of group feedback analysis, which uses general empirical social science findings in concrete organizational settings. For example, to reduce perceived skill gaps between two levels of management in an organization, Heller collects information and then feeds it back at different stages along with the data from similar research, e.g. on a national or industry level. This has been effective in its application, and in the long run the researcher's use of the theory in concrete settings may encourage theoretical advances.

4. Collaboration in action research

Lisl Klein works in the tradition of action research, trying to join social science theory with empirical research through collaboration on specific problems. Her book, *A Social Scientist in Industry* (1976) documents and analyses her five years of experience as the in-house social sciences adviser for Esso Petroleum. In her long narrative account, Klein (1976: 17–201) richly details both the development of her role within the company and her work on specific projects. She treats her experiences in company politics as data to be analysed. Klein notes that social scientists may easily become involved in political conflicts already existing in an organization. The role of social scientists in an organization is relatively ill-defined and their knowledge is a potential source of power, so they may be threatening to some. Being confined to the employee-relations department reduced Klein's power.

During Klein's employment, Esso hired a US research team to change leadership styles in a large-scale research project. Klein reports that this involved using standard techniques to change the behaviour of individuals, an approach which ran counter to her work focusing on organizational structures and technology. The struggle between Klein's existing operation and the incoming Americans' was both theoretical or methodological and territorial (Klein, 1976: 236–41). The heavy organizational support Esso gave to the Americans undermined Klein's stature within the company. She had more trouble gaining access to research settings and the company eventually abolished her position.

A common model of research utilization consists of a transfer from a 'resource system' (providing knowledge) to a 'user system' (taking action). Klein generalizes from her Esso experience to call this model inadequate. User systems have their own resources and resource systems have their own action needs, like the need to protect professional territory against other consultants (Klein, 1976: 214–20). She also argues that social science lacks professional norms, which sometimes allows social scientists to exploit clients (Klein, 1976: 211–14).

Other action researchers describe different problems with collaboration. Alfred W. Clark (1976) identifies the client and 'practitioner' as interdependent systems, and says the trick is to maintain, creatively and simultaneously, enough independence and enough inter-dependence. The main thing holding the two systems together is the shared task of changing the client, which requires shared information and action. Clark also describes how differences and similarities in the external environments and value, reward and power systems can help regulate the correct level of inter-dependence. In trying 'to create enough overlap . . . for communication and action to take place', it is essential not to give up 'the differences that enhance the possibility of a creative tension' (Clark, 1976: 127). Clark believes that initial differences in values and skills need not doom the collaboration, and that greater differences can lead to more creative organizational changes.

But others argue that extreme differences in values have subverted action research. Stanley Seashore (1976) complains that in action research there is often a trade-off between action and research, and that this is going increasingly in favour of action. This is because funding and institutional links with non-academic, 'service-buying' sources are increasing faster than those with academic sources. Also, the new generation of action researchers accepts the scientific legitimacy of mere consultancy (Seashore, 1976: 104).

To encourage more focus on the scientific potential of action research, Seashore lays out a model of action research 'design properties' which affect its scientific contribution. For example, the theoretical orientation can drive the choice of action, or vice versa. The researcher can create theories either grounded concretely in the case under study (and its context), or related to generalized abstractions. Besides theoretical orientation, choices are available in the information or data base, the degree of action orientation, the role of time, and the independence of inquiry and intervention (Seashore, 1976: 105-11). Seashore also categorizes types of scientific contribution as being theoretical, methodological, technological (as in recording and retrieving data) and educational (teaching managers or new researchers, for example).

According to Stephen Town (1973), action research faces special difficulties in contributing to social science if the problem it is to deal with is vaguely defined and the power structure within which it must work is incoherent. He reviews two large British projects in education and urban poverty. Although an important intent was to generalize the findings from a limited geographical area to the whole nation, more action than research resulted. Town tries to be optimistic about the situation, and suggests using these experiences to understand the process of doing action research in broad policy areas. For example, since researchers on such projects must frequently change their roles, the presuppositions of those roles could be better examined. This kind of action research could be a precursor of the kind which successfully solves well-defined problems (Town, 1973).

Trist (1976a) sees an especially pressing need for more action research. Technological change is producing an increasingly uncertain environment for organizations and highlighting the need for 'adaptive planning'. Such planning judges values and selects areas of action rather than taking them as given. It aims at building self-regulating systems and enhancing organizational learning. It operates through collaboration on a basis of shared values, and Trist sees the processes of adaptive planning as identical with those of action research. Trist (1976a) relates the argument for adaptive planning to much other literature, especially the book *Towards a Social Ecology* (Emery and Trist, 1972).

Most of these writers seem to offer their theories as insights or methodological tips for other action researchers. They report their own experiences or cite other cases of action research, but do not offer the kind of systematic evidence (e.g. for the effectiveness of collaboration in effecting organizational change and producing social science knowledge) which might convince a sceptic that action research is preferable to other kinds.

5. Linkages in evaluation research

Action research is not the only type of social science concerned with collaboration. Many researchers are interested in 'linking' or 'bridging a gap' between researchers and users, with outright collaboration as the limiting case. They see the research utilization problem as one of closely matching research produced with the requirements of users, so they focus on improving the interaction between the two. This perspective lacks the action research emphasis on advancing a theoretical social science which stands outside the relationship of researcher to user. Most of the following contributions present this view while seeking to increase the utilization of 'evaluation research'.

A vast amount of US social science evaluates the federal government's social programmes. Evaluation research was a by-product of the boom in social programmes in the mid-1960s. Congress set aside a small fraction (less than 1 percent) of most budgets for evaluating the programmes. Evaluations have not been very conclusive but they generally show that programmes do not achieve their aims (see, for example, Mullen et al., 1972). Evaluations were intended to help make systematic decisions about how to fund or reform programmes. However, any uses at all were rare until the Nixon administration used evaluation findings to justify its decisions to eliminate many programmes. With another round of social programme cuts in the early 1980s, funds for evaluation research itself are in danger (Heilman, 1983: 707). There has been widespread criticism of the quality of many evaluations, and some complain that it is hurting the reputation of social science.[10]

Typical of the field is Michael Quinn Patton's (1978) book, which suggests ways in which evaluations can be made 'utilization-focused'.

Patton draws on his experience with thirty evaluation projects and on forty interviews with federal evaluators in reaching his conclusions. He says it is vital to aim the research at specific people, not diffuse audiences. The researcher should continually consider these users' needs, consulting with them at various stages, such as during decisions about research design, how to analyse and present data, and so on. Patton sees this as a creative process based on mutual respect, but believes that evaluators must always put the user's needs ahead of the demands of social science. He warns against those who insist on framing research questions in social science terms. They may be pursuing their own interests while masquerading as evaluators in order to get some of the available money (Patton, 1978).

Efforts to reform evaluation research have been vigorous if unsuccessful. A 1974 conference included about one hundred government officials and researchers. The resulting book describes their efforts to find ways to improve 'the scientific quality and policy utility' of evaluations (Abt, 1976: 11). Like much of the literature on the utilization of evaluation research, it is intimately connected to the technical criticism of aspects of evaluation methodology. The following briefly reviews some of the most central and influential of these works.

The 1400-page *Handbook of Evaluation Research* (Struening and Guttentag, 1975; Guttentag and Struening, 1975) tries systematically to improve the quality of evaluations. They explain that evaluation research consists of many steps, at any one of which it is easy to go wrong. They suggest that evaluators use the *Handbook* as a set of experts 'between hard covers' since many research teams lack access to such expertise in flesh-and-blood form. The overall impression is of a field where the work has grown much faster than the available skill or competence, and which is trying desperately to control quality. The first volume runs through the steps of doing research and the second deals with cost-benefit analysis and mental health evaluations. There are also a few articles on the politics of utilization, which are reviewed in part 6 of this chapter.

Another major publication is *Evaluation Studies Review Annual*, which seeks to include the year's best evaluation research. Most of it is in particular areas of policy, with little work on theoretical issues or utilization. The editor of the first volume said he was unable to find much theoretical work worth including, because most of it is dull and repetitious (Glass, 1976: 10).

One article he did include was the Stanford Evaluation Consortium's (1976) critique of the *Handbook*, which provides an alternative view of evaluation research. The authors prefer the early involvement of researchers in studies for planning new programmes, rather than their inclusion later when everything is in place. They think researchers should be free to change their research designs as they proceed rather than be locked in by detailed contracts. They do not fear making findings known as soon as possible to programme administrators to help them improve their practices. When they report their final results, they try to find many different uses for them, reverting to their initial role in planning.

The study of evaluation research has affected more general studies of utilization. Jack Rothman (1980) surveyed the in-house research functions of twelve London social service departments. He draws on evaluation literature to support the conclusions he makes from this small sample. Rothman proposes better linkages between the 'two worlds' of the researcher and the administrator. He divides these into structures (like meetings of various kinds or legitimation from a high-level board), processes, attitudes and relationships, and research report characteristics (Rothman, 1980). Like the others in part 5, Rothman's evidence consists of examples and very limited studies, which he treats as complete, positive tests of his hypotheses.

6. Politics, policy-making and social sciences

Writers who propose 'linkage' solutions view utilization as a technical problem to be solved by applying the right techniques, practices, structures, etc. Others are most interested in the political aspects of utilization, and some think it is almost completely a political matter. Under this approach, attempts to solve the utilization problem are limited by the existing understanding of the relevant politics. Part 6 reviews the literature which has a political bent.

Like Rothman, Andrew M. Pettigrew (1975) writes about research in organizations. Pettigrew notes that organizational politics are based on a division of labour; career, reward and status systems; and conflict over resources. The effectiveness of internal consultants depends on their control and use of five kinds of power resource: their technical expertise; control over organizational information; sensitivity to matters of power in their personal relationships; their stature as assessed by others; and the support of other consultants or members of their research group. For example, if consultants spend their energy in rivalry, they may undermine each other in relation to the rest of the organization. Pettigrew gives examples to illustrate his argument, but no evidence or suggestions for testing his theory.

In action research in an organization, the client's support for the research is obviously essential. But it is not always simple to maintain it. Clark (1972) describes an action research project to improve morale at an industrial site. Initial top-level sanction had led to an agreement on a new management philosophy, but managers blatantly violated it and when the researchers objected, they lost organizational support. Clark concludes with what are effectively hypotheses: that sanction must be continual and broad, for example including support from the shop-floor workers, the trade unions and the government, that it must be based on shared values and objectives, not just official legitimation, and that initial success is sometimes necessary to get support for more controversial interventions.

More writers are interested in utilization by government, especially in making national policy. Beverly Russell and Arnold Shore (1976) describe, although somewhat superficially, how US government institutions limit the use of social science theory, however much empirical data they may use. Congress depends on compromise and coalitions of interests to pass legislation. These processes use social science as 'political ammunition', as when economists testified both for and against the supersonic transport programme. The Congressional Research Service employs 400 researchers to provide whatever information, consultation and expert witnesses Congress wants. The President often uses social scientists in forming comprehensive domestic policy programmes like Johnson's Great Society (which had fourteen task forces), but there is no conclusive evidence that any social science gets used. Both the civil service and the White House selectively employ social scientists, for example to study the public response to political information (Russell and Shore, 1976).

Social scientists often want radical changes, say the authors, but since only incremental ones are possible, they are liable to be disappointed. They urge researchers to remember that short-term political feasibility is very important in the government, and to study the details of policy and especially policy history as carefully as they research the substantive area of policy. Finally, the authors suggest that large-scale political crises, such as those faced by Presidents Roosevelt and Johnson, might help the chances of utilization.

James Q. Wilson (1978) agrees that there is an important difference between using social scientists and using social science. The former usually give personal opinion, while the latter must include well-stated theories and tested propositions. He claims to have seen many instances of the former, and none of the latter. For example, Cloward and Ohlin developed untested theories that the cause of youth delinquency lay in the structure of community opportunities. Politicians used this to create the Mobilization for Youth programme, aimed at reducing delinquency rates. The programme did not achieve this (Wilson, 1978). Wilson's article uses personal stories and other anecdotes to sound a pessimistic note about research utilization.

Most researchers seem to find the similarities among different countries' utilization problems to be more striking than the differences (e.g. Weiss, 1977; Kallen, 1982). But L.J. Sharpe thinks that studying the literature on US utilization is misleading for understanding the situation in Britain, where the nature of politics is very different. In Britain, there is a general tendency to rely more heavily on practical than on academic knowledge. Civil servants and politicians like to practise 'intellectual self-sufficiency' (Sharpe, 1978: 308). In contrast, US social science is more highly institutionalized, has more status, is more empirical, and can more easily gain access to politicians, who are used to consulting a range of experts. In short, Sharpe seems to say that US social science is better integrated with the government. Unfortunately, he gives little evidence for his interesting claims.

Weiss (1982) traces the prevalent high expectations about utilization to a view of governmental decision-making as rational. She extracts five elements from this view of decision-making, by which authoritative individuals make decisions according to a linear process which calculates alternatives in relation to fixed goals, in a way that takes account of the consequences of decisions. Of course, this rarely happens in practice, because one or more of these elements is missing or almost missing. Weiss details a number of alternative methods, including following customs, innovating on the basis of past practices, negotiating conflicts and adjusting to others' decisions (Weiss, 1982).[11]

Such 'diffuse' policy-making would seem to have little use of social science. But Weiss points out that social science remains popular with government officials. They say they like it, and they pay for a lot of it. Social science may provide information for control, as when administrators use programme evaluations to see whether local agencies are spending money the way they are supposed to. Or officials can use research to justify current policies (Weiss, 1982), something easy to do with the ambiguous mass of evidence available in most evaluation studies.

Berger (1980) thinks that policy-makers use social science for 'legitimation' or 'partisanship' as well as for knowledge, and backs up her claim by citing several case studies of national policy. For example, changes in housing policy occurred before the results of social experiments in that area were known (fully described in Field, 1980: 276). In many cases, social science may not make a difference in decisions, but may be desired for its 'scientific presence'. The result is often little more than 'scientifically decked-out opinion' (Berger, 1980: 12). In commenting on the famous riot commission report, Michael Lipsky calls this the 'paprika role', where social sciences add colour but no substance (Lipsky, 1971: 81, quoted in Berger, 1980).

More optimistically, social science may make a conceptual contribution, according to Weiss. It may affect ideas and discourse, though often after long delays. For example, evaluations of California prisons showed that rehabilitation had little effect. For a long time the government did not use these findings. In recent years, the research results were important in convincing the state to give up on rehabilitation and make punishment the purpose of imprisonment (Weiss,1982).

Although the optimism of this model of conceptual utilization, or 'enlightenment' has appealed to many writers, it may be deceptive. There is no reason to expect that the research used in this way will be of the highest quality, the most relevant or the most up-to-date, says Weiss. In the case of the California prisons, social scientists will disagree on the validity of the conclusion that 'nothing works' in rehabilitation. Conceptual utilization may result in 'endarkenment' rather than enlightenment. Further, even if changes in ideas and discourse are positive, they may not translate into changes in action (Weiss, 1982). 'Conceptual utilization' seems to be a badly flawed concept.

Finally, as Daniel Weiler pointed out in the discussion following Weiss's presentation, the use of social science terminology by policy-makers may devalue them as social science concepts more than it changes policy-makers' ideas. The jargon comes to stand for the research conclusions, regardless of whether they are worth anything. If every policy opinion can be supported with social science jargon, then the ideal of systematic, objective knowledge loses meaning (Kallen, 1982: 314–15).

Weiss would not disagree. She says that direct, conceptual utilization would always happen because ideas are important in the world, but more rational policy-making would mean more chances for utilization. She also points out that since social science is necessarily value-laden and most social scientists are left-wing, conservative governments understandably resist using much social science. Finally, social science has no monopoly on policy-relevant knowledge, both because much research is not that good and because policy-makers know a lot themselves (Weiss, 1982).

Weiss concludes that conceptual utilization implies certain strategies for researchers. It makes possible a role for social science as an autonomous social critic. Social scientists should do conceptually and methodologically sophisticated work from an independent position and not worry so much about speedy application (Weiss, 1982). Weiss seems to be willing to settle for conceptual utilization, despite its difficulties.

Charles E. Lindblom and David K. Cohen, in *Usable Knowledge* (1979), seek a more general view of the relation of knowledge to 'social problem-solving'. They see the utilization problem as an opportunity to explore deep questions about the nature of knowledge and problem-solving, and think that much of the current effort in this field is misdirected. They suggest that most of the difficulty lies with social science's understanding of itself, and therefore want to turn the discipline *on* itself.

One point at which the authors think most researchers have gone wrong is in failing to see that understanding a problem is not the only way to go about solving it. Action or 'interaction' are quite common substitutes for 'analysis', as when economic markets use buying and selling activity to solve the problem of what price to set. Coin tossing is an alternative to using a rational, scientific analysis of a problem, and in many circumstances it may be more efficient and no less reliable. Most social scientists think that analysis is the main route to problem-solving and this leads to them wasting much energy. People solve problems by acting far more often than through analysis alone.

However, because people never stop thinking for long, all interaction contains with it some analysis. The important relationship between analysis and interaction is largely unexplored, though often referred to in catch phrases like 'the political context of social science'. But interaction can be economic or social, not just political. Social science has ignored this whole area (Lindblom and Cohen, 1979: 10–29).

Unfortunately, the way Lindblom and Cohen have set up this problem makes more difficult the work they are calling for. They give examples but no real definitions of the central concepts 'analysis' and 'interaction', and 'social problem-solving' is defined in a way that includes just about anything. It will be hard to study how these phenomena relate to each other in detail if even these authors cannot say more about exactly what they *are*.

Another major social science mistake Lindblom and Cohen identify is in discounting the importance of ordinary knowledge. Ordinary knowledge consists of common sense, speculation, analysis, and so on, which does not use the methodologies of professional social science. Social science often ignores or tries to replace ordinary knowledge, but ordinary knowledge is usually far more useful. Futher, it is basic to all social science knowledge, and social scientists must rely on some ordinary knowledge even when they are arguing against another part of it. Social science can normally only supplement or refine ordinary knowledge. Overall, social science makes only a relatively small contribution to knowledge (Lindblom and Cohen, 1979: 10–29).

The authors seem to ignore the role of science in structuring ordinary knowledge, for example through the statement of testable causal theories which are then related to statements of evidence. Most of the knowledge used may be 'ordinary', but organizing it to maximize criticisability is not.

Lindblom and Cohen argue that social science may act as an obstruction to social problem-solving rather than as aids. Social science is scarce and expensive, so society must direct it to those problems where it will be most useful. This is not the same as the most important problems, because some problems are more amenable to social analysis than others. 'Noise' is another unfortunate by-product of misdirected social science. Science is so highly institutionalized and popularized that it gets too much attention regarding decisions on social problems such as schools and race. Its noise level distracts society from applying ordinary knowledge and interaction to many problems (Lindblom and Cohen, 1979: 76-96).

The authors say that they do not try to reach conclusions from the literature so much as to outline a wholly new research programme based on a few crucial assumptions. Yet their argument amounts to a sharp, radical critique of social science, warning that it is not and cannot be as important to policy-making as most social scientists think.

Martin Rein and Donald Schon (1977) are less pessimistic about the potential value of social science. They argue that policy research can affect 'problem-setting' as well as problem-solving. A process of selecting information and questions, and of finding patterns among them converts 'worries' into problems. The authors describe methods for doing this, such as aggregating related worries from different policy areas. This 'framing' of a problem both explains empirical data and suggests possible action. The frames often result in metaphors which generate new understanding. Making a system 'healthy' or winning 'victories' (e.g. in the 'War Against Poverty') are common metaphors in policy research. Story telling becomes useful at this point, as do analytic tools for understanding stories, like 'maps' and models (Rein and Schon, 1977). Rein thinks these methods contain possibilities for a meaningful social science contribution to policy, and gives examples of how it can work.

Like many writers, however, he is also aware of the possibilities of political manipulation. He describes the 'interplay' between research policy rather than the 'utilization' of research (Rein, 1980). With Sheldon White, he describes four 'neglected pathways' between research and policy (Rein and White, 1977). Politicians may use research to 'contain' policies, as when the opponents of 'Head Start' limited its growth. Research may be used as an instrument of power and political positioning, e.g. as a symbol or a delaying tactic. It may also be used to 'police' programmes by revealing the flow of money. For example, black militant groups used evaluations of Title I education programmes to show that funds were not reaching those they were supposed to (Rein and White, 1977). Finally, social reformers may use social science. In a recent case, the attempt to replace welfare programmes with negative income taxation led to social experiments in New Jersey (described in detail in Heclo and Rein, 1980).

Others point out how politics constrain evaluation research more subtly and profoundly. Richard A. Berk and Peter H. Rossi (1977) criticize evaluation research for ignoring fundamental issues of wealth and power and for supporting only incremental change while claiming to be above politics. Evaluation research has not helped social science to counter the charges raised in the 1960s that it had sold out and was irrelevant. But Berk and Rossi think evaluation still has potential. One important function is 'de-mystifying', as when it showed that most social programmes fail. But since evaluation is unavoidably political, evaluators should build political considerations into their research designs. For example, it may be statistically verifiable that children who watch the 'Sesame Street' television programme can count a few numbers higher than children who do not watch it. But that fact is probably not of any substantial (e.g. political) importance (Berk and Rossi, 1977).

More interesting is the authors' proposal for making political judgements about aspects of research design, like which statistics to use. 'Decision theory' can guide judgements about the political risks of different kinds of errors. Selecting appropriate statistics for data analysis involves judgements about different risks, because in a given situation some statistical tests can minimize the chance of certain kinds of errors. Berk and Rossi extend this principle to include political considerations like the probability of data being misinterpreted in a particular way (Berk and Rossi, 1977).

Weiss (1975) also sees evaluations as politically constrained, but calls for broader research to counter the problems. She explains that while evaluations are rational, they are also political in several ways. The social programmes themselves are creatures of legislative and bureaucratic politics, and higher-level decision-makers use the results of evaluations in selective ways for their tactical purposes. But most important are the political assumptions and biases which underlie evaluation research. By judging programmes according to their stated goals, evaluators legitimate the programmes. Large-scale social experiments must ignore most of the variables they could include, implying that they are not affected or are not important. Well-established programmes are not usually evaluated, and neither are those that challenge the distribution of income or power. Researchers always operate from the perspective of the agency, not the client. Finally, evaluation has a distinct reformist bent, since it tries to improve practices within existing structures (Weiss, 1975).

Weiss finds these biases especially disturbing because the research shows that few programmes achieve their goals, and the history of utilization shows that policy-makers do not pay attention to the findings unless it suits them. Weiss concludes that the current approach of programmes and evaluation will not solve these social problems. Instead, social science should step outside the current framework to study the institutional structures and social arrangements which frame the problems and make existing programmes ineffective. Study should be comprehensive, rather than fragmented into different government programmes (Weiss, 1975).

Gideon Sjoberg (1975) attacks evaluation methodologists for ignoring politics and ethics. Such considerations are an inevitable part of research because it is itself a social process. Further, social scientists are part of the research design and their outside political and ethical commitments affect their research. Evaluation occurs in the context of the increasing bureaucratization of society. Bureaucracy is based on hierarchy and is fundamentally in conflict with the value of equity. Evaluation helps to maintain the hierarchy, for example by insisting on simple organizational goals instead of complex or multiple ones which can serve different interests. By reforming practices, evaluation helps to maintain the power structure and may help administrators to manipulate their staff. The recent move towards 'social indicators' helps to sustain class power. For example, the widely quoted Uniform Crime Reports do not include white-collar crime like embezzlement, and the system of educational testing serves to bar lower-class people from higher education. In general, evaluators assume the existing structural constraints and align themselves with the dominant groups in society (Sjoberg, 1975).

He also sees this as an ethical problem. Evaluators commit themselves to the nation-state and its bureaucracies, often forgetting their commitment to science and therefore to human dignity. Human dignity requires the availability of 'structural choices'. Sjoberg recommends that social criticism be part of evaluations. One difficulty is that existing programmes are normally compared only with themselves. Researchers should develop 'counter-system' or utopian models of society so they can compare programmes to something outside the given structural arrangements (Sjoberg, 1975).

Many writers think that social science is misused. Some carry their criticism to the politics within the social science establishment itself. In *The Fallacy of Social Science Research*, Pablo Gonzalez Casanova (1981: ix–xiii, 1–3) says that international social science co-operation is irrational. It avoids conflict by selecting research groups which are ideologically homogenous and which enforce research designs on subordinate teams in the various countries. As a result, the most important, contradictory alternative hypotheses of this century are never included in the same research design. The present situation is born of the desire to avoid social conflict and preserve the status quo. But it is itself an irrational manifestation of conflict. Casanova wants to deal with ideological conflict by giving it a role in research models. His book analyses, in technical detail, the political and theoretical assumptions of two contrasting social science methodologies and applies his conclusions to the case of research on economic development (Casanova, 1981).

Careful qualitative analysis must precede quantitative research. This involves the selection of primitive categories, hypotheses, dimensions and variables. For example, primitive categories in studying economic development have traditionally been wealth, power, consciousness and exploitation. Qualitative tasks are the most important part of social science, but receive little attention. Mathematically precise yet conceptually ambiguous simulations result. For example, Casanova shows how the statistical technique of factor analysis depends heavily on earlier, qualitative decisions (Casanova, 1981: 4–15).

Often, most of the qualitative decisions are made implicitly. Imposing such partially articulated research designs on other researchers obscures ideological conflicts (Casanova, 1981: 4–7).

Casanova argues that the tendency to emphasize quantitative methods and downplay qualitative tasks is related to the researchers' ages and cultural backgrounds (US social science is heavily quantitative), but more importantly, to their politics. Those aiming for social change use qualitative analysis to compare society to its alternatives. Quantitative analysis is more useful for measuring the existing relations, perhaps with the aim of stabilizing it but certainly not of changing it. Normally this means that there are distinct Marxist and non-Marxist research styles, but central planning in socialist countries attracts quantitative Marxists (Casanova, 1981: 8–15). Unfortunately, Casanova does not give any systematic evidence for his interesting ideas about political ideology and research style.

Political ideology, says Casanova, affects also choices of primitive categories and research design. Marxists focus on exploitation and analyse it in relation to time, in order to take history into account and to propose change. Conservatives are more interested in consciousness or values, and ignore history by focusing on the 'eternal present'.

Casanova's despair over the scarcity of qualititative work resembles Meehan's argument that researchers do not produce the necessary instruments for rational policy-making. Both see research results as instruments for achieving human purposes. But while Meehan says that his scrutiny of economics literature reveals it to be useless, Casanova claims (with less evidence) that the type of instruments currently produced have distinct political functions. When the connection between primitive categories or concepts and data is missing or misleading, research is necessarily geared toward supporting the status quo rather than criticizing it. Meehan might argue that this work is useless. Casanova's perspective, however, offers to explain why it is still done.

If Casanova is right, the qualitative foundation of social science is mostly implicit. Under-use of research could then be explained by reference to hidden problems in these structures, due to lack of articulation and criticism. If Meehan is right, the qualitative underpinnings are not simply ignored, but are missing altogether because social science has failed to develop them. In this case, the non-use of research is the best course open to policy-makers. The difference between these two positions can be formulated as empirical questions about the research products of social science.

Like Casanova, Nevitt Sanford (1976) believes that the established powers are not interested in effective social science, in this case action research. Action research continues in areas like public health, criminology and community psychology, but mainstream social science has frozen it out by institutionalizing the separation between action and research. Social science is fragmented by its division of labour and has becom so separated from its subject that it risks irrelevance. Like most modern industries, it heavily pollutes its environment, both in the way it exploits research subjects and through the publication of worthless research (Sanford, 1976).

But Sanford believes the specialized interests want to keep things that way. Social science is an élite establishment, economically and politically dependent on a larger establishment. Sanford calls for an autonomous social science, supported by broad subsidy instead of the current system of project grants. Action research by academics on academics would also help, and would be easy to do.

This literature has not reached any firm, notable conclusions, nor does it seem to be moving towards them. However, one ironic message may be implicit in it. If social science in general is no better conceptualized, is based on theories which are no more testable, and is no more strongly supported by empirical evidence than utilization research is, then a factor in research under-utilization may be like the water is to the fish that swims in it: omnipresent but invisible. It is hard to see how this field will progress unless its researchers develop more rigorous, meaningful definitions of what utilization is, construct testable theories, and test them in the field(s): the organizations of research, business, and government.

At the same time, questions about research use are not trivial ones. Research is sometimes used in important ways, e.g. when economic theories about secondary labour markets influenced the federal labour policy 'paradigm'. Clearly, social science has a political role — but is it one of legitimating existing policies, engineering solutions already chosen, scientifically developing policy, or what? The social science study of the political possibilities of and constraints on utilization might start by investigating the historical development and relations between institutions of research and policy-making.

Notes

1. 'Utilization' contains eight more letters and four more syllables than 'use', and means almost exactly the same thing. Its extra bulk may lend 'utilization' a kind of scientistic authority. At any rate, most of the writers reviewed here use the longer word, particularly those trying to develop a more precise, technical definition. In discussing each author, I have been faithful to their particular conventions. Elsewhere, I use the words interchangeably for the sake of variety.

2. Other surveys and literature reviews not reviewed here include: National Science Board (1969), which relates social science to the professions, the federal government, business, labour, community organizations and the public; National Research Council (1968); National Academy of Sciences and Social Science Research Council (1969), which surveys the social sciences generally and devotes several chapters to their bearing on policy; and Human Interaction Research Institute (1976) which summarizes 266 works and 'distils' many more, mostly in the area of mental health research but including some more general contributions. Havelock (1972) assembled and partially annotated a bibliography.

3. Leviton and Hughes (1981) set out to review the literature on the utilization of evalution research, but in the face of its paucity they extended their scope to the utilization of social science research. The definitions they develop are relevant to the more general field. The emphasis on 'utilization by policy-makers' or decision-makers describes the field more narrowly than, for example, 'use by society' would, but this is a bias shared by most of the writers reviewed here. A notable exception is Charles E. Lindblom and David K. Cohen (1979).

4. First reported in Caplan et al. (1975).

5. Meehan examined important books in economics, the works of major figures in the field, all the articles in four major journals, and one quarter to one half of the articles in fourteen others. He covered the period 1970–80, and analysed mostly American economics literature, though he included some from Western Europe (Meehan, 1982: 16-18).

6. Meehan develops his theory of knowledge in more detail in *Reasoned Argument in Social Science: Linking Research to Policy* (1981).

7. Briefly, they are: that the theory of knowledge can 'account for what has been accomplished intellectually in the past, particularly in such areas as physical science'; that any discipline can use it as a critical basis to improve the usefulness of its knowledge for policy; and that the educational content and strategies it implies enhance the intellectual performance of young students. Meehan claims preliminary success for the third test though he does not give evidence here (Meehan, 1982: 21).

8. Berger's article draws on the nine case studies which it introduces. These cover major areas of US government policy. Academic social scientists report on: Negative Income Taxation experiments (Hugh Heclo and Martin Rein); the development of dual labour market theory (Michael J. Piore); and the non-use of economists' expertise in the Clean Water Act of 1972 (John Zysman). Social scientists in government describe: housing experiments (Charles G. Field); social science in the Department of Labour (K. Guild Nichols); experiments in health policy (Larry L. Orr); and employment policy and criminal offenders (Charles W. Phillips). Sitting more or less astride the two groups of case studies is Nathan Caplan's empirical study of how federal administrators use social science research, first reported in Caplan et al. (1975).

9. Michael J. Piore (1980) reports at length on this case.

262   *The use and abuse of social science*

10. Weiss (1977: 1-22) describes this viewpoint.
11. This model of 'diffuse' decision-making is partly based on the work of Charles E. Lindblom (1965).

References

Abt, Clark C. (ed.) (1978) *The Evaluation of Social Programs.* Beverly Hills and London: Sage.

Argyris, Chris (1968) 'Some Unintended Consequences of Rigorous Research', *Psychological Bulletin*, 70: 185-97.

Argyris, Chris (1970) *Intervention Theory and Method: A Behavioral Science View.* Reading: Mass: Addison-Wesley.

Berger, Suzanne (1980) 'Introduction', pp. 7-25 in Organization for Economic Co-operation and Development, *The Utilisation of the Social Sciences in Policy Making in the United States.* Paris: OECD.

Berk, Richard A. and Peter H. Rossi (1977) 'Doing Good or Worse: Evaluation Research Politically Reexamined', pp. 77-90 in M. Guttentag (ed.), *Evaluation Studies Review Annual, Vol. 2.* Beverly Hills and London: Sage.

Boehm, Virginia R. (1980) 'Research in the Real World — a Conceptual Model', *Personnel Psychology*, 33 (Autumn): 495-503.

Bulmer, Martin (1982) *The Uses of Social Research: Social Investigation in Public Policy-making.* Boston and London: Allen and Unwin.

Caplan, N., A. Morrison and R. Stambaugh (1975) *The Use of Social Science Knowledge in Policy Decisions at the National Level.* Ann Arbor: Institute of Social Research.

Caplan, Nathan (1980) 'The Use of Social Science Knowledge in Policy Decisions at the National Level', in Organization for Economic Co-operation and Development, *The Utilisation of the Social Sciences in Policy Making in the United States.* Paris: OECD.

Caplan, Nathan (1982) 'Social Research and Public Policy at the National Level', pp. 32-48 in D.B.P. Kallen et al. (eds), *Social Science Research and Public Policy-Making: A Reappraisal.* Windsor: NFER Nelson.

Casanova, Pablo Gonzalez (1981) *The Fallacy of Social Science Research: A Critical Examination and New Qualitative Model.* New York and Oxford: Pergamon.

Ciarlo, J.A. (ed.) (1981) *Utilizing Evaluation: Concepts and Measurement Techniques.* Beverley Hills and London: Sage.

Clark, Alfred W. (1972) 'Sanction: A Critical Element in Action Research', *Journal of Applied Behavioral Science:* 713-31.

Clark, Alfred W. (1976) 'The Client-practitioner Relationship as an Intersystem Engagement', p. 119-34 in A.W. Clark (ed.), *Experimenting with Organizational Life: The Action Research Approach.* New York and London: Plenum.

de Mey, Marc T. (1982) 'Action and Knowledge from a Cognitive Point of View, pp. 185-96 in Kallen et al. (eds), *Social Science Research and Public Policy-Making: A Reappraisal.* Windsor: NFER Nelson.

Emery, Frederick E. (1976) 'Professional Responsibility of Social Scientists' pp. 11-18 in A.W. Clark (ed.), *Experimenting with Organizational Life: The Action Research Approach.* New York and London: Plenum.

Emery, Frederick E. and Eric L. Trist (1972) *Towards a Social Ecology.* New York and London: Plenum.

Field, Charles G. (1980) 'Social Testing for United States Housing Policy: The

Experimental Housing Allowance Program', pp. 235–81 in Organization for Economic Co-operation and Development, *The Utilisation of the Social Sciences in Policy Making in the United States.* Paris: OECD.

Glass, Gene V. (ed.) (1976) *Evaluation Studies Review Annual, Vol. 1.* Beverly Hills and London: Sage.

Guttentag, Marcia and Elmer L. Struening (eds) (1975) *Handbook of Evaluation Research, Vol. 2.* Beverly Hills and London: Sage.

Guttentag, Marcia (ed.) (1977) *Evaluation Studies Review Annual, Volume 2.* Beverly Hills and London: Sage.

Havelock, Ronald G. (1969) *Planning for Innovation through Dissemination and Utilization of Knowledge.* Ann Arbor, Michigan: Institute for Social Research.

Havelock, Ronald G. (1972) *Knowledge Utilization and Dissemination: A Bibliography.* Ann Arbor: Institute for Social Research.

Heclo, Hugh and Martin Rein (1980) 'Social Science and Negative Income Taxation', pp. 29–66 in Organization for Economic Co-operation and Development, *The Utilisation of the Social Sciences in Policy Making in the United States.* Paris: OECD.

Heilman, John G. (1983) 'Beyond the Technical and Bureaucratic Theories of Utilization', *Evaluation Review* 7(6): 707–28.

Heller, Frank A. (1976) 'Group Feedback Analysis as a Method of Action Research', pp. 209–22 in A. W. Clark (ed.), *Experimenting with Organization Life: The Action Research Approach.* New York and London: Plenum.

Human Interaction Research Institute (1976) *Putting Knowledge to Use: A Distillation of the Literature Regarding Knowledge Transfer and Change.* Rockville, MD: National Institute of Mental Health.

Kallen, D.B.P., G.B. Kosse, H.C. Wagenaar, J.J.J. Kloprogge and M. Vorbeck (eds) (1982) *Social Science Research and Public Policy-Making: A Reappraisal.* Windsor: NFER Nelson.

Klein, Lisl (1976) *A Social Scientist in Industry.* Epping, Essex: Gower Press.

Larsen, Judith K. (1981) 'Knowledge Utilization: Current Issues', pp. 49ff in Robert F. Rich (ed.), *The Knowledge Cycle.* Beverly Hills and London: Sage.

Leviton, Laura C. and Edward F.X. Hughes (1981) 'Research on the Utilization of Evaluations: A Review and Synthesis', *Evaluation Review*, 5(4): 525–48.

Lindblom, Charles E. (1965) *The Intelligence of Democracy.* New York: Free Press.

Lindblom, Charles E. and David K. Cohen (1979) *Usable Knowledge: Social Science and Social Problem-Solving.* New Haven and London: Yale University Press.

Lipsky, Michael (1971) 'Social Scientists and the Riot Commission', *Annals of the American Academy of Political and Social Sciences*, 394 (March): 72–83.

Meehan, Eugene, J. (1981) *Reasoned Argument in Social Science: Linking Research to Policy.* Westport, CT and London: Greenwood Press.

Meehan, Eugene J. (1982) *Economics and Policy-Making: The Tragic Illusion.* Westport, CT and London: Greenwood Press.

Mullen, Edward, James Dumpson and Associates (1972) *Evaluation of Social Intervention.* San Francisco: Jossey-Bass.

National Academy of Sciences and Social Science Research Council (1969) *The Behavioral and Social Sciences: Outlook and Needs.* Englewood Cliffs, NJ: Prentice-Hall.

National Research Council (1968) *The Behavioral Sciences and the Federal Government.* Washington DC: National Academy of Sciences.

264 The use and abuse of social science

National Science Board (1969) *Knowledge Into Action: Improving the Nation's Use of the Social Sciences.* Washington, DC: National Science Foundation.

Patton, Michael Quinn (1978) *Utilization-Focused Evaluation.* Beverly Hills and London: Sage.

Pettigrew, Andrew M. (1975) 'Towards a Political Theory of Organizational Intervention', *Human Relations,* 28(3): 191–208.

Piore, Michael J. (1980) 'On the Conceptualization of Labor Market Reality', pp. 67–95 in Organization for Economc Co-operation and Development, *The Utilisation of the Social Sciences in Policy Making in the United States.* Paris: OECD.

Rapoport, Robert, N. (1970) 'Three Dilemmas of Action Research', *Human Relations,* 23: 499–513.

Rein, Martin (1976) *Social Science and Public Policy.* Harmondsworth, Mddx: Penguin Books.

Rein, Martin (1980) 'The Interplay of Social Science and Social Policy', *International Social Science Journal,* 32(2).

Rein, Martin and Donald Schon (1977) 'Problem Setting in Policy Research', pp. 235–51 in C.H. Weiss (ed.), *Using Social Research in Policy Making.* Lexington, Mass.: D.C. Heath.

Rein, Martin and Sheldon White (1977) 'Policy Research: Belief and Doubt', *Policy Analysis,* 3(2) 239–71.

Rich, Robert F. (1977) 'Use of Social Science Knowledge by Federal Bureaucrats: Knowledge for Action versus Knowledge for Understanding', in C.H. Weiss (ed.), *Using Social Research in Policy Making.* Lexington, Mass.: D.C. Heath.

Rothman, Jack (1980) *Using Research in Organizations: A Guide to Successful Application.* Beverly Hills and London: Sage.

Russell, Beverly and Arnold Shore (1976) 'Limitations on the Governmental Use of Social Science in the United States', *Minerva,* 14(4): 475–95.

Sanford, Nevitt (1976) 'Whatever Happened to Action Research?' pp. 19–32 in A.W. Clark (ed.), *Experimenting with Organizational Life: The Action Research Approach.* New York and London: Plenum.

Seashore, Stanley (1976) 'The Design of Action Research', pp. 103–18 in A.W. Clark (ed.), *Experimenting with Organizational Life: The Action Research Approach.* New York and London: Plenum.

Sharpe, L.J. (1978) 'The Social Scientist and Policy-making in Britain and America: A Comparison, pp. 302–12 in M. Bulmer (ed.), *Social Policy Research.* London: Macmillan.

Sjoberg, Gideon (1975) 'Politics, Ethics and Evaluation Research', pp. 29–51 in M. Guttentag and E. L. Struening, *Handbook of Evaluation Research, Vol. 2.* Beverly Hills and London: Sage.

Stanford Evaluation Consortium (1976) 'Review Essay: Evaluating the *Handbook of Evaluation Research',* pp. 195–215 in G. V. Glass (ed.), *Evaluation Studies Review Annual, Vol. 1.* Beverly Hills and London: Sage.

Struening, Elmer L. and Marcia Guttentag (eds) (1975) *Handbook of Evaluation Research, Vol. 1.* Beverly Hills and London: Sage.

Susman, Gerald I. and Roger D. Evered (1978) 'An Assessment of the Scientific Merits of Action Research', *Administrative Science Quarterly,* 23(4): 582–603.

Town, Stephen (1973) 'Action Research and Social Policy: Some Recent British Experiences', *Sociological Review* (4): 573–98.

Trist, Eric L. (1976a) 'Action Research and Adaptive Planning', pp. 223–36 in A. W.

Clark (ed.), *Experimenting with Organizational Life: The Action Research Approach.* New York and London: Plenum.

Trist, Eric L. (1976b) 'Engaging with Large-scale Systems', pp. 43–58 in A.W. Clark (ed.) *Experimenting with Organizational Life: The Action Research Approach.* New York and London: Plenum.

Wagenaar, Henk C. (1982) 'A Cloud of Unknowing: Social Science Research in a Political Context, pp. 21–31 in Kallen et al. (eds), *Social Science Research and Public Policy-Making: A Reappraisal.* Windsor: NFER Nelson.

Weiss, Carol H. (1975) 'Evaluation Research in the Political Context', in Struening and Guttentag, *Handbook of Evaluation Research, Vol. 1.* Beverly Hills and London: Sage.

Weiss, Carol H. (ed.) (1977) *Using Social Research in Policy Making.* Lexington, Mass.: D.C. Heath.

Weiss, Carol H. (1982) 'Policy Research in the Context of Diffuse Decision-Making', pp. 288–314 in Kallen et al., *Social Science Research and Public Policy-Making: A Reappraisal.* Windsor: NFER Nelson.

Wilson, James Q. (1978) 'Social Science and Public Policy: A Personal Note', pp. 82–92 in L. E. Lynn (ed.), *Knowledge and Policy: The Uncertain Connection.* Washington, DC: National Research Council.

Conclusions

Frank Heller

A word of caution

The case examples and theories described in the preceding chapters illustrate a wide but unavoidably incomplete range of experience of social science utilization. Nevertheless, they present important lessons for researchers and their clients as well as for funding bodies.

In this final chapter, I shall attempt to draw on these lessons to reach a few tentative conclusions. My objective is twofold: to reduce frustration and widen the scope for research utilization. To reduce frustration one has to set realistic expectations and these have to include the realization — briefly referred to in the opening chapter — that throughout the long history of mankind and in almost every field of endeavour, there are many examples of discovery and knowledge being misused or not implemented for long periods of time. Knowledge that the earth was round rather than flat was reasonably well demonstrated when Christopher Columbus reached America in his search for a short route to India, but the immediate consequence was the cruel and deceitful extermination of advanced ancient civilizations.

Printing was invented in China in approximately the seventh or eighth century A.D., but it was only in the late Sung Dynasty, 300 years later, that it was put to practical use and it had to be reinvented in Europe in 1454. There are innumerable recent examples of useful discoveries followed by long infertile periods. I will mention one which every reader can check from experience. In 1909 Frank Gilbreth published a book called *Bricklaying System* (Gilbreth, 1953). In it he describes in some detail how bricklaying can be improved from a haphazard, relatively slow, exhausting and back-breaking, low-quality activity to an accurate, fast, relatively relaxed high-quality handicraft. There are many facets to his ingenious redesign, but one essential structure consists of a simple portable height-adjustable scaffolding which allows the bricklayer to work comfortably and quickly without back-breaking muscle strain and fatigue. Gilbreth's method improved the bricklayer's productivity without greater effort from 120 to 350 bricks per hour. Go to any building site today, and you will see bricklaying done by the exact method Gilbreth set out to eradicate seventy-five years ago.[1]

In a recent analysis of modern technology, a high-powered team of experts concluded that there is at least a ten to twenty year delay between the discovery of a new technical approach and its implementation (New Technolgy, 1981: 70). Weiss, in her chapter, makes a similar observation of the social sciences.

These examples are given to caution rather than to discourage. Funding bodies, clients and researchers have a difficult task in attempting to assess the cost-benefit of their investment. Several further caveats are appropriate, particularly to remind social scientists of some of their own more firmly established findings. One relates to the well-documented tendency to behave non-rationally, or with what Simon (1957) has called 'bounded rationality'. Carol Weiss goes so far as to argue that policy-makers are very well aware that their policies are 'not the problem of rational problem-solving.'[2] The other caveat is the equally well-documented literature on the difficulty of achieving attitudinal and behavioural change.[3] Both these very human characteristics mitigate against an easy and rapid acceptance of research outcomes. Within the literature on resistance to change, one must also mention the socio-psychological dynamic of power, which will support some but oppose other social science evidence, irrespective of its merit. It is unrealistic to expect power-holders to accept findings which are against their perceived interest. The chapters by Cherns, Eldridge and Berry et al. show this very clearly and a recent critical evaluation of research on modern policing methods gives further support (Weatheritt, 1986). Major changes, first from foot patrols to police cars, and a later reversal back to emphasis on foot patrols, were based on hunches supported by a powerful mythology. Research evidence was either excluded or distorted. The real reasons behind these changes were economic considerations, while senior police officers pretended that the changes were designed to reduce crime and improve relations with the public. In the 1960s there was a dire shortage of police recruits and by putting them in cars, they tried to cover wider areas. However, with the steep increase in the cost of petrol in the late 1970s, patrolling by car became expensive and this ushered in new emphasis on community patrolling. In both cases, research evidence was put to one side (Weatheritt, 1986).

The chapter by Berry et al. shows how traditional accounting philosophies supported by several groups of people who hold powerful positions in the coal board and the accountancy profession can secure decisions which have substantial national repercussions. The critically important role of accounting practices in almost every sphere of modern life stands in sharp contrast with the profession's reluctance to consider research evidence or alternative conceptual frameworks proposed by academic accountants. It is the profession, not the researchers, who impose solutions. This struggle is neatly described by Hopwood (1985).

Given these difficulties, social scientists are at times inclined to cut corners or force the pace. These temptations also exist when one or other interest group, client or funding body, expect too much, too rapidly. Dahrendorf warned some time ago that when clients become impatient and ask for practical or comprehensive solutions, social scientists may 'forge the currency' (Dahrendorf, 1959). Lévy-Leboyer makes a very similar observation in her chapter, saying that social science is often too easily and too loosely applied, and she gives several examples. Gill argues that the very people who are sceptical about social science (senior administrators, for instance), are often quite keen to use well presented packages, frequently out of date or based on poor evidence. Weiss shows that, at least in the United States, programmes that had been positively evaluated, were cut back and some of those that were criticized were expanded; consequently, biased findings and out-moded ideas have often been absorbed.

How to win influence . . .
Popularity in social science may not always be a guarantee of quality. The extraordinary case of *In Search of Excellence* (Peters and Waterman, 1982) selling about 4 million copies since being published and translated into many languages, improbably even into Chinese, is worth considering. Its lack of novelty is probably its only virtue. It presents readers with simple check-lists, based on interviews with only the highest level of organizations, whose self-serving answers are unlikely to include any critical data. Consequently, all the companies described in this book are paragons of virtue. Few researchers and consultants familiar with even the most outstanding companies will find this credible. The authors worked with McKinsey, the consultants, but also teach at the Stanford Business School and one wonders whether a lack of critical faculty is now acceptable in some seats of learning.[4] This question is pertinent, since the book is openly hostile to business schools and to formal research, and quotes with approval comments about young business graduates: 'People with degrees like Harvard BA and a Stanford MBA last about seventeen months. They can't cope' (Peters and Waterman, 1982:35) But they are inconsistent, because when its suits them they will use evidence from academic research to support their arguments in favour of one of the eight basic practices which are alleged to lead to excelllence.[5]
    In a different context, a political philosopher put the case very well when he said:

> The success of ideas in taking root in society and becoming a driving force for men and history does not depend upon their form, upon how scientific they may be, it depends upon the degree to which they are capable of elucidating and motivating the vital aspirations of individuals and social groups. (Djilas, 1972: 45)

When there are so many traps to avoid and hurdles to clear, success, or even the less ambitious avoidance of failure, becomes an important subject for analysis.

The three constituencies

Our examples and the literature show that there are three major constituencies which share responsibility for success or failure of research utilization: the research community, the research funders and the potential users.[6]

Most of the lessons we can learn from the experiences and theories described in the various chapters of this book address themselves to researchers and, to a lesser extent, to those who fund research. The user constituency is referred to indirectly and by implication, but even where user problems are identified, remedies remain elusive. Very much more systematic evidence has to accumulate before a coherent framework of analysis can be devised for such a variegated and complex area as consumer behaviour, and even more knowledge and ingenuity will be required to integrate the three constituencies in such an analysis. Is this a realizable ambition?

For instance, we are told that government interest in research fluctuates over time and seems to be a function of changes in political ideology (see chapters by Haveman, Brannen, Cherns and Weymann et al.).[7] Is it possible that changes within the funder-research community can adequately compensate for the troughs in government interest? Let us take two examples: first Gill argues that unintelligibility of academic social science writing, as measured by the Fox index, is a major obstacle to utilization and may be a result of the competitive need for prestige and promotion in universities. Secondly, we know that funding bodies are often opposed to supporting either replication or action research, although our chapter writers believe in both (Ansoff, Wilkins, Lévy-Leboyer and Gustavsen). Is it therefore sensible to suggest that during a depression of the government-interest cycle, researchers should upgrade their Fox intelligibility index and funding bodies should switch from traditional to replication and action research? But if these measures are effective, why wait for a downturn in the economic cycle?

Other cycles of interest and fashion may be even more difficult to handle; organizational research can serve as an example. Ansoff identifies two recent trends of mistaken emphasis. One is leadership research, which has all too often taken the easy path and followed managerial preferences, opting for the virtues of consensual behaviour and loyalty, rather than the more intellectually challenging virtues of critical analysis which may occasionally lead to rocking the boat in a good cause. Secondly, he identifies the large and related area of participation research which assumes that 'individuals share a common ideology and seek a maximum of self-determination in decision-making'. These value preferences, says Ansoff, are in conflict with the reality of post-industrial society, which requires attention to differentiation and ideological polarization.

The problem of values

Researchers, clients and even funding bodies have values, though they may not always be aware of them. The *pros* and *cons* of values have been extensively debated, but the problems identified in these debates do not disappear. It is one thing to say that values are inevitable — which thay are — it is quite another to extol their uninhibited virtue or argue that as long as they are disclosed, no harm is done.[8]

Values, like ideas, are powerful agents in society. They are organized either in support of the status quo or in opposition to it. Maynard Keynes's famous message at the end of his General Theory book graphically draws attention to the power of ideas. He argues hat economists, whether they are right or wrong, are more powerful than the general public believes and that the ordinary man in the street, who would never consider himself to be subject to intellectual influences, is frequently enslaved by the value preferences of some defunct economist. Ideas, says Keynes, for good or evil are more powerful than vested interests.

In social science, values and ideas are not always easy to keep apart. Hypotheses, subject to disproof, are close to what we normally call ideas, but hypotheses are frequently formulated as if they had some intrinsic goodness which should be sustained by the research. In this case hypotheses, like ideas, can be enveloped in a net of values. When values become very strong, they are imbued with emotions and — in extreme conditions — the envelopment becomes a strait-jacket. Somewhere along the line one must call a halt. The fact that there is no agreement on the exact position where values become counter-productive to the research process is no reason for pretending that the problem does not exist.[9]

Most of the thirty-four cases of scientific falsification of data exposed by Broad and Wade (1985) were probably due to excessively strong value judgements. This was certainly the case with the life-long passions of Sir Cyril Burt and Dr Morton described in Heller's chapter. Values about the intellectual superiority of a chosen élite had become an obsession, but the fact that even when the frauds were exposed, scientists with similar value preferences failed, at first, to accept the fraud for what it was, is revealing about the strength of the perceptual distortions which can occur.

It is significant that nearly all cases of falsification were committed by single researchers working in isolation. None of them involved comparative research carried out by a collaboration between different research centres. I believe that adequate safeguards can usually be built into the research process, particularly when the topic carries substantial political overtones.[10]

It is for this reason that we must be critical of recent trends mentioned in several chapters (for instance Weymann, Lengyel, Berry et al. and Heller) for fact-finding activities to be carried out by, or directly on commission to an interested party with strong values. Tobacco research is, of course, a clear example. The proliferation of economic 'research' institutes affiliated or close to a political party is a regrettable trend and consultants have also started to stray into the field. A consultancy specializing in training or Quality Circles is not in an ideal position to carry out research into these fields. One well-known consultancy, for instance, has claimed that their 'package' which was originally used for training, will now also improve physical and mental health and the same package is claimed to be a statistically significant indicator of 'heart attacks, asthmas, ulcers, cancer and so on' (Blake and Mouton, 1978: vi)

The media do not often report social science research, and when they do, seem to find it difficult to separate the wheat from the chaff.[11]

Gresham's Law

Current trends support Ansoff's criticisms and explain why a form of Gresham's Law is now operating. Sir Thomas Gresham, a sixteenth-century financier, believed that bad money always drives out good money.[12] This notion can be tested in many other areas of social life and seems to apply to cycles and fashions in organization research. In the 1960s, the publication of two very prestigious reports which criticized the quality of research and teaching in American business schools led to very extensive changes (Pierson, 1959; Gordon and Howell, 1959). They drew attention to the fact that loose, anecdotal, purely descriptive case studies had replaced more objective types of research. This trend was sharply reversed after the publication of the two books and this is an excellent example of the effectiveness of research-based reports. However — as so often happens — the trend went to extremes. Abstract mathematical models and increasingly complex statistical procedures were applied, often to inferior raw data or over-simplified assumptions. Factor analyses and multiple correlations became surrogates for understanding priorities and complex relationships.

Just as uncorroborated descriptive case studies had driven out, or at least reduced the more objectively oriented research in some major American business schools in the 1950s, so the exaggeratedly 'scientistic' research[13] which replaced it in some schools, tended to denigrate the worthwhile results of work carried out with less sophisticated methods, even if the quality of the data was superior.

Now, in the 1980s, we observe yet another turn of the cycle, probably in protest against positivistic excesses. We seem to witness a regression to the earlier, largely descriptive, anecdotal stage of organizational research which favours slogans and check-lists as a way of making an impact on users. This simplistic work is highly successful in terms of economic reward and may push the more painstaking, careful research, including the examples collected in this book, into the background. Will the 'bad' once again drive out the 'good'?

The outstanding example of the new trend, the book *In Search of Excellence: Lessons from America's Best-Run Companies* has already been criticized, but it has spawned imitators in several places. One called *The Winning Streak* by Goldsmith and Clutterbuck (1984) quite openly acknowledges having been modelled on the *Excellence* book (as it is now familiarly known in board rooms). Like its predecessor, it lists its conclusions under eight headings and quotes with approval some extraordinary guidelines from top executives, like: 'I attach more importance to integrity than to ability' (p.123); and, from Sir Michael Edwardes, the proud circular aphorism: 'Success is about leadership and leadership is about success' (p. 13).[14]

Is it possible for serious researchers to compete for the attention of the user community against the persuasiveness of eight point check-lists and glib sayings more appropriate to after-dinner speeches than to books designed to improve organizational efficiency? The academic community tends to puts on an embarrassed smile when these pot-boilers appear, but say very little by the way of criticism. Since the pot-boilers are very profitable, criticism could be interpreted as envy, and who wants to be accused of that? And so it seems that Gresham's Law on debased currency may apply to all social science and leads to the absorption of untested nostrums.

Do-it-yourself social science

A senior economist from the OECD (Organization for Economic Co-operation and Development) has recently come out with a somewhat similar analysis by stressing the difference between the amateur and the professional.[15] David Henderson (1986) gave a series of lectures in which he coined the phrase 'Do-it-yourself Economics' or DIYE. He describes this as a constellation of beliefs and judgements 'about the working of the economic system and about national interests and the welfare of the community, which owe little or nothing to the economics profession' (Henderson, 1986:14). Henderson did not discover DIYE among politicians or in his local tennis club, but in Her Majesty's Treasury, a government department with special responsibility for the formulation of economic policy. The doctrines he came across were 'intuitive and self-generated: those who held them thought that what they were saying was plain common sense which needed no prompting or authority' (p.15). As a consequence of the prevalence of these unchallenged beliefs, he felt that the professional economists in the Treasury were grossly under-used. Do-it-yourself Economics has a universal character; it is timeless and respects no frontiers.

William Niskanen, a member of the President's Council of Economic Advisers in Washington, is quoted as complaining about a similar syndrome. While managers generally respect the views of most special disciplines with a professional base, like lawyers and engineers, they constantly

> override the judgements of economists on economic matters ... basically every senior manager and board member ... thinks of himself as an economist, as having a democratic right to make his own judgement about economic phenomena. (Henderson, 1986: 16)[16]

If this is the situation in the oldest and most respected of the social sciences, we should not be surprised that the Do-it-yourself tendency prevails even more strongly in all the other areas of social science, including those covered by our chapter writers. From the point of view of research utilization, this phenomenon justifies an acronym. We will call it DYSS: Do-it-yourself Social Science. Government officials, Ministers, consultants and managers in every field of activity are tempted to practise DYSS as a divine right.

The question for social science is whether we are prepared to accommodate to DYSS, as the authors of *In Search of Excellence* appear to have done, or whether, like Henderson, we challenge the divinity as well as the right to make DYSS judgements in those cases when better evidence is available or when DYSS generalizations apply only to a limited set of circumstances.

This brings us back to the complaint by Ansoff about mistaken emphasis in some of the social science literature, and in particular about consensus leadership and participative decision-making, two areas where DYSS is heavily entrenched. The danger of forging a closely-knit consensus at the top is never emphasized in the DYSS literature, but it was at work in UNESCO (see Lengyel's chapter) and in the National Coal Board (Berry et al.). In a different context, consensus by eliminating critical analysis bears a heavy responsibility for some of the scientific frauds mentioned in Heller's chapter.

A much more scientifically powerful demonstration of the consensus danger is analysed by Janis's work on 'Groupthink'. He describes major catastrophes, like Japan's destruction of a large part of the American fleet at Pearl Harbor in December 1941, Kennedy's disastrous Bay of

Pigs decision to invade Cuba, and Neville Chamberlain's appeasement of Hitler. These figure among many other examples of the negative consequences of group loyalty and consensus which ignored external evidence that should have been considered and which might have avoided calamity (Janis, 1982; Janis and Mann, 1977).

In recent years, the DYSS literature has used a superficial analysis of Japanese decision-making in support of the benefits which can be achieved by obedience to high-level policy decisions. This is based on a serious misunderstanding of two safety mechanisms in the Japanese decision process. One is called *nemawashi* and consists of extensive preliminary sounding-out processes to test all available evidence before a policy is adopted; the other is the highly participative process known as *ringi* (Heller and Misumi, 1986). The Japanese *ringi* is a complex method of communication and decision making which encourages initiatives at lower levels of organization. These initiatives are gradually taken upward through the organization and if they successfully reach the top, are then implemented by the lower level initiator. Obedience and loyalty are beside the point. If consensus is achieved, it is through arguments and evidence. But, in many cases, the *ringi* stops when no agreement is reached. Managers who indulge themselves in wish fulfilment will lap up over-simplified DYSS ideas about organizational consensus and ignore other research evidence.

Realism or Utopia

In conclusion, it may be worth speculating for a moment on three alternative philosophies about research utilization. We assume for the purpose of this comparison that we have a successful research outcome, meaning that the findings are fairly reliable and valid and point to firm conclusions.[17] We can now set up three sets of expectations. The most natural, common sense approach and the one most widely followed in the utilization literature, is to expect the client or user system to accept the findings and take the necessary steps to implement them. This is the *engineering model*. When a better or more efficient machine is designed in the laboratory and has passed the necessary tests, it will be produced and used. In cases where these common sense outcomes do not occur, one is fully justified in complaining, or at least being disappointed.

The alternative is to look at the evidence of what actually happens to social science in the real world. Some of this evidence has been documented in this book and would justify quite different expectations to those derived from the engineering model. This approach would expect the results from reliable and valid research to be frequently subject to one of three different treatments.

One treatment is to ignore the research, at least for long periods of time, and to turn one's attention to other issues.

An alternative is to criticize the research or some part of it. This is very easily done, most usually by raising doubts about some aspects of methodology. Having raised doubts, it would be unwise to take the matter further until these doubts are satisfactorily resolved.

The third treatment is to accept the findings as quite interesting and sensible, but to doubt whether they apply in all circumstances and probably not in those which the client perceives as prevailing at the time. Under this treatment the research will be praised for its success, but it will be considered that implementation in the existing circumstances cannot be justified.

These three methods of implementation avoidance are not new and they do not exhaust all possibilities, but they seem to explain a substantial part of the total variance. In addition, we have already seen that several chapters document the existence of national differences and cycles of receptivity to research from decade to decade. A well-known American academic and consultant, Fritz Steel (1977), substantiates the view of several chapter writers when he says:

> Quite simply, I have never been able to negotiate an effective organization development contract with any firm in the UK. I have had a large number of lunchtime 'exploratory discussions' but none has ever gone past the gastronomic stage. (p. 23)

If we add all these symptoms together, we arrive at a situation quite distinct from the *engineering model* and I will call it the *Pyrrhonic model.* Pyrrho founded a sceptic philosophy in the third century before the birth of Christ, which upheld the doctrine of the impossibility of attaining certainty of knowledge. Derivatives of this doctrine have gained many adherents over the centuries.

A third set of expectations can be called the *investment model* and, in one form or another may explain most utilization successes, for instance those described by Lévy-Leboyer, Gustavsen, and Wilkins, and the Glacier project described by Heller. Investment is characterized by a measure of optimism and enthusiasm on the part of the researcher as well as the client, moderated by a recognition of risk. Once investment has been agreed and has taken place, both researcher and client will be inclined to strive for amortization. The cash nexus does not dominate the model. Investment and amortization in ideas, values and emotions are probably more significant. The research-action method, which I mentioned in the Introductory chapter, may be particularly appropriate for creating the optimism, enthusiasm and tolerance to risk which this model seems to require.

The successful case examples in preceding chapters suggest that fairly close relations between user and researcher are always helpful and some joint role in the phase beyond the data collection may be necessary.

Weymann's evidence points in this direction and Gustavsen's 'generative principle' makes even more stringent demands as a way of creating a process of on-going mutual learning which cannot be hurried to fit into a prearranged timetable, as the engineering model would suggest.

Accepting realism

The case for limiting our expectations about the role of social science research is strong and may require a substantial readjustment in the policy thinking of funders, users and researchers.

Adapting Argyris' and Schon's (1978) terminology, one could say that we espouse the engineering model, while we act on the philosophy of Pyrrho. Among the contributing considerations in this dilemma which stretches back over the whole history of mankind, five are worth summarizing:

1. our drastically bounded rationality
2. the almost universal agony of change
3. the distorting effect of power
4. Gresham's law of the 'bad' driving out the 'good', reinforcing a tendency for DYSS (Do-it-yourself Social Science), and
5. the danger of abuse from unbridled values.

I am tempted to infer from the evidence, that rapid research utilization will always be the exception rather than the rule, and that we would do well to accept this as the norm. It does not mean, of course, that we cannot strive for improvements. One is not talking of miracles which are beyond the wit of man; only exceptions which can be assiduously cultivated.

I hope that this excursion into realism will not be misunderstood, though I realize that for some constituencies it will be tempting to do so. The problems I have mentioned are not unique to social science; few of them are insoluble and by identification we have already started the battle to defeat them. We are fortunate in having been able to assemble a convincing range of 'successful' research, which in each case has enjoyed the confidence and interest of a user community. Each author, even those who have reported utilization failures, has made suggestions for improvement — either directly or by implication. We must also remember Wilkins' astute observation that his greatest success grew out of a series of preceding failures.

I have previously drawn attention to a measure of convergence in the success stories: close contact, active and continuous communication, involvement of the client or potential user in all phases of the project and particularly during implementation. These are common features for most user-friendly research. In the Introduction I described a six-fold scheme and identified the positive characteristics with what was called 'Building bridges between researcher and user'. 'Research action' was a particularly promising method within this scheme, and this has received support from the evidence of many case examples (particularly Lévy-Leboyer, Wilkins, Gustavsen, van de Vall and Karapin). But I also showed that some of the most widely-used theories and practices are based on a variety of methods. There are several roads to success.

Failures also teach us important lessons. For instance, Lengyel's answer to Unesco's incompetence in research is to restructure the enterprise with a clear focus. Unesco's pusillanimity is not unusual in the United Nations family. Most agencies have very limited funds and split this up into ridiculously tiny sums to produce the largest possible number of projects, on the assumption that their governing bodies will equate effectiveness with the number of reports listed in an appendix.

Realism is quite different from pessimism. One cannot build a firm edifice on euphoria and half truths; patience may be a virtue we have to encourage. Instant solutions and quick applications are not always feasible. Printing was a solution to the problem of communicating the fruits of calligraphy in an enormously large country. It took 300 years to gain a firm foothold in China and another 300 years before its benefits reached Europe. Few would dispute that it was worth it.

The reader of the preceding chapters will have derived several ideas about how to provide some of the necessary conditions to nurture the delicate seed corn and reduce its mortality rate.

Since I acknowledge that change is always difficult, unless it happens to be in the direction we want to go anyway, I would not expect funders to discard overnight their adherence to the engineering model or users to throw off their long-standing addiction for Pyrrho's tempting escape routes. But one could, perhaps, ask researchers to be more persuasive and open in their defence of the conditions that underpin the structure of investment, and particularly its built-in margin of risk and uncertainty. Researchers must think of themselves more as entrepreneurs than as managers and therefore more in need of long-term venture capital than fixed-term money or overdrafts.

Notes

1. By using this example of bricklaying, I do not want to signal approval of the so-called scientific management movement which Gilbreth and F.W. Taylor ushered in at the beginning of the twentieth century. Most of the 'scientific' prescriptions were lacking in a rudimentary understanding of human nature and have caused much harm.

2. For other psychological evidence of non-rational behaviour, see for instance Kahneman et al. (1982); Nisbett and Ross (1980); and Pitz and Sachs (1984).

3. See for instance Goodman and Dean et al. (1982); Seashore et al. (1983); Smith (1982); Lippitt et al. (1985) and Plewis (1985).

4. Neither Peters nor Waterman is on the full-time faculty of Stanford. Both are closely connected with McKinsey and Company, the consulting firm which also

provided the major back-up to the investigation. Peters has now opened his own consulting business.

5. For instance, they quote several research studies to support their sixth principle of 'sticking to the knitting', that is to say avoiding or limiting branching out into new fields for diversification (pp. 294–6). This is a direct attack on the economic justification of conglomerates and rests on sound findings. Even so, takeover fever has not diminished since the book was published.

6. Sometimes the funders are also users, but the distinction is nevertheless useful. A government department, through its research section, may commission or carry out research, but a different section, often at a higher level, is the potential user.

7. Although occasionally, maybe miraculously, continuity is achieved in spite of sharp political changes, as in the German Humanization of Work programme (see Chapter 9).

8. While this argument is frequently used to justify a free rein for value judgements in research, actual formal and overt disclosure is very rare. In the cases of fraud described in Heller's chapter, for instance, there was no disclosure of the researchers' value position and, as we saw, important national policy decisions were based on their findings.

9. One can imagine that some of the contributors to this book have found the dividing line difficult to draw. The work of Eldridge and his colleagues (Glasgow University Media Group, 1976 and its follow up, Philo et al., 1982) has been subjected to criticism on grounds of value and methodology (see Harrison, 1985; Hetherington, 1985; Schlesinger, 1979; and Tunstall, 1983). This dispute about methods and values has led to an active debate and correspondence in *The Times Higher Education Supplement*, March 1986.

10. I have pointed out elsewhere that there are important advantages and safeguards in cross-national research (Heller, 1985a; 1985b). Cross-national teams tend to represent a plurality of values and this will usually eliminate substantial bias (see IDE, 1981). Even when one member or one team attempts to impose its own value interpretation, disclaimers can be incorporated (see Tannenbaum et al., 1974: Ch. VII; and MOW, 1986: Ch. 14).

Even in a single country research, it should be possible to assemble some value plurality. For instance, research on alcohol should not be carried out by heavy drinkers. It sounds obvious, but in practice these important details are often ignored.

11. It is not unimportant to recognize that while newspapers and television all have specialist correspondents in a wide range of topics from science, medicine, agriculture, politics, to horse racing, motor racing, cricket, chess and so on, the only social science discipline represented is economics. When they need somebody to give a specialist view on a behavioural science problem, they usually call on a medical doctor or psychiatrist.

In science reporting, very important biases operate which have nothing to do with short-term utility which normally guides media priorities. A part of a skull, possibly belonging to an ancient hominid, or a mural in an Egyptian tomb, will receive many column inches of coverage, but I guess that in terms of the research covered in this book, only the UNESCO story or possibly one of the frauds would receive mention.

12. In its original formulation, it meant that a government which introduced debased or adulterated coinage drove out the purer coins which were then smelted down for their value as metals.

13. The term 'scientistic' comes from Hayek (1942), who uses it to criticize

attempts by social scientists to imitate the methods of the physical sciences where this is inappropriate.

14. The Goldsmith and Clutterbuck book is in at least five respects superior to *In Search of Excellence:*

1. it makes an attempt to analyse unsuccessful companies,
2. it adds a chapter on success in small companies,
3. it admits that success often does not last,
4. it accepts contingency thinking, admitting that retailing is very different from manufacturing, and
5. it publishes their Interview Schedule.

Nevertheless, a large amount of their case description is superficial and they take almost no account of well-documented evidence.

15. An amateur in this context does not have to be a person without qualification. He may have a university degree or even a doctorate in the relevant subject, but his 'Do-it-yourself' approach is based on political or other value judgements rather than those of a professional economist.

16. Henderson is, of course, aware that economists do not always agree on either analysis or remedies, but he claims that in many areas of their field, disagreements are limited and clear majority views exist. One could, of course, make the same point about lawyers and medical doctors.

17. By 'reliable' we mean that findings are repeatable or are in line with previous outcomes; by 'valid' we mean results that are substantially above chance and explain a significant percentage of the events under investigation. Of course, only a minority of social science can claim to fall within this description, but the purpose of my argument is to show that even when fairly reliable valid outcomes occur, utilization does not follow quickly and automatically. This is almost equally true of the medical-biological sciences.

References

Argyris, C. and D.A. Schon (1978) *Theory in Practice: Increasing Professional Effectiveness.* San Francisco: Jossey-Bass.

Blake, Robert and Jane Mouton (1978) *The New Managerial Grid.* Houston, Texas: Gulf Publishing.

Broad, William and Nicholas Wade (1985) *Betrayers of the Truth: Fraud and Deceit in Science.* Oxford: Oxford University Press.

Dahrendorf, Rolf (1959) *Class and Class Conflict in an Industrial Society.* London: Routledge and Kegan Paul.

Djilas, Milovan (1972) *The Unperfect Society: Beyond the New Class.* London: Unwin Books.

Gilbreth, Frank (1953) *Bricklaying System.* New York: Myron C. Clark.

Glasgow University Media Group (1976) *Bad News.* London: Routledge and Kegan Paul.

Goldsmith, Walter and David Clutterbuck (1984) *The Winning Streak.* Harmondsworth, Mddx.: Penguin Books.

Goodman, Paul and James Dean Jr. (1982) 'Creating Long Term Organization Change', in Paul Goodman and Associates, *Change in Organizations.* San Francisco: Jossey-Bass.

Gordon, R.A. and J.E. Howell (1959) *Higher Education for Business.* New York: Columbia University Press.

Harrison, Martin (1985) 'Whose Bias', *Policy Journals.*

Hayek, F.v.A. (1942) 'Scientism and the Study of Society', *Economica*, 9: 267–91.

Heller, F.A. (1985a) 'Some Theoretical and Practical Problems in Multinational and Cross-cultural Research on Organizations', in Pat Joynt and Malcolm Warner (eds), *Managing in Different Cultures*. Oslo: Universitets Forlaget.

Heller, F.A. (1985b) 'Some Problems in Multinational Research on Organizations', in Susumu Takamiya and Keith Thurley (eds), *Japan's Emerging Multinationals*. Tokyo: University of Tokyo Press.

Heller F.A. and J. Misumi (1986) 'Decision Making', in Bernard Bass, Pieter Drenth and Peter Weissenberg (eds), *Organizational Psychology: An International Review*. Beverly Hills, Ca: Sage.

Henderson, David (1986) *Innocence and Design: The Influence of Economic Ideas*. London: Basil Blackwell.

Hetherington, Alistair (1985) *News, Newspapers and Television*. London: Macmillan.

Hopwood, Anthony (1985) 'The Tale of a Committee that Never Reported: Disagreements on Intertwining Accounting with the Social', *Accounting, Organization and Society*, 10: 361–77.

IDE (Industrial Democracy in Europe Research Group) (1981) *European Industrial Relations*. Oxford: Oxford University Press.

Janis, Irving and Leon Mann (1977) *Decision Making: A Psychological Analysis of Conflict, Choice and Commitment*. New York: Free Press.

Janis, Irving (1982) *Groupthink*. Boston, Mass.: Harcourt Brace.

Kahneman, D., P. Slovic and A. Tversky (1982) *Judgement Under Uncertainty, Heuristics and Biases*. Cambridge: Cambridge University Press.

Lippitt, Gordon, Peter Langseth and Jack Mossop (1985) *Implementing Organizational Change: A Practical Guide to Managing Change Effects*. London: Jossey-Bass.

MOW (Meaning of Working) (1986) *The Meaning of Working*. London: Academic Press.

New Technology: Society, Employment and Skill (1981) 'Report of a Working Party of the Council for Science and Society'.

Nisbett, Richard and Lee Ross (1980) *Human Inference: Strategies and Shortcomings of Social Judgement*. Englewood Cliffs, N.J.: Prentice-Hall.

Peters, Thomas and Robert Waterman Jr. (1982) *In Search of Excellence: Lessons from America's Best Run Companies*. New York: Harper and Row.

Philo, Greg, John Hewitt, Peter Beharrell and Howard Davis (1982) *Really Bad News*. London: Writers and Readers.

Pierson, F.C. (ed.) (1959) *The Education of American Business*. New York: McGraw Hill.

Pitz, Gordon and Natalie Sachs (1984) 'Judgment and Decision: Theory and Application', *Annual Review of Psychology*, 35: 139–63.

Plewis, Ian (1985) *Analysing Change: Measurement and Explanation Using Longitudinal Data*. Chichester: John Wiley.

Schlesinger, Philip (1979) *Putting Reality Together*. London: Sage.

Seashore, Stanley, Edward Lawler III, Philip H. Mirvis and Cortlandt Cammann (eds) (1983) *Assessing Organizational Change: A Guide to Methods, Measures and Practices*. New York: John Wiley.

Simon, Herbert (1957) *Models of Man, Social and Rational*. New York: John Wiley.

Smith, Kenwyn (1982) 'Philosophical Problems in Thinking about Organization Change', in Paul Goodman and Associates, *Change in Organizations*. San Francisco: Jossey-Bass.

Steele, Fritz (1977) 'Is the Culture Hostile to Organization Development?', in Philip Mirvis and David Berg (eds), *Failures in Organization Development and Change*. New York: John Wiley.

Tannenbaum, A., B. Kavcic, M. Rosner, M. Vianello and G. Wieser (1974) *Hierarchy in Organizations*. San Francisco: Jossey-Bass.

Tunstall, Jeremy (1983) *The Media in Britain*. London: Constable.

Weatheritt, Mollie (1986) *Innovations in Policing*. London: Croom Helm (in association with the Police Foundation).

Index

Aaron, Henry 78, 83, 83n.1
Abrams, Philip 182
Abuse of social science 123–6: in consensus decision-making 20–1, 269, 273–4; 'Do-it-yourself Social Science' 272–3; 'packaged' social science 99, 100, 268, 272; political 54–5, 271; of theories and techniques 13, 26; *see also* Social research: implementation avoidance
ACAS (Advisory, Conciliation and Arbitration Service), UK 17n.2
Accountancy (journal) 88, 90, 91
Accounting methods, study of, 13–14, 267
Ackoff, R. 118
Action Research and Consultancy, UK 282
Adult education 67–8
Advertising 27, 120
Advisory, Conciliation and Arbitration Service (ACAS), UK 17n.2
Advisory Council on the Penal System, UK 53n.3
Alcoholism, project on 12, 27
Allison, G.T. 222
American Correctional Association 43–4
Annan Committee on the Future of Broadcasting, UK, 179
Ansoff, H. Igor 7, 11, 12, 14–15, 101, 269–70, 271, 273
Argyris, Chris 8, 101, 103–4, 243, 276
Aspen Institute for Humanistic Studies 129, 130, 139n.4
Association for Learned Societies in the Social Sciences 283
Automobile industry 29, 154n.3

Banbury Committee, UK 119
Banks, J.A. *see* Scott et al.
Bateson, G. 151
BBC (British Broadcasting Corporation) 9, 179–82
Beatrice Foods Company 139n.8
Beck, Ulrich 64

Beckhard, R. 108
Belgium 139n.7
Benson, Sir George 41, 42
Berger, Suzanne 246, 253
Berk, Richard A. 256–7
Berry, A. J., T. Capps, D. Cooper, T. Hooper and E. A. Lowe 9, 13, 267
Berthoud, Richard 192
Blackler, F.H.M. 128
Blum, Léon 54
Boehm, Virginia R. 243
Booth, Charles 245
Boyatsis, R.E. 108
Brand, J. 189
Brannen, Peter 10, 16, 283
Britain *see* United Kingdom
British Institute of Mangement 183n.1
British Social Survey 42
Broad, William 125, 138, 270
Brown, Alan 140n.22
Brown, C.A. 128
Brown, Wilfred 131–2
Bullock Report 164
Bulmer, M. 185, 245–6
Burns, Tom 179
Bursk, E.C. 209
Burt, Sir Cyril 124, 125, 270
Business administration 201

Cannon, I.C. 164
Caplan, Nathan 239
Capps, T. *see* Berry et al.
Carter, President 77–8
Casanova, P.G. 124, 258–9
Caswill, Chris 121n.4
Centre for Research in Industrial Democracy and Participation, UK, 283
Chad 63n.3
Chamberlain, N.W. 209
Cherns, Albert 16, 100, 101, 267, 283
Child care studies 211n.1
Churchman, C. West 22
Clark, Alfred W. 247–8, 251–2
Cloward, R.A. 252
Clutterbuck, David 272, 279n.14

29–31: Germany 67; Netherlands 207–10; Norway 144–50; UK 131–4, 171–7, 247
Industry and Employment Committee, ESRC, UK 119, 120, 121n.6
Inner-city regeneration 129
Institute of Chartered Accountants of England and Wales (ICAEW) 86, 91
Institute of Cost and Management Consultants (ICMA), UK 92
Institute of Economic Affairs, UK 196
Institute for Labour Market and Occupational Research, FRG 68, 71
Institute for Research on Poverty, US 76, 282
International co-operation in research 14, 54–63, 128–31, 258, 278n.10
International Labour Organization 57
International Social Science Council 59, 62
International Social Science Journal 124
International Sociological Association 284
International Workshop on Educational Research and Public Policy-making 238

Israel 129–31, 139n.7
ITN *see* IBA

Janis, Irving 273–4
Japan 129–31, 139n.6, n.7, 274
Jaques, Elliot 131–4
Jobs in the 80s project 124, 128–31, 138
Johnson, President 75, 77, 252
Joseph, Sir Keith 191–2, 197n.2
Joseph Rowntree Memorial Trust 139n.9
Juvenile delinquency 67, 252

Kallen, D., G. Kosse, H. Wagenaar, J. Kliprogge and M. Vorbeck 186, 187, 188
Kamin, Leon J. 124, 125
Karapin, Roger 2, 8, 124
Kennedy, President 222, 273
Keynes, Maynard 10, 270
Klein, Lisl 247
Klein, Rudolf 191–2
Kliprogge, J. *see* Kallen et al.
Koestler, Arthur, 124

Kolb, D.A. 108
Kosse, G. *see* Kallen et al.
Kuhn, T. 152

Labour relations *see* Industrial relations
Language of social science 2, 4–6: and prestige 83n.1, 101, 254, 269; unintelligibility 14, 22, 100, 137
Laos 63n.3
Law (discipline) 76
Lazarsfeld, P. 179
Lengyel, Peter 9, 14, 124, 277
Leviton, Laura C. 237–8
Lévy-Leboyer, Claude 7, 8, 10, 11, 12–13, 268, 275, 282
Lewin, K. 24
Leyden Institute for Social Policy Research 283
Likert, R. 10
Lindblom, C. E. 223, 231, 254–6
Lipsky, Michael 253
Liverpool University 171
Lockheed 44–5
London School of Economics 245
Low, J. O. 172
Lowe, E. A. *see* Berry et al.
Lupton, T. *see* Scott et al.
Lyman, S. *see* Vidich et al.

McGregor, D. 10
McGregor, Ian 98n.3
McKinsey and Company 268, 277n.4
McNamara, Robert 74–5
Maheu, René 57
Management and Industrial Relations Committee, SSRC, UK 104, 110–11, 119
Management science 21–2, 101
Mannheim, Herman 42
Manpower studies: Jobs in 80s 124, 128–31, 138; projects in 67–70, 127; work schedules 11, 29–31
March, J. G. 226
Market research projects 37–41
Marketing (discipline) 113
Marketing social research 21–3
Marshall Fund, FRG 139n.8
Marx, Karl 10
Maslow, A.H. 10, 26
Mayo, E. 172

About the contributors

Igor Ansoff is Distinguished Professor of Management at US International University, San Diego and Visiting Professor at Stockholm School of Economics, Sweden. He has been a pioneer in the development of Long Range Planning, Strategic Planning, Strategic Management and Strategic Issue Management and is the author of more than sixty articles and books on planning, strategy and management. In addition to his contributions in the fields of management writing and research, Professor Ansoff has spent many years as a practising manager and consultant.

Anthony Berry is Senior Lecturer in Management Control at the Manchester Business School. He was Director of the Operational Management course for four years and was Director of the International Teachers' Programme, an eight-week international management teacher-development programme, in 1980 and 1981. From 1983–85 he was Director of Studies of the MBA Programme. He is an ex-editor of *Management Education and Development* and has published papers and articles on management control and on management development. His research interests are in management control processes. He also works as a consultant in group relations training.

Peter Brannen has held posts at the Universities of Durham, Bradford and Southampton where he has undertaken research into social stratification and industrial relations, worker participation and the organization of medical care. Since 1973 he has been Chief Research Officer in the UK Department of Employment. His publications include *Entering the World of Work—Some Sociological Perspectives* (HMSO, 1975), *The Worker Directors* (Hutchinson, 1976) and *Authority and Participation in Industry* (Batsford, 1983).

Teresa Capps, having spent six years in academic life at Sheffield Polytechnic and the University of Sheffield, is now a divisional management accountant in the UK Brewing Industry. Her current research interest is in furthering the development of management accounting theory.

Albert Cherns, having retired in 1984 as Professor and Head of the Department of Social Sciences at the University of Loughborough, is now a visiting Fellow at Science Policy Research Unit, University of Sussex and an independent consultant. He is President of the Socio-technics Research Committee of the International Sociological Association. Professor Cherns' publications include *Using the Social Sciences* (Routledge and Kegan Paul, 1979) and some fifty articles mostly in the fields of organization and utilization of the social sciences, quality of working life and alienation.

David Cooper is Price Waterhouse Professor of Accounting and Finance at the University of Manchester Institute of Science and Technology. Prior to his appointment in 1984, he held appointments at the University of Manchester, East Anglia, British Columbia, California (Berkeley) and Copenhagen School of Business. He has published widely in scholarly journals on the organizational and social aspects of accounting and is the joint editor of three books, published by the Institute of Cost and Management Accountants, which seek to forge links between management accounting research and practice. As a result of the research on the National Coal Board reported in this volume, he has chaired an independent enquiry into the proposed closure of Polkemmet colliery and provided evidence to the Select Committee on Energy and the collier review procedure. He is currently involved in a major study of 'Accounting Regulation as Corporatist Control' funded by the ESRC as part of their corporatism and accountability initiative.

John Eldridge is Professor of Sociology, University of Glasgow, former President of the British Sociological Association and first Chairperson of the Association for Learned Societies in the Social Sciences. He is a founder member of the Glasgow University Media Group and Director of the Centre for Research in Industrial Democracy and Participation at Glasgow. He has published extensively in the fields of industrial sociology and the mass media.

John Gill is Reader in Management Studies at Sheffield City Polytechnic, having formerly lectured at the University of Bradford Management Centre and held managerial posts in the chemical industry. Most of his research has a basis in organizational analysis, design and change in manufacturing industry. He has also for some years conducted research into research utilization, particularly through action research and consultancy. Currently he is managing a major research project into the management of stringency in public sector higher education. He is Chairman of the CNAA Committee on Business and Management research and has published more than forty papers and contributions to books on management subjects.

Bjørn Gustavsen is Professor at the Swedish Center for Working Life and Research Fellow, previously Director, of the Work Research Institute in Norway. His main fields of research and publication are sociology of work and organization and the role of action in developing social knowledge. He is currently engaged in developing a new generation of union–employer development programmes in Sweden and Norway and also concluding a book on the role of action in social research titled *Sociology as Action: on the Construction of Alternative Realities.*

Robert H. Haveman is John Bascom Professor of Economics at the University of Wisconsin-Madison and Research Associate at the Institute for Research on Poverty. His research is in the areas of economics of poverty and income distribution, benefit-cost analysis and the incentive effects of government taxes and transfers. He has published several journal articles on these topics, and most recently has authored *Poverty Policy and Poverty Research: 1965–1980* (University of Wisconsin Press, 1987), from which the chapter in this volume is derived.

Frank Heller, currently Director of the Centre for Decision Making Studies, has been with the Tavistock Institute since 1969 after two years as Visiting Professor at Berkeley and Stanford Universities. He is now also Visiting Professor at the University of Surrey; Visiting Fellow of the Management College, Henley; President of the Organizational Psychology Division of the International Association of Applied Psychology and Executive Editor of the Wiley series of International Yearbooks of Organizational Democracy (to be followed by a Handbook series published by Oxford University Press). Dr Heller was previously Head of the Department of Management at the Polytechnic of Central London and then for six years was consultant to the ILO and the United National Special Fund in two South American countries. He was originally trained as an engineer before qualifying in economics and psychology.

Trevor Hopper is a lecturer in Accounting at the University of Manchester. Prior to this he was a management accountant in industry and a lecturer at Wolverhampton Polytechnic and Sheffield University. He is currently editing, with David Cooper, a book *Debating Coal Closures,* Cambridge University Press, which brings together the major economic and financial analyses by academics pertinent to the recent coal dispute.

Roger S. Karapin now studies in the Department of Political Science at the Massachusetts Institute of Technology. His research interests include US political participation in policy making, organization theory, political economy and technological change, and the development of methods for qualitative modelling in the social sciences.

Peter Lengyel is an Australian economist trained at London University and Harvard. He joined Unesco in 1953 and ten years later became the editor of its quarterly *International Social Science Journal* (ISSJ), a position he retained until his resignation in 1984 in protest against Unesco's mismanagement and de-professionalization. During his time at Unesco Peter Lengyel was also responsible for projects on social science data and documentation; he acted as economic advisor to a number of conferences and it was under his editorship that Arabic, Chinese and Spanish editions of the ISSJ were launched. Lengyel is the author of *Failure in International Social Science: The UNESCO Experience* (1986) and was the editor of *Approaches to the Science of Socio-Economic Development* (Unesco, 1971).

Claude Lévy-Leboyer is Professor of Psychology and Vice-President of the Université René Descartes, Paris V. She is also President of the International Association of Applied Psychology. Her research work deals with applied social pscyhology, mainly in the work and environment fields and, more recently, in health psychology. Among her recent and forthcoming publications are *Psychology and Environment* (PUF, translated into English, Italian, Spanish), *Vandalism, Behaviour and Motivation* (North-Holland), *La Crise des Motivations* (PUF), and *Traité de Psychologie du Travail* (PUF).

Anthony Lowe took early retirement in September 1986 from his post as Professor of Accounting and Financial Management at the University of Sheffield and is presently engaged as a research associate full-time on an ESRC research study on accounting regulations in the UK. Previously he held permanent academic posts at the Manchester Business School, University of Bradford Management Centre and School of Economic Studies, University of Leeds; and visiting posts at Harvard Business School; Sloane School of Management; Massachusetts Institute of Technology; University of California, Berkeley; Faculty of Commerce and Business Administration, UBC, Vancouver; and the University of Nairobi. He is a graduate of the London School of Economics (1957) and started off working life in 1945 as a sixteen year old office boy in a City of London firm of chartered accountants. Subsequently he qualified as an accountant and chartered secretary and built up a professional accountancy practice 'from scratch'. His academic interests are built round a concern for the effectiveness of management in relation to societal welfare and human survival.

Mark van de Vall is Professor of Sociology, University of Leyden, The Netherlands, and Adjunct-Professor at the Department of Sociology, the State University of New York at Buffalo. He is Director of the Leyden Institute for Social Policy Research (LISPOR) and Vice-President of the Sociotechnics section of the International Sociological Association. His research and publications are in the areas of industrial and labour relations, social policy research and knowledge utilization.

Carol Hirschon Weiss is a sociologist on the Faculty of the Harvard Graduate School of Education. Her publications include *Evaluation Research, Evaluating Action Programs, Using Social Research in Public Policy Making, Social Science Research and Decision-Making* and numerous journal articles. Most recently she has studied the channels through which findings from research and evaluation travel, including the mass media *(Reporting of Social Science in the Media,* forthcoming) and Congress-focused issue networks.

Ansgar Weymann is Professor and Head of the Department of Sociology, University of Bremen. He has served as Chairman of the German Sociological Association Section on Education and Head of the Sociological Research Center, University of Bremen. In 1984–85 he was a Fellow at the Netherlands Institute for Advanced Study. He studied sociology, psychology and philosophy at the Universities of Saarbrucken, Munich and Munster and was an Associate Professor in the Faculty of Sociology at the University of Bielefeld. He has published a number of books and articles.

Leslie Wilkins has, since June 1981, been Research Professor (Emeritus) at the State University of New York, Albany, where he was a member and one time Chairman of the Faculty of the Graduate School of Criminal Justice. Prior to taking up the appointment in New York he was Dean of the School of Criminology at the University of California at Berkeley. Leslie Wilkins has received many awards, including the Francis Wood Prize of the Royal Statistical Society, The Sutherland Award of the American Criminological Society, and the Durkheim Award of the International Society of Criminology. He is also listed among the Distinguished Educators of America. He has published widely on criminology and social policy in the United Kingdom and the United States.